T H E

TEN BEST
OPPORTUNITIES

FOR STARTING

A HOME BUSINESS

TODAY

T H E

TEN BEST

OPPORTUNITIES

FOR STARTING

A HOME BUSINESS

TODAY

658.041
T289 B

The New Careers Center, Inc.
with Reed Glenn

Live Oak Publications
Boulder, Colorado

Live Oak Publications
P.O. Box 2193
Boulder, CO 80306
(303) 447-1087
Distributed by Publishers Group West

Library of Congress Cataloging-in-Publication Data
New Careers Center, Inc.
      The 10 best opportunities for starting a home business today/The New Careers Center, Inc. with Reed Glenn.
            p. cm.
         ISBN 0-911781-10-2 : $14.95
            1. New business enterprises. 2. Home-based businesses--Management. I. Glenn, Reed, 1947- . II. Title. III. Title: Ten best opportunities for starting a home business today.
HD62.5.N478 1993
658'.041--dc20
                                                            93-19008
                                                               CIP

Disclaimer

Every attempt has been made to make this book as accurate and complete as possible. There may be mistakes of content or typography, however, and the author and publisher make no guarantees, warranties, or representations of any kind. This book is designed as a general guide to the subject. The reader is urged to investigate and verify information and its applicability under any particular situation or circumstances.

The author and publisher shall have no liability or responsibility to anyone with respect to contacts, negotiations, or agreements that may result from information in this book, or for any loss or damage caused or alleged to have been caused directly or indirectly by such information. If legal advice or other expert assistance is required, the services of a competent professional person should be sought.

Contents

1. Choosing Independence Through a Home Business
The Opportunities Have Never Been Better 1

2. Opportunities in Word Processing Services
Lucrative and fast-growing 19

3. Opportunities in Independent Publishing
Newsletters, books and more 39

4. Opportunities in Educational Services
Teaching without the bureaucracy 59

5. Opportunities in Child Care Services
Much-appreciated help for working moms 79

6. Opportunities in Research and Information Services
New markets with growing demand 97

7. Opportunities Growing Specialty Plants
Home greenhouse businesses and more 115

8. Opportunities in Writing and Editing Services
Specialization is the key 135

9. Opportunities in Cleaning Services
Solid profits for the energetic 153

10. Opportunities in Lawn and Garden Services
Definitely "growth" oriented 175

11 Opportunities Making and Marketing Gift Baskets
Turning a profit from an artistic bent 195

Resource Guide 215

Chapter 1
Choosing Independence Through a Home Business

The American Dream used to be a starter home. Now, for many it's a home-based business — a successful one, of course. As people burn out from the daily commute, traffic, office politics, and life slipping away from them in the service of someone else's business, many are turning to self- employment. Single parents find it hard to juggle a job and home life simultaneously. Married couples with eight-to-five jobs and a commute — the national average is 40 minutes round trip — have little time and energy left for their children, family life, hobbies, recreation and each other. And then there are those who are forced out of their regular jobs — such as the geologist laid off by a boom-and-bust oil company, mentioned in a later chapter here — who pursue an alternative and quite different career than they ever imagined for themselves.

This book is designed to give you a taste of what it's like to run 10 home-based businesses—businesses that offer realistic opportunities for earning at least a reasonably good income (and sometimes much better than that) while discovering a new balance in your life.

How this book came about

In 1985 the New Careers Center (NCC) was founded with the mission of helping people to find or create "whole" work—work that is personally satisfying as well as financially rewarding. Hundreds of books and other materials were evaluated on topics such as alternative careers, self-employment, new work options, job hunting and working from home, and the best were selected to be included in the first "Whole

Work Catalog."

In the years since, millions of Whole Work Catalogs have been distributed. Tens of thousands of people interested in improving their work situations have written or called NCC. Inevitably, certain patterns began to emerge.

For one thing, it became clear that there was a growing interest in working at home, coupled with an increased interest in entrepreneurship and wide-spread dissatisfaction with available jobs. In response, more books and tapes on home business opportunities were added to the catalog, and "Working From Home" became one of the most popular sections in the catalog.

Over the years, some home business opportunities emerged as clearly superior to others, realistically offering more growth potential and less risk. These are opportunities that have stood the test of time, unlike others that become suddenly popular, and then just as quickly fade away.

This book doesn't attempt to be the final word on these opportunities, by any means. In fact, the Resource Guide in the appendix lists entire books devoted exclusively to each of the opportunities that we cover in only one chapter. Our goal is simply to share what we've learned about the best home business opportunities, giving you enough information for you to decide if you want to seek more information on any particular home business.

For a free trial subscription to the "Whole Work Catalog," you can call 1-303-447-1087 from 8 a.m to 5 p.m. Monday through Friday, Mountain Standard Time. The 24-hour fax number is 1-303-447-8684, and the address is The New Careers Center, Inc., 1515-23rd Street, P.O. Drawer 339-TB, Boulder, CO 80306.

Working at Home or Home-based?

Some of the businesses covered in this book–such as word processing services and home child care businesses–can be operated entirely from your own home. Others–such as cleaning services and lawn and garden services–are operated outside the home but are still "home-based," because it's not necessary to lease an office or other commercial space. In this book the terms "home business" and "home-based business" are used interchangeably.

The Nuts and Bolts of Starting Up

But how do you start a home business? We're all familiar with the grim statistics of small business failure rates. These numbers needn't discourage those who really want to make a go of it and are willing to do their homework, however. This book tells how and presents real-life success stories for inspiration, including:
• a homemaker who turned her money-saving ideas into a national newsletter that netted her a six-figure advance to write a book, a 12-city speaking tour and an appearance on the Donohue show.
• a semi-retired woman who turned a road-side stand into a booming business with a four-star restaurant, 250 classes and a mail-order catalog.
• a lawyer and a psychotherapist husband-and-wife team who abandoned a hectic corporate life along with their original professions to make the business of home-based businesses their own cottage industry — writing books and columns, giving seminars and speeches and hosting their own radio shows from their home.

Is self-employment really the new American dream? "Twenty- five years ago the 'Great American Dream' was the mail-order business, and that was self-employment, too, says Barbara Brabec, author of *Homemade Money* and a recognized authority on home-based businesses. "So maybe it's an old dream rediscovered."

Historically speaking, the home-based business boom began in America with the 13 colonies, Brabec notes. "To many people, of course, it is new, but the idea of working for yourself has been here for as long as the colonies were settled." In the original 13 colonies, everybody had a little cottage business in his or her home — the silversmith, potter and shoemaker. People worked at home and bought goods from other people who worked at home making life's necessities in little shops in the back of their houses — "that was really the start of all of it."

In those simpler, pre-industrial times, the home-based business was a common commodity and not some wishful thinking as seen by many today. In more recent history, the home-business industry got its start with many mothers and other women saying, 'I'm tired of my job and I want to break out on my own,' Brabec says. "They start the business and then the husbands sit back and say, 'this is nothing, you're just playing around.' Then one day it takes off, and the husband says, 'You know, maybe I could quit my job.' More and more I'm seeing that. There's no question we have a real home-business bandwagon going here. All the major consumer publications are talking about the work-at-home movement — mothers especially. Everybody needs extra income, so the economy has really given a boost to the movement, and the media's picked up on the things that have been happening with everybody losing their jobs and saying, 'Is this really a possibility?' And yes, it really is."

Most Likely to Succeed

"I would never say, 'Oh, anybody can be a success in a home-based business,' because it takes some special personal qualities," Brabec continues. "It takes, if not business experience to start with, the willingness to acquire those business management and marketing skills that are essential to the success of any company, small or large. A lot of people that just start out with the idea of making a little extra money don't go very far and they drop out and go back and take a job, because it takes a lot of dedication, a lot of time spent on self-education, a lot of reading and research and networking with other business owners. People take courses and go to conferences. These are the people that are most likely to succeed."

What else do successful home-based business people have in common? "Lack of money, lack of time, lots of great ideas, persistence, creativity and stress," Brabec says. She should know; she has been self-employed most of her adult life, has written four books and numerous articles on home-based

4

businesses and publishes a newsletter entitled, "National Home Business Report," now in its 12th year. Those who do succeed, she says, "have given serious consideration to a product or service that they've pinpointed the need for. They don't just make products that give them pleasure and then try to sell them, and they don't just offer a service because, 'Oh, gee, this would be fun.' They look around and they see that niche in the market that no one else is filling, and then they jump in. Those are the people that are most likely to succeed."

This type of niche marketing is the secret of successful home-based businesses. "It's interesting how creative people can be in digging up these little pockets of opportunity that large companies just can't afford to go after. It's right in line with the low budget, the lack of money for advertising that home business owners have. They target these little pockets and go in there with the rifle-shot technique of marketing one by one and pick off their customers and clients and build very nice little businesses with this kind of strategy."

A prime example of this is Peggy Glenn's firefighter's bookstore catalog. Glenn, who is married to a firefighter and runs a word processing business — mentioned later in this book — started her catalog business several years ago and is doing quite well sending it to every firehouse in the country. Her catalog lists books on fire fighting and related topics.

Making the Break

"Our lives were full and exciting. Paul was a chief executive officer for a corporation. Sarah was an administrator for a government agency. We both spent too many hours flying across the country, keeping tight schedules, and waving goodbye to each other in airports. We were smoking too much, sleeping too little, and leading the ulcer-prone lives that have come to characterize what our society calls success," write Paul and Sarah Edwards in their book, "Working From Home."

In the 1960s, Sarah said she struggled with trying to combine a career with motherhood, was dead tired all the time and felt she was not doing either with the dedication she wanted. One day, she visited two consultants she worked with

5

who operated their business from home and "I knew with certainty, 'This is for me!'" Two years later, with a new master's degree, she quit her secure government job and began a psychotherapy practice at home.

"Most people I knew predicted that I would miss my government job and regret my decision. But they were wrong. I haven't regretted my decision for one day in the 16 years since I left the hallowed gray halls of the Federal Building.

"Working at home was like having flowers delivered to me every day. I felt healthier immediately. For the first time in my son's young life, I could be a real mother and still pursue my career. I was more relaxed, and I relished working in an environment with windows and trees and the out-of-doors just a few steps away."

Paul was concerned about the image a home-based office might create in his new political consulting firm and that he might not be able to get work done at home. So initially, he rented a downtown office with a secretary. He found himself working at home more and leaving later and later each day — some days not going into the office at all. Finally he set up an office in the home recreation room with a place for his secretary. Initially she felt uncomfortable about working in someone's home, but the fact that she would be only two miles from her own home and closer to her own children made her decide the situation was a good one.

"Working at home meant having all my files and books in one place," Paul writes. "It meant saving a lot of time that used to be wasted commuting and a great deal of money that used to be spent on overhead. It meant being free to put those resources into making my home as pleasant as I wanted it to be. After all, I was working there! Most important, the saving on overhead has meant I can afford to pursue the kind of work I want to do instead of taking business just to pay the overhead."

It all worked beautifully. That was 1976, and as time went on and people kept asking the Edwardses how they were able to keep major clients and work together at home, they decided to write a book on the topic. That book, "Working From Home," is now in its third edition. Over time, the Edwardses

6

book publishing and other home-business-related activities
made them decide to focus on the business of home business.
In 1983 they founded the Working From Home Forum on
CompuServe Information Service. Today, from their home in
Santa Monica, California, they co-host the weekly "Home
Office" show on Business Radio Network and the Los Angeles
radio show, "Here's to Your Success." They are contributing
editors and columnists for "Home Office Computing" magazine and give speeches, seminars and workshops. They refer
to themselves and other self-employed people as "open-collar"
workers.

Myths and Realities

"One of the myths is that successful home-business
people have to be entrepreneurs," Paul Edwards says, "That
you have to have an entrepreneurial personality, which means
that you are a risk taker, had parents who were self-employed,
that you were doing this from the time you were a little kid and
have already had a lot of businesses, you're very quick to make
decisions, you're really great at spotting opportunities — the
full constellation of features the tests have arrived at to
determine that someone's an entrepreneur. Generally speaking they center around the fact that they (entrepreneurs) are
real high in terms of wanting stimulation and create a stimulating environment around them.

"What we've found is that most home-based business
people — four out of five — are not entrepreneurs. They're
'propreneurs,' people who make good employees." The Edwardses coined the term "propreneurs" and define it as "individuals engaged in business enterprise not for its own sake, or
even for the profits per se, but for a purpose beyond the
enterprise. Propreneurs want to create a livelihood for themselves that enables them to do more meaningful work, enjoy
life more while doing what they know how to do best, and doing
it the way they want to do it. They're more interested in doing
the work of their business than in running a business."

"But," he emphasizes, "they had the necessary self-
discipline and the necessary flexibility to adapt to the needs of

being self-employed — for instance, they're able to market themselves — which is a set of learned skills."

The most important thing in being self-employed is to be motivated, Sarah says. On a scale of 0 to 10, with 10 being totally motivated and 0 being not motivated at all, you need to be at a 7 or above, she says. "You have to really want to do it, and secondly you have to be willing to learn and master new skills that are required if you don't already have them, such as marketing or communications, because you do have to be good at talking to people and building relationships." Fortunately, she says, those are both skills that people can develop by reading and taking classes and seminars.

Are You Experienced?

In addition, say the Edwardses, people need to be reasonably good at whatever it is that they're offering — not necessarily the best or even outstanding—but reasonably good. "The reason you don't have to be the best is because the marketplace — whether you're serving businesses or consumers — is at all places along the spectrum in terms of how much money they have to pay and the level of quality they anticipate." So, consequently, someone who's an average word processor, but is able to market him-or herself, will do fine, he says. "They don't type 120 words per minute and make fewer than five mistakes per minute, they do not have to be able to win a contest in their community or beyond in order to make it as a word processor."

The Two Types of Readiness

Two different factors determine how quickly someone will be able to succeed in a home business, Sarah says. "One is how ready they are, meaning how well positioned they are right now — do they already have marketing skills and know people/have contacts that can lead them directly into business? In other words, are they already ready or is there going to be a substantial learning curve? And two is how ready is the market or community for what they have to offer?"

8

In some instances a community or market may not be ready or need certain services, for instance information brokering. Or that community may not understand or realize what this service is and how it could benefit them — so therefore, there is not a perceived need. In that case, those skilled in and wanting to offer these services in such a community would have a big job of education and promotion ahead of them.

Obviously, some types of services are more marketable and need less promotion and marketing skills than others. The 10 home businesses discussed in the following chapters have varying degrees of requirements in marketing skill. Information brokering would be high in its requirements for marketing skill; child care would be relatively low. Cleaning services would also be low in terms of marketing skills required, whereas writing and editing or independent publishing would be high.

In some cases, people who want to offer services that are less marketable, such as educational services or consulting, are often better prepared to do so. "In terms of readiness for the market place, people going into educational services or consulting are probably jumping off from their paid or salaried vocation," Paul says. "So that they probably have been prepared in the job world to be able to do that on their own. Approximately half of the people that are out on their own are doing something that was related to or the same as they were doing in the world of salaried employment."

Someone starting a gift basket business, for example, who has previously worked in a gift store, buying association or a large chain that carries gifts will make the transition much more quickly than someone who has been working in a bank, but makes pretty baskets. Though the person who worked in the bank may make great gift baskets, they probably don't have any contacts yet and "They don't necessarily know the mindset or have an idea of the pricing sensitivity of the marketplace," Sarah says. "They're going to have to arrive at that, do more research and build relationships first. So that will take more time."

Or someone going into word processing — even if they have excellent skills — will take longer to become established

9

if they're brand new to a community. On the other hand, there are people like Peggy Glenn, who worked at the local university for 20 years and had lots of contacts in the community. When she began working from home, her success came quickly. Glenn, whose tips and information are given in this book's word processing chapter, is now considered the biggest name in word processing, and her book, "Word Processing Profits at Home," is the most popular in the field.

So, you can't always compare yourself to someone who has immediate success. Chances are they had a head start either in contacts or experience. Depending upon how ready you are it can take anywhere from a few months to a few years to get your business rolling.

Other Degrees of Success: The MBA or the SBA

Having what the Edwardses call an MBA, "Marginal Business Attitude," won't help in a home based business. It's one that unfortunately arises — "not on purpose, but simply because people are not very well-prepared to go into business for themselves," Sarah says. "They don't take it terribly seriously. So they don't get a separate business (phone) line, they don't get adequate equipment, they don't get their business license, they don't set up a separate space — they put their business on the kitchen table. They have their kids answering the phone. They don't get a business card or they go to the printer and get pattern No. 1 out of two patterns in stock. They pick a business name that does not work for them at all. They say, 'My initials are TRB, so I'll be TRB Enterprises.' People who operate with an MBA have a much, much harder time. They're the ones who struggle along—you'll find them in every business." Many businesses are prone to this, such as child care, cleaning services or even gift basket businesses, because people come into them without a business background.

The SBA, on the other hand, is what the Edwards describe as the "Serious Business Attitude." These are people that do the opposite of all the above. "They get a separate business line, they have a professionally done letterhead and stationary, they chose a name that works for them that's memorable, that is easy to pronounce and that has a benefit as a part of it. The get a separate business bank account. They take all of the steps. They answer the phone in a businesslike manner. They go ahead and invest in the equipment that's going to save them time and give them the competitive edge. They don't say, 'Oh, well, I can't afford that.' Instead, they say, 'I can't afford not to do that' — if it's something that's really going to propel their business forward."

Reasons for Failure

In larger businesses, typical causes of failure are financial issues. But in the case of the home business, Paul says, "I do not believe that's the case." Instead it's related to all of the above. Sarah identifies three specific things:

A. Finding the right business. For those who fail she says, "They've either chosen the wrong business — one that doesn't have a market in their community or it's really not suited to them." You may chose one of the top 10 most successful businesses, "but if you don't like doing any of them or have no aptitude, it will be a difficult row to hoe," she says. "If they view it only as an opportunity to make money, it will be more difficult to motivate themselves and to do the distasteful and difficult things and to see themselves through the tough times that most businesses experience somewhere along the line," Paul adds.

B. Developing a Marketing Mindset. Getting business to come to you instead of you always having to go get the business is the end result of the marketing mindset. "It's a matter of learning how to really market your business, so there's a momentum of it coming to you rather than you're having to spend 50 percent or more of your time each week — or indefinitely — getting business.

"Of course, you'll have to do that in the beginning. That's another mistake that people make related to marketing. They assume because they have done more passive marketing activity (such as) direct mail advertising — or because they're good — that business will come to them. And that's not the case. At the outset they're going to have to be working full time to market that business. But then to develop the kind of revenue they will be comfortable living with, they're not going to be able to spend 80 percent of their time marketing. They'll have to switch to 80 percent revenue-producing activity as the business matures." The Edwardses say it was a few years before their own home-business publishing efforts started producing any income. In their case, they were ahead of the market.

C. The third reason for home-business failure is the "MBA" — or not being able to run your business in a business-like fashion. Part of the problem is that many home-business owners don't have a clue what their overhead is and charge less than they would need to charge to make a profit. For instance, a person might not realize she should include the cost of packaging in her price.

"The problem is that many people, even after they strike out on their own, are still operating from a paycheck mentality that we all have — which is to show up for work and do a good job. People don't realize they need to put on a new mindset."

Statistics: Are You Working More Now and Enjoying It Less?

How do home-based business people match up with their salaried counterparts? In a series of 108 interviews done by the Edwardses, the average, successful home-based business person was working 61 hours a week. That's also the average number of hours that an executive or manager works on the job, according to various surveys.

The Edwards found in their interviews that the people who do best work in the 40- to 70-hour range. The people who work more than 70 hours tend not to do as well, Paul says, and other studies have corroborated this. "All the workaholic research shows that those people don't do as well, they burn themselves out and lose their creative freshness." With a home business, "You're still working harder than the classic 40-hour week — if that still exists. It's been eaten away by many companies trying to save money by splitting jobs and hiring part- time workers so they don't have to pay full fringe benefits and by consciously understaffing — down-sizing the company — spreading the same amount of work out with fewer people."

According to LINK Resources, a New York-based research firm that studies the home-business phenomenon, the median income for the "successful" home-business person (probably working about 61 hours a week) is $61,000 a year. For the less "successful" average full-time, home-based business person, the average is $27,500 (probably working less than 61 hours a week). The national average income of a salaried worker from the U.S. Bureau of Labor Statistics is $23,600. So the average home-based business person is actually making more than his or her salaried counterpart — but probably working more hours.

Franchises

Another option for a home-based business is a franchise. Franchises offer the freedom of operating from your own home and being your own boss, but with the security of being connected to a larger company that can offer training, guidance and support — a welcome safety net for those out on their own. Buying a franchise, however, is generally a lot more costly than starting your own home-based business. In her book "Franchises You Can Run From Home," author Lynie Arden says people considering a franchise should ask the following questions:
1. How long has the franchisor been in the industry?
2. How long has the firm offered franchises?
3. How many franchises are there? How many are in your area?
4. Does the firm seem interested in a long-term relationship, or does its interest end with the initial fee?
5. Is the franchisor concerned with your background and abilities?
6. Are you required to purchase supplies from the franchisor? If so, are the prices competitive? If not, are other suppliers available?

7. Who is responsible for warranties and guarantees?
8. What are the terms covering renewal rights? Can you sell, trade, or convert your franchise?
9. Does the franchisor have the financial resources necessary to provide continuing assistance in the future?

Franchises related to specific businesses will be discussed in greater detail in the following chapters.

Future Predictions

Barbara Brabec thinks home business will "keep growing at a phenomenal rate in the future simply because of the shift that we're seeing in our economy from manufacturing to services and the fact that there are no guarantees for jobs anymore. People are realizing that they're going to have to make their own future. It's going to have to keep growing, because there just aren't a lot of options for a lot of people." She calls the self-employment movement "a sleeping giant."

"I don't know where the growth curve is going to end. I suspect it's going to be somewhere around half the work force," Paul Edwards says. "At the turn of the century 50 percent of the population was self employed mostly in agriculture or small mom and pop businesses. We now see the pendulum swinging back. Of economic necessity most people will be self-employed at home. It may stop short of 50 percent. It bottomed out at 7 percent in the late 70s, but has potential to get back up to 50 percent, depending upon whether or not there are breakthrough technologies that create new industries in the United States that would employ people.

"Based upon the restructuring that we're seeing now occurring and the absence of growth in industries that employ lots of people, I think it could hit 50 percent around 2010," Paul says. Despite this, most people today are ill-equipped and the schools currently are not preparing people with the self-employment skills needed to become self-sufficient. "They are preparing people for the old corporate model. And the corporate world is no longer offering job opportunities. Nine million jobs have been lost in Fortune 1000 companies alone."

"Right now the economic climate — and what appears to

be the economic climate in the near future — is that it's much more cost-effective for companies to either be small, or if they're large, to out-source to independent contractors or other small businesses than to take on the responsibility of permanent employees," Sarah adds.

Currently the self-employment rate is 13 percent, a doubling since 1977. There are 11.8 million part-time home-based self-employed people and 12.1 million full-time, according to LINK Resource's annual Work at Home Survey.

Disadvantages

For some people, the demands of running one's own business can outweigh the benefits. Though it sounds great, sometimes being in control of your own destiny can be unnerving — especially since there's no one else to fall back on or ask for help, when things begin to go awry. As even the Edwards admit, "The biggest advantage is that you can set up everything exactly the way you want, and the biggest problem is that you can set up everything exactly the way you want" — one and the same. Which brings up the question of structure. Those who have difficulty with a lack of structure and have trouble creating one should think long and hard before tackling their own self-operated enterprise. That's not to say a person can't take a time-management course or attend seminars and read books on starting one's own business to learn how. A strong sense of organization and discipline are also some of the job requirements for working at home.

Everyone hails the great advantage of being your own boss and not having anyone looking over your shoulder. But, not only are you your own boss, you're also your own receptionist, filing clerk, secretary, mail person, delivery person, bookkeeper, accountant, marketing and promotion department and payroll office — all in addition to producing the product or service. It can be overwhelming and exhausting.

It's important to analyze your personality, temperament and lifestyle needs before launching a home-based business. What can be the perfect situation for a career-minded mother who wants to work at home to be near her children and

15

have more energy and time for her family and husband, can be the death knell for the outgoing single person, who lives alone and needs the stimulation of co-workers — and finds working at home alone all day akin to a prison sentence. Likewise for a single parent or a divorced "empty-nester" with children grown and off to college or beyond. Gone is the easy camaraderie of peers in the office along with people nearby to bounce ideas and questions off of. Compatible work-at-home couples seem to function very well because they can share some of the difficulties and offer support and companionship.

One way for single people to overcome the isolation of working at home is to find or start a support/networking group that meets regularly. One such group of free-lance women writers even has their own "office Christmas party," despite having no office.

Advantages

Many feel that when they're working on their own, there's less stress, they can work at their own pace and have control of their own destiny. With that sense of control comes a reduction in the amount of stress that people experience.

According to the 1992 "Home Office Computing" magazine reader survey (4,100 people), the top five benefits of working from home that home-business people expressed were
1. I feel more relaxed.
2. I have a healthier diet.
3. I take more time off.
4. I exercise more often.
5. I have a better marriage and sex life.

The same survey found that 98 percent said they were happier working from home; 96 percent would recommend working from home to others; 88 percent would never return to the corporate world; 77 percent expected revenues to grow in the coming year.

Another very important benefit for many is having more time to be involved with their children and raising their children. Even when supplemental child care is involved, parents still have more flexibility and can more easily be the

16

primary care givers than can a person with a regular job. For others, another positive benefit is the opportunity and freedom to do more meaningful work.

Recent technological advances with computers, modems, fax machines and telephone options have made it much easier for home-based businesses to operate — and even compete with larger businesses in speed, efficiency and quality. Technology often allows money-saving shortcuts like the ability to have two separate phone numbers, with two distinctive rings, both coming in on only one phone line — a much less expensive option than paying for two separate lines. This allows you to know when a business call is coming in so you can answer in an appropriate manner, even though you only have one phone line. Beepers can call people out in the field, and cellular phones can help you keep your business running smoothly when you're on the road.

People lacking a lot of money to start up shouldn't be discouraged about starting a home-based business. As one successful 10-year, home-business veteran quips "However much money you've got, you're going to blow. Because you don't know what you're doing when you start out. So if you don't have the money you're not going to blow it." He says he wouldn't hesitate to encourage anyone to really give it a try if they have the right attitude to do it in the long term and are willing to really "bootstrap" the operation. "Don't move out of your home until you absolutely have to," he advises, "and then get the cheapest space you can find. I'm constantly shaking my head at new businesses that are starting up with ridiculous overhead — it's just outrageous."

Although starting a home business doesn't necessarily take a lot of money, what it does take is time. For most people, starting a home-based business will take considerably longer than they think. It's a long-term project, and needs to be viewed that way. Those who view it as a "get rich quick" scheme will likely be disappointed. More realistically, one needs to assume the attitude that starting your own business is a bit like getting a college education — something that takes most people several years to achieve. In truth, people probably learn as much starting their own business as they do in four

17

years of college. So it's important to take the attitude that this is a long-term commitment and it may take years. If you do go into it with such a long-term attitude, you're likely to ultimately be successful.

The Bottom Line

Those who are working at home no longer have the huge division between their personal life and their work life, which can be so much more efficient and relaxing given all the time saved by not commuting and the money saved by not needing full-time child care. Another great advantage is dressing the way you're most comfortable and not having to budget money for an expensive work wardrobe. Then there's that perfect spring or summer day when there's nothing pressing to work on, and all you want to do is go fishing. You can do it!

Nevertheless, with all of the difficulties, extra hours and stress of being responsible for one's own livelihood, you may wonder what makes people stick with their home-based businesses. "Love of doing," Barbara Brabec answers without a moment's hesitation. For many people, she says their greatest idea comes when they finally say 'If I had a choice and could do whatever I want versus what's going to make the most money, what would I do?' "And they come up with the idea, and it turns out that that IS the most profitable thing to do because they love it so much they can put their whole heart and soul into it. The key is picking that enterprise that fits your personality and your lifestyle and your secret dreams — the thing that gives you that great kick—that makes you feel creative and productive, boosts your ego. Those are the things. And when you find what's right for you, you don't care if you're not making as much money as somebody down the street because you're a lot happier than they are."

Chapter 2
Opportunities in Word Processing

"It saved my life. I wish I'd done it 10 years earlier.
I just love it!" —Julia O'Rourke

After being ordered by her doctor to "get out or die," Julia O'Rourke began to evaluate her job, her career, her entire work life. "At first I thought he was an alarmist," she said, even though she had been hospitalized twice in four months for stress-related asthma. "I was burned out, and that was before it was even a recognized syndrome." When she won a car in a lottery, she decided that "this is my chance." She sold the car back to the dealer and gave her two-week notice.

O'Rourke took the summer off to think about what it was she really loved doing. "I decided it was secretarial work, even though I had been promoted several times and was a manager within the criminal justice system," O'Rourke says. She had started out as a police officer and her last title was training coordinator, a position for which she herself had received no training. "I realized that I didn't like managing people, I didn't like meetings, and I didn't like crisis management." This led her to start a home-based word processing business, especially after a few of her ex-colleagues became independent consultants and asked for her help. Today, she accepts new clients only by referral and has a life she thoroughly enjoys.

Before You Begin

Whether it's to escape office politics or to be your own boss, starting a home-based word processing business can be an opportunity with unlimited potential. Some owners go on to hire employees and even move out of their homes altogether. Others, like O'Rourke, are more comfortable controlling the growth of their business, keeping it always manageable with just their own efforts.

Regardless of your goal, it's important to take a word processing business seriously and do some important ground-work before you formally open your doors to clients. "I see a lot of people who think this kind of business means they can stay home and make easy money," says Deb Ibis of Alternative Office Services. That kind of attitude doesn't lead to success. "You should make sure you have the secretarial background, then research the market, have a plan, and start out as if you mean to go on," she says. This last piece of advice — starting as if you mean to continue — was some of the best she ever got, Ibis claims. "Even if you can't have everything you want immediately, start out with a vision of how you want it to be five years from now and make your decisions based on that." Creating a business plan isn't a complicated procedure. It just takes some time, effort, research, and thought. You can obtain a business plan outline by calling the Small Business Administration (SBA) in your area. The SBA publishes a wealth of information on starting and managing a business. Or refer to one of the excellent books on business planning listed in the appendix of this book.

Do Your Homework

Basic market research is the first step in developing a business plan, and you don't have to hire a professional marketing research firm to do it. Mostly it requires only time and a curious mind. By conducting your own market research you'll discover what's really required to run a successful word processing business and whether that's the kind of business that suits you. And, by finding out in advance what your competitors offer, how much they charge, and what services are needed by potential clients in your geographic area, you'll be way ahead of the game when you're ready to start the business. Thorough research minimizes the mistakes you'll make once you're actually in operation.

Your research tasks will fall into three categories: the word processing business in general, your competitors, and your target market. Uncovering information in one area will lead you to additional information in another area until you get an overall picture of what you're getting into.

For detailed information about the word processing business you can use a combination of published literature and personal contacts. Excellent books on the subject include *Word Processing Profits at Home*, by Peggy Glenn, and *Word Processing Plus: Profiles of Home-Based Success* by Marcia Hodson (listed in the appendix of this book).

You can get the name of the local word processing or professional secretarial association from your librarian or from your local Yellow Pages and attend a meeting or two. Interview the members, asking them why they started their business, what they like about it, what they don't like. Kathy Mandy, owner of Select Word Services and member of the Association of Professional Office Support Services (APOSS) in the Minneapolis/St. Paul area says, "People who come to APOSS for start-up information often decide this isn't the business for them, or they become certain that it is and now know what they have to do." If there is no professional group in your area, you'll need to call business owners directly. This can be combined with competitor research.

Talking with your competitors can be handled in two ways. You can call a word processing business across town and be up front about your situation. Tell them you're thinking about starting a business like theirs and want to know more about it. Most owners who don't see you as an immediate competitor (and you probably aren't a competitor if you're in a different geographic area) will be happy to talk with you. Have a list of questions ready, from specifics to generalities. "Years ago when I started," O'Rourke says, "I was shut out. People didn't want to talk. Today, it's different. In fact, now I rely on my 'competitors' to handle jobs I'm too busy to take on."

The second approach to learning about your competitors is to call them with a proposed project. You'll see how they work with customers, how much they charge, and the services they offer. Some people are comfortable calling competitors with a fictitious job; others actually have a small project such as a resume or term paper for the competitor to complete.

Determining what type of client to go after and what services to offer involves looking at your own interests, the competition and the market. Would you enjoy helping an individual shape a resume into an eye-catching, readable document that will get them an interview and, ultimately, a job? Is your background in the medical industry, giving you an edge on handling jargon in dictation that needs to be transcribed? Or maybe you empathize with other home-based businesses such as manufacturer's reps, who are on the road and need support services.

You can call a small sampling of businesses and ask them if they ever need outside secretarial or word processing services. Continue your questioning with "how often?" "how much?" and "exactly what?" Those interested in the academic market can check the bulletin boards of nearby college campuses for word processing services. Who is offering to do what, for how much?

After researching the competition, your interests, and your potential clientele, look at all the information together. In your review of the college bulletin board, for example, you may have discovered that few people in your area are providing students and professors with word processing services, combined with expert editing. If your background fits, this might be a target market. Or, a local clothing boutique may want to do monthly or quarterly mailings, but may not have the necessary equipment or personnel. You could create a personalized database for the store, entering customer names and addresses from the customer's check written at the time of the last purchase. With the right equipment and expertise, you could even expand into desktop publishing (see related chapter) and produce the flyer for them as well.

Here's a quick look at some of the services you might

offer:

- Resume writing and editing
- Mass mailing of resumes
- Manuscript word processing, including books, papers, and theses
- Direct mailings, including mailing labels, personalized sales letters, flyers
- Dictation and tape transcription
- Fax service
- Copying service
- Data entry
- Invoicing for small businesses
- Notary public
- Checkbook balancing
- Photocopying
- Calligraphy
- Translating

Once you know what you enjoy doing and what your clients want, you're free to decide what specific services to provide. Then you can go on to flesh out the rest of your business plan, including the financial projections.

Making the Commitment

After doing the research, there comes a time when you'll need to say yes or no. "If you're going to last," O'Rourke says, "you have to be committed to the business." You have to want to make it happen. Being committed helps you weather the ups and downs that are sure to come, and it can free you to truly enjoy the work, because you know you're doing what you love.

A commitment also helps you feel more relaxed about the financial investment required to get started.

How Much Will It Cost?

Before you dive in, it's a good idea to make an assessment of your total expected start-up expenses, covering everything from computer equipment to stationery. This will help you get off on the right foot, either by saving the amount

23

required, getting a business loan or finding another source of financing. Starting with less than you need can leave you strapped for cash just when you want it most. For example, maybe you didn't budget for or buy transcription equipment, and suddenly you find yourself with a client wanting tapes from a business meeting to be transcribed.

Most home-based word processing business owners agree that you'll need the following minimum of equipment to get started:
• computer and printer
• software
• business cards and letterhead
• basic office supplies
• telephone
• license, if required by your municipality

The next group of items should be considered near-essentials and should be purchased as soon as possible:
• laser printer
• fax machine
• transcription equipment
• business telephone line
• back-up computer
• accounting services
• legal services

Additional equipment, depending on your budget and services offered, might include:
• modem
• scanner
• photocopier

Prices are continually dropping on computer hardware and software, so keep a lookout for a few weeks or months to get an idea of price ranges. If you're new to computers, it's an especially good idea to buy locally, rather than through mail order, so you can get the support and service you need. O'Rourke, who taught herself how to use a computer, found that having a knowledgeable, friendly salesperson at a nearby computer store was of critical importance.

In addition to letterhead, second sheets, envelopes, and business cards, you'll need general office supplies such as various paper stock for client projects, a calculator, pens and pencils, a stapler, diskettes, diskette holders, paper clips, file folders, mailing labels, clasp envelopes, printer cartridges, and fax paper. You might wander through an office supply store or thumb through one of the many catalogs available from mail-order office supply firms just to note what you'll need and how much it costs. Don't forget reference books (dictionary, thesaurus, and specialized volumes for your particular clients), as well as basic equipment such as a chair with good back support, desk, and copy stand. If you're "bootstrapping," i.e., buying items over time from the profits of your business, look at what you absolutely must have immediately, the next desirable purchase and so on. Routine office supplies are one area where you can save money by shopping for the best price, or look for a retail store that will let you set up an account.

After determining your initial budget, you'll know how much money to pull from savings, start saving or otherwise finance. "I know 18% credit card interest is high," says O'Rourke, "but if it's the only way you can do it, I think it's worth it. At least it gets you started." She strongly warns, however, not to overspend on equipment you think you must have right away. You can plan for it, as Ibis does, but don't get too far in debt. When she does use her business credit card for an equipment purchase, Ibis pays it off completely within a year. Leasing equipment is an option, too, if you need to minimize your front-end costs.

If you decide to obtain a bank loan, ask your accountant for a referral, says Mandy. Her first attempt at a loan required her husband's signature and their car as collateral. "That was 1981," she says, "when banks didn't treat women fairly. Maybe they still don't."

Just four years ago, when she decided to buy a laser printer, the bank required her husband's co-signature, even though she had been successful in business for more than seven years. She went to another bank, where she met with a female officer and got the loan in two hours time on the basis of the business alone.

Selecting Hardware and Software

Take the time to carefully research and evaluate the computer hardware and software that's available. Products change rapidly and get better all the time, so you'll need to make the best decision you can at the time you're ready to start, then plan to upgrade regularly. Make visits to retailers, check computer magazines such as "Home Office Computing" and talk to other computer users to get the information you need.

In choosing a computer remember that you'll need at least 640K of memory (anything less will not be enough to run higher-end software), two disk drives—preferably both 5-1/4" and 3-1/2", a hard disk drive and expansion slots for peripherals you'll be adding (e.g., modem, printer), a good monitor (you'll be looking at it most of the day), a mouse and a high-quality printer (impact, ink jet, or laser).

Your most crucial software purchase, of course, will be your word processing package. Look for features such as bolding, underlining and manipulating blocks of text; ability to change type styles; easy importing of other file formats; easy page formatting; spell-check and thesaurus; search and replace; and mail merge.

Other software you may need will depend on the services you plan to offer. You might want a database, for example, or spreadsheets, or a package unique to a client's needs (for example, O'Rourke has just started using Harvard Graphics to do not-to-scale architectural drawings for a client who consults on jail design and construction). If you need a modem, consider one with fax capabilities so that data from a client can go directly to your computer.

What to Charge

Deciding how much to charge for your services is an area of difficulty for many business owners. A number of factors come into play: how much income you want, what your competitors are charging and what the market will bear. The end result is usually somewhere in the middle.

Peggy Glenn, author of *Word Processing Profits at Home*,

recommends the following exercise as a starting point: Take the average wage for a word processing operator in your area (e.g., $9/hour), add one-third of that amount ($3) for your own employee benefits, and then add approximately one-half ($4) for inflation and capital improvements. In this example, you arrive at $16 an hour. Compare this to the competition in your area. Is it still in the same price range? Does it add up to the amount of annual income you want?

Another approach suggested by Glenn is to calculate your monthly expenses (household and business) and divide the total by the number of working hours in a month (that amount's up to you; for a full-time employee, it's usually figured at 176 hours). You'll arrive at an hourly rate required to meet your expenses. From there, you can raise the rate to account for slow weeks, business reinvestment, and time off.

Pricing often varies according to type of work. Some owners have a carefully determined system, with one price for word processing, another for transcription, and another for direct mail (down to the cost of labeling and sealing an envelope). Others stick with one hourly rate for all projects. Again, check your competitors. If all medical transcriptionists are charging by the line rather than by the hour or page, there's a reason for it (in this case, probably because little page formatting is required).

Here are some common methods of charging:
• Resumes — Flat rate per resume page (based on type size, type style and margins)
• Manuscripts, Papers, Theses — Rate per finished double-spaced page
• Direct Mail — Separate prices for data entry; printing letters; printing envelopes or labels; folding, stuffing, stamping, and sealing
• Dictation, Tape Transcription — Hourly rate

Factoring in "what the market will bear" is generally best done after you've been operating awhile or by relying on others in the business. "Here in the Minneapolis area," says Ibis, "we see people in the south part of town charging more than those in the north." While you'll need to be within the price range of your competitors for most services, if you offer

27

something unique, try charging a bit more. Chances are your clients will be so pleased to have the service, they'll gladly pay the price. Also consider surcharges for rush work, pickup and delivery, or illegible handwriting.

The most important thing is to avoid undercharging, says Mandy. "When people start out, they tend to under price," she says. "You find out this doesn't work: you work for nothing, they refer someone else to you and you feel obligated to work at the same low rate." It's an endless cycle. "The market will pay what you need; there is a fair price." Mandy says she'll never undercut on price again, that it's the worst way to get a job. "You may have learned something in the process, but it's a disgusting experience." She says first-time customers never object to a price for a first-time, high-quality job.

Ibis agrees: "In the beginning, developing the confidence to set prices was hard. I used to quote a price in an apologetic tone of voice, but no longer. Now I say, 'If you want good service, you should hire me.' "

The National Association of Secretarial Services, an organization you might consider joining, publishes national standards for pricing. Their address is 3637 Fourth Street North, Suite 330, St. Petersburg, FL, 33704-1336.

When to Start Your Business

By the time you've researched your market and developed your business plan, you'll undoubtedly be eager to open the business. Some times of year, however, are better than others for starting. If you can take advantage of these natural cycles, you'll have a better chance of getting clients early on in your business. If you're going after the commercial market, start your service during a good weather season. By the time the blizzards, tornadoes, or hurricanes arrive, your clients will be sold on you and won't object to driving across town for service they can trust.

Starting at the beginning of a semester or quarter will be best for reaching the academic market. It will give you enough time to advertise regularly so that when term papers are due, students will have you in mind, or at least will have seen your name repeatedly.

If you'll be personally visiting legal and medical firms to promote your business, you'll want a time of year when you can look your best. Humidity, below-zero temperatures, and torrential rains can make you look and feel less than great–not the best situation for personally promoting your services.

Getting Clients and Keeping Them

A regular client base is essential for a healthy, steady business. O'Rourke is a prime example. Providing excellent service for her long-time contacts in the criminal justice system kept her from ever having to get out and "hustle" for work.

Most business owners, though, don't start with an instant client base. "I find it to be the toughest part of the business," Ibis says. "Because we're not professional marketing people, this tends to be our weakest point," she says about word processing business owners. Mandy agrees, saying she's more production-oriented and still finds getting customers a challenge, even after years in business. Both she and Ibis overcome their marketing shyness by developing a regular schedule and forcing themselves to carry it out. "I read somewhere that you should devote four hours a day to promotion," Ibis says. She admits to not matching that level, but believes regular marketing efforts, even cold-calling, are essential for building up a client base. Without such regular marketing efforts, business can seem like a perpetual feast or famine affair.

A marketing plan consists of both "the basics" and the unique factors that depend on your services and geographic area. The basics include deciding what type of client you want to serve and how you might reach them. College students read the campus newspaper, for example, and new businesses consult the Yellow Pages. The variable factors are determined by what you're willing to do and what's effective in your market. Ibis gets the best results from the Yellow Pages, particularly her local united telephone directory. She also relies on referrals, cold calls, and some mass mailings. Newspapers have not been a successful vehicle for her. She started out with advice from a marketing consultant as well as a marketing director she had worked for in the past. Now she updates her plan regularly based on the responses she gets and what others in her professional association have tried.

One of the advantages of using direct mail, says Mandy, is that there's no personal rejection involved as there is with cold calling. "I conclude that the reader isn't rejecting me personally–they just don't need me right now." Direct mail has been quite successful for her. She believes that marketing in today's world is changing: "Businesses want you to pursue them. They expect you to be assertive." Consequently, she's cutting back on her Yellow Pages advertising, which is expensive and isn't drawing right now, and is putting that money into more promotional pieces, which she designs on her computer and prints in large quantities. She'll also be visiting more companies personally, particularly the ones that produce the most profits for her, such as marketing firms.

"When you start a business," Mandy says, "you'll get calls from salespeople who want you to advertise in their newspapers, magazines, or other publications." She recommends avoiding spending money on these. Newspaper advertising is expensive, she says, and doesn't seem to pull. "Spend your money on good handout pieces that you can deliver in person or by direct mail. Passive advertising today isn't going to do it."

How you go about getting new clients is really limited only by your imagination and creativity. Here are some approaches used by seasoned veterans:

Yellow Pages advertising
Campus newspaper advertising
Bulletin board flyers
Personal visits to print shops and office supply stores for referrals
Chamber of Commerce networking
Targeted direct mailings to businesses
Discount coupons for first-time customers
News releases
Advertising promotions (e.g., calendars, rulers)

Telephone marketing
Writer's Digest classified advertising
Display booths at business meetings

Once you have clients, keeping them is important. Otherwise, you'll be back on the street trying to round up some more. The key? Quality. "Quality service and products is what will set you apart," Mandy says. It's what makes clients keep coming back. Be flexible to accommodate client needs, and pay strict attention to deadlines. Consistently put out a high-quality document on time and you're most of the way there. To accomplish this, you may have to occasionally subcontract work to other home-based word processing services. If you're subcontracting to an individual, Mandy recommends bringing that person into your home to complete the job (if you have the additional equipment) so that you can supervise the work. "On one job I sent out to an individual, I missed two deadlines — hers and mine — because she didn't make the commitment that a true home-based business would."

You may find that services you thought necessary to keep clients happy, such as pick-up and delivery, aren't so important. "They really only care about the product," O'Rourke says. Provide a good one and you'll see repeat business.

Avoiding the Pitfalls

No one said running a business is always easy. Both Ibis and O'Rourke warn that much of your business and personal growth will occur by "making every mistake in the book." But by listening to the voice of experience, you can avoid many of the common mistakes beginners make.

The first danger is not taking the business seriously. While home-based businesses are getting a better reputation, you'll still need to work hard to overcome the bias of "just a typewriter on the table." View your word processing service as more than just a job or a source of income. Be a professional. That means children don't answer your business phone, your advertising and stationery are well-designed and printed, and, if you're seeing clients that day, you have a dressed-for-the-office look. Without this approach, you'll be losing the battle for clients who expect you to be thorough, committed, and professional.

Another area to watch for is overspending or incorrect spending. Think equipment purchases through carefully, and don't just go for the cheapest. Look for service and other support you'll need — good relationships with your local computer and office supply dealers are invaluable. For a top-quality letterhead design, consider bartering with a graphic designer. Make sure your advertising purchases match you business objectives. If you have a written marketing plan, you can respond to advertising sales reps with, "I'm sorry, that doesn't fit in with my marketing strategy."

Managing the business to preserve your own well-being is the other major area of precaution. You'll need to take client deadlines very seriously, but also pay attention to your own tendency to work too many nights and weekends. Contact other word processing services for overload help when you're swamped. You can subcontract to them and still keep your client. For more ideas see "Keeping Your Sanity," in this chapter.

Perhaps one of the most frightening experiences is not having enough cash to meet your expenses. Don't give up. In the beginning, you'll need to make steady efforts and the results may not always be immediate. If you've planned carefully, you'll know that you have enough money to live for six months or a year, until business starts rolling. An unexpected major expense, however, or time out for a major illness, can leave you with large bills and little client work. Consider this an exceptional situation and call a temporary agency. You'll probably quickly and easily get a short-term word processing assignment that will ease your mind and your cash flow. After a couple weeks, say goodbye and get back to business. This shouldn't be a regular occurrence, but it can help in a pinch.

Managing the Home Life

Many business owners choose to set up operations in

their homes so they can care for children or aging parents. For this to work, your spouse will need to be at least mildly supportive of what you're doing. The last thing you need when working to meet client deadlines are constant battles over household chores and child care, things you're "supposed to do" just because you're at home.

Mandy, who loves the flexibility, peace, and quiet of working at home, strongly recommends that the office be in its own area, ideally with a door. The office space should be separate from the family area, or at least from the television. The physical boundaries also help create psychological ones: Children know the area is "hands-off," although they may feel free to enter, and at the end of the work day, you can remove yourself from the day's tasks by physically leaving your office behind.

Mandy also suggests a separate business line if you have children in the home. "Children should never ever answer the telephone if it's your business line," she says, "and if you have real small children, it's better to have them in day care." Ibis has found at least part-time day care to be an essential. "Three years ago, when I had my third daughter, I found myself taking care of her in the day and doing my office work at night and weekends, which didn't leave much time for the rest of the family or myself," she says. "To be professional, I couldn't have a screaming child in the background." By taking her youngest to day care four mornings a week, Ibis was able to meet her deadlines and cut down on after-hours work, and her daughter had someone to play with. "That really made things start to work," she says, "Even one or two days a week helps." The tactic helped her refocus her time, and reduced her stress factor by 100 percent. Ibis's second daughter didn't attend day care or preschool, and the computer became her competition. "She would stand by my chair and cry 'I don't want you to work anymore.'" When kids get out of the house, Ibis says, they feel they've had something special for themselves that day.

O'Rourke, with a live-in 80-year-old mother, finds that hiring a cleaning service to come in every other week is a tremendous help. "I have them do the floors and stuff I just can't get to, like baseboards." Since where you live is where you

33

work, it's doubly important to keep it clean and pleasant. When trying to do it all has you burning the candle at both ends, getting help is a wise choice.

Even if you're occasionally forced to work in the evening or on weekends, you can minimize the demands on family time by keeping these times off-limits for client visits. Strictly controlling your client interactions, either by setting specific hours when they can drop by or by establishing an appointment-only rule, will keep you and your family much happier. Your clients should have the same respect for your time as if they were working with a traditional nine-to-five office outside of the home.

Keeping Your Sanity

The advantages of a home-based business are many: flexibility for children's events or an invalid's medical appointment, setting up the office the way you want, staying out of traffic in bad weather, casual dress, and even working by yourself, if that's your preference. But like anything else, there are a few disadvantages to be aware of. Luckily there are ways to get around them.

"I love being with people," Mandy says, "so it gets lonesome once in a while." She counters this by attending a monthly meeting of her secretarial group and making frequent (often daily) phone contacts with members during the month. "A support group is very important," Ibis says, "because you can get too isolated, especially during the first couple years when clients are few." It's good to see other people who are successful, or are even right where you are, to keep you from getting discouraged. Some people find that the client interaction alone is enough social exchange for them. Others appreciate a part-time high school student coming in a few times a week to help with routine filing or direct mailings.

A set schedule with regular breaks is also important. "I start at nine and always take a full hour for lunch," Mandy says. "I try to get out of the house — run errands or go to a restaurant." She takes a 20-minute break at 3:30, when her daughter arrives home from school to talk about the 14-year-old's day. O'Rourke starts her work at 6 a.m. "Six to eleven are my power hours," she says, "and by 2:30 I'm done." Whether it's a split schedule (8 a.m.- 2 p.m. and 6 - 8 p.m.) or a regular nine to five day, find one that works best for you and then stick to it. Get out of bed, shower, and dress as though you were heading out of the house to work. You can also establish the right frame of mind by setting the day's priorities the evening before.

The peaks and valleys of client work can sometimes be unnerving. You can ride with the flow if you're prepared. Have subcontractors lined up to handle jobs during the peaks when you can't take on any more projects. During the lulls, hit your marketing hard, and catch up on bookkeeping or those professional magazines you haven't had time to read.

One of the best things to do during a predictable slow time (e.g., summer, if you're serving the academic market) is to take a vacation. After you've tracked your business for awhile, you'll see that some times are better than others for getting away. Tell your clients six weeks in advance, and factor in a day before and after to pack and readjust. If you have a particularly special client who can't delay tasks until you get back, arrange for an associate you trust to handle the work. If you've been providing good service to the client over a period of time and have a reputable subcontractor, the account will still be yours when you return.

Growing and Changing

For your own satisfaction and your clients', you'll want to keep current on business activity and changes in the word processing industry. Publications and meetings are two of the best ways to keep up to date. You'll find about the latest and best equipment and software that can help you attract new clients or do your job more efficiently. You may discover a new market after reading a new business profile in your local newspaper. Mandy subscribes to "Home Office Computing," "Word Perfect Magazine" and other business periodicals. Ibis attends computer classes to get the most out of her word processing package. O'Rourke hired a consultant to help her learn Excel inside out. Women's business groups and chambers of commerce are also possible ways to expand your world and take the pulse of the business community.

Over time, your interests and needs will change. The delight of being a business owner is that you can adjust your work life to accommodate those changes. This is where periodic assessment and planning comes in. "I make a yearly plan," Ibis says. She looks at her personal goals (e.g., will I work part time when the new baby arrives?), equipment needs (e.g., should I get the new printer this year or next?) and financial goals (e.g., did my marketing efforts bring in the results I wanted?).

In your evaluation session, ask yourself:
• were my expenses in line with my budget?
• which clients or type of clients brought in the most revenue at the least amount of effort?
• which assignments did I enjoy the most?
• what seems to be my best work schedule?
• which skills do I have that I wish I could use more?
• what new equipment would be helpful to have?
• if I bought that equipment, how much would it increase my profits?
• are there clients I'd rather not work with anymore?

With this information, you can adjust your goals and budget for the following year. You may discover that 30 hours a week would give you the income you need and free your time for other activities. Or your thoughts may turn to expanding or changing the business in ways that are more exciting for you. You might have a hidden desire for self-publishing a monthly newsletter, for example, or producing stunning brochures using a desktop publishing package. Would you love to provide private computer lessons for children, or teach at your local community college, or speak to mothers' groups about home businesses or write newspaper articles? There's no reason you can't. Being your own boss means you set the agenda, one that suits your unique goals, dreams and personality. And don't limit your planning sessions to once a year. Monthly mini-reviews will keep you on top of your finances and your goals.

A significant change for home-based business owners is moving to a new home, because much of the service is based on geography. Ibis plans such a move in a couple months. She and her husband are building a house in a nearby Minneapolis suburb, with a design that includes a first-floor office. "I'm working on a written plan for how I'll saturate the area when I get there. I'll be increasing my mailings and doing cold calls," she says. Her Yellow Pages ad is already in for her current location, so she won't count on it to be an effective promotion for her new location. Many clients have said they'll continue to use Alternative Office Services even though it may mean a longer drive. With couriers and fax machines, distance is becoming less important.

The Final Test

In deciding to start a home-based word processing business or keep one going, you'll find the most important factor is enjoyment. It's the litmus test. If you're doing what you love, you'll have a natural enthusiasm for getting new clients and keeping up with the industry. Your self-confidence will soar as you accomplish what you thought you couldn't and gain respect as a successful business owner.

Chapter 3
Opportunities in Independent Publishing

Once considered taboo by serious writers, self-publishing has become a respected, profitable activity. Self-published books such as *50 Simple Things You Can Do To Save the Earth*, by John Javna have even joined the bestseller list, and John Muir sold close to one million copies of his self-published *How to Keep Your Volkswagon Alive*. Desktop publishing software and affordable laser printers now allow entrepreneurs and writers to efficiently get the word out in an attractive format. Home-based business owners are publishing everything from newsletters to books, creatively promoting and distributing their own work.

Publishers in Profile

The routes to independent publishing are as varied as the individuals involved. Some successful publishers looked for a business to start at home, others wanted to produce a book they didn't think a large publishing house would accept and others simply followed a love of literature and the arts.

Nancy Edwards of Paintbox Studio Press was always involved in art. She won awards in high school and continued her studies in college, despite her parents' admonition that it wasn't a practical pursuit. Edwards properly earned her degree in elementary education, but hated teaching. Ten years ago she was asked to illustrate a Christmas book written for women. Today she has sold over 250,000 of her own "write your own" books.

Bob Bellotti has developed a highly sophisticated system of analyzing a basketball player's statistics to determine the worth of the player. It seemed unlikely, he concluded, that time-sensitive information like this, designed for a highly select audience, would be picked up by a traditional publisher, so he set off producing it himself. Bellotti just finished his fourth volume and has hired an agent to negotiate with a publishing house for future volumes.

Amy Dacyczyn and her husband Jim found their dream home in rural Maine, an ideal location for raising children, but not so convenient for employment as a graphic designer. Eschewing a one-hour, one-way commute, Dacyczyn searched for a home-based business and settled upon the idea of a monthly newsletter she named "The Tightwad Gazette." Twenty-seven issues later, Dacyczyn is still loving the work and has added a remote office that houses eight full- and part-time employees who fulfill over 80,000 subscriptions.

To be a successful home-based publisher, you'll need to have some background in at least one aspect of the business, and be willing to acquire the other skills with study and experience. Edwards was a specialist at her craft from years of art work. Bellotti had been a writer and editor for a small newspaper, as well as a technical writer for a large corporation, where he saw the steps involved in publishing. Dacyczyn did graphic design for very big accounts (e.g., Polaroid) in Boston, which she feels is not reflected in her folksy newsletter but helped her start the publication inexpensively, with her own illustrations and paste-up. Although she was not a professional writer, the popularity of Dacyczyn's personal letters convinced her that her writing would be well-received. Finally, Dacyczyn saw her father's success at publishing a newsletter and decided she could do one of her own.

You must be very interested in your project and feel it's worthwhile, Bellotti says, because self-publishing requires a huge amount of work and long hours. There's the research and writing, of course, but there are also printing schedules, advertising schedules and the overall management of the business. Sometime in the future you may be able to hire people to do the tasks you don't enjoy, but in the beginning, it's

40

usually all up to you.

The rewards can be worth it. Both Dacyczyn and Edwards are pleased with the financial return on their efforts and will continue their businesses as long as it's enjoyable. "What else would I do?" Edward says. "It can become fun - even intoxicating," Bellotti says.

What's To Publish?

The type of product publishable is limited only by your imagination. Edwards started with recipe cards, gift enclosure cards and note cards, all carrying her carefully rendered drawings. Her company's mission is to produce "beautifully illustrated books that people fill in with their own information." Edwards' product line now consists of a write-your-own cookbook, a menu-planner, a day-planner and a write-your-life-story book. Other volumes are in the works.

Marilyn and Tom Ross, in their book *How-to-Make Big Profits Publishing City & Regional Books*, list the following possibilities:
• travel/tourist guides
• consumer books
• activity guides
• nature field guides
• special interest books
• historical books
• regional cookbooks
• photography books
• trivia books
• folklore books
• list books
• maps
• Yellow Page directories
• Who's Who publications
• media source guides
• real estate directories
• collectibles directories

In addition to newsletters, independent publishers are

41

finding success with magazines and newspapers. Others are putting information into booklets that can be sold via mail order. Public speakers are packaging their presentations into audio and video formats, and some entrepreneurs are publishing computer software.

It's not uncommon to start with one product, such as a newsletter, and repackage the information into another format, such as a book. Occasionally a traditional publishing house will cast a favorable eye on such a project. Dacyczyn, for example, recently received a six-figure advance from Villard Books, a division of Random House, to produce a book containing information from the first 24 issues of "The Tightwad Gazette."

Where To Start

When first considering a publishing project, most people think about creating the content of the book, newsletter or directory. In reality, however, the creation stage is but a fraction of the total publishing effort. Other phases precede and follow this one creative surge.

The important key is remembering that publishing is a business. That means a logical first step is assessing the market. Your market research will vary with the type of project you have in mind. If your endeavor is a book, is your subject one readers will be interested in?

In *How To Make $100,000 A Year In Desktop Publishing*, Thomas A. Williams recommends choosing books that will be sold in a limited geographical area to a clearly identified customer. He identifies the prime opportunities as an illustrated history of your town or county, an institutional history, historical narratives and documents, reprints of out-of-print books, oral histories, buying guides and anything mysterious or supernatural. A particular favorite for Williams is the information booklet, which is inexpensive to produce and can be marketed through the mail.

Dan Poynter, author of *The Self-Publishing Manual*, agrees that nonfiction is the best venue. Poetry and fiction can be very difficult, if not impossible, to sell for at least a reasonable profit. Subjects with the best sales potential, Poynter says, are self-improvement, hobbies, how-to's, money, health, sex and psychological well-being. His advice is textbook marketing wisdom: "find a need and fill it."

If you are considering a newsletter, you could serve a very narrow market without the geographic constrictions. "What makes a newsletter unique," Dacyczyn says, "is that you can reach people all over the country for the price of a postage stamp. You can write a newsletter that would appeal to a very small segment of the population (model railroading for example), and you could get enough subscribers to make it."

Dacyczyn recommends writing about something you know well, something you've been doing for years. In her case, it was saving money. Her tactics ranged from reusing aluminum foil to calculating the cost of drying a load of laundry. In less than seven years she and her husband had saved $49,000, made major purchases of $38,000 and were debt free. This kind of experience, combined with good timing (the U.S. economy and an ecology awareness), led to her success with "The Tightwad Gazette."

Newsletter publishing also requires regular news. When evaluating your topic, consider whether you have enough material to write issue after issue. You must keep the subscriber interested and happy. A newsletter on the subject of how bad television is may seem worthwhile at first, Dacyczyn says, but is there really enough to say about it? "Before I attempted my newsletter," she says, "I carried a wad of paper around and put each idea on a separate sheet of paper. Finally, I had a couple hundred ideas for articles and decided I had enough to say to put out a newsletter. Some subjects just don't have much to say."

For directories, look carefully at the potential buyer: do you have a business customer or a consumer? A media guide, listing all the newspapers, magazines and radio and television stations in your city, is an example of a business-oriented publication. A bed and breakfast directory is a consumer volume. Carefully look at what is already available — you probably won't have much success trying to differentiate yourself from someone who publishes the same information.

For idea-generation, look through the "Directory of Directories" at your local library. It's a national listing that can inspire you to publish a regional version of any of the directories described.

As with any business, the more research you do before you begin, the more successful your enterprise is likely to be. "I didn't know what I was getting into," Bellotti says. "I initially thought I could write a marketing plan in one night. Now I know better. Start with as much planning as you can."

Finding Information to Publish

After you've assessed the market for your publication and carefully refined your idea to meet that market, you're ready to start the actual creation process.

Coming up with article ideas for a newsletter can be a treasure hunt in itself. While some publishers simply gather information published in other sources and reorganize it into a newsletter format, you'll be most successful taking a more creative approach.

"The material shouldn't be easily found in other sources," Dacyczyn says. "Why would anyone subscribe to an eight-page newsletter if they can read the same information in "Woman's Day" at the library or doctor's office?" She says that's why you won't see articles about investing in her newsletter, even though it's a publication about saving money. Investing information is available in many places. "I want to provide information that's off the beaten path," she says. "If 'Woman's Day' runs an article on how to feed a family of four on $80 a week, my readers want to know how to do it on $35-45 a week."

Assuming you're starting a newsletter on a topic you know and love, your own life history will provide you with many ideas. "I didn't think I was qualified to write a book or teach a course," Dacyczyn says. She decided a newsletter was within her range and, like many publishers, believed she could research and write new topics as she went along, a type of "we'll all (readers and author) learn together" attitude. But she realized it wasn't a successful approach. It's better to write about what you know.

Dacyczyn discovered that she had plenty of expertise to write a newsletter. But it was the right combination of skills, subject matter and experience that brought her success. Even now, when over 20 other "how to save money" newsletters have appeared, some with a slicker format than "The Tightwad Gazette," Dacyczyn holds to her original strategy. "We write about ourselves," she says. "What do you know about Heloise? Nothing. I want to reveal something about myself as a person. That's what's working for me - people want to know that." As a result, her readers gain not just a collection of tips, but a clearer sense of what the lifestyle of frugality is like.

Because newsletters are usually written for a very narrow readership, you can afford to write directly to their interests - no need to please the average consumer. Much of what's available in media today, even in newsletters, is "mainstream" material. What makes "The Tightwad Gazette" so successful, Dacyczyn says, "is who we are as people, the romance of where we live, the balance of material, the upbeat tone and my ability to produce drawings rather than using clip-art." Perhaps most important of all is her creative approach to material. "Who else would go through the work of inventing a chart for how much a cup of flour costs?"

Dacyczyn mentions balance of material. This means a mix of theoretical and practical articles. For example, the topic of how to make your marriage more romantic may appear captivating - everyone's interested in romance. But if all the articles are theory-oriented, the reader will probably lose interest after a couple issues. Spice it up with things you or others have tried, not just psychological treatises on staying in love.

Gathering information for a book requires a slightly different set of skills because of the large amount of material involved. Organization and discipline are vital. Armed with a research plan and a daily work schedule, you can proceed through the book in a smooth, enjoyable manner. In *Finding Facts Fast*, Alden Todd explains how you can use the skills of a reference librarian, a university scholar, an investigative reporter and a detective to ferret out your information. He also discusses the four ways of finding out what you need to know:

45

reading (including multi-media), interviewing, observing and reasoning.

A well-thought-out research plan may involve each of these activities and can save wasted hours or days. If you're looking for printed material, for example, ask yourself, "who would know? who would care? and who would care enough to have it put into print?" This will quickly take you to the best and most complete source.

Dan Poynter, author of *The Self-Publishing Manual* and many other books, has a clever exercise for clearly defining your book's objective and thereby focusing your research efforts. Simply write the back cover copy before you begin writing the book itself. He suggests drafting a paragraph on each of the following:
• a headline addressed to potential buyers
• sales copy: what the book is about, benefits of reading it
• author
• testimonials and endorsements
• sales closer, asking the browser to buy
• price (don't go too low)

Allow room for the bar code and ISBN, which will come later. Use the back of Poynter's book, or others, as a guide.

It may be helpful to divide your information gathering into two phases: primary research (i.e., conducting interviews or surveys) and secondary research (i.e., investigating what already exists in written, audio or visual form). Some authors start with primary research, others with secondary, but usually everyone's first step is a visit to the local library. Here you'll uncover books previously published on your subject, as well as a myriad of other tools. Consult the library's card catalog, periodical indexes, newspaper indexes, association directories and telephone books. Your goal is to track down not only material to be used in your book, but also to find leads to information outside the library, including potential interviewees. Don't be afraid to use the entire range of media in your search, including computers, microfiche, videos and audiotapes.

If you're unfamiliar with research techniques or want to brush up the ones you have, refer to a good book on the subject such as Todd's, mentioned earlier, *Where to Go for What*, by Mara Miller, or the classic work, *The Modern Researcher*, by Jacques Barzun and Henry F. Graff.

Collecting information for a directory is most quickly and easily done by starting with an existing database such as the Yellow Pages or a membership list. You may be able to purchase a list, enter it into your own database and then gather the additional information you'll need to make the directory worthwhile. A "who's who" of area business women, for example, might be constructed by compiling membership lists from women business associations and then interviewing these women by mail or phone. Or, a guide to restaurants could be formed from a Yellow Pages listing, followed by visits to each dining establishment. To learn more about publishing a directory, refer to *Directory Publishing: A Practical Guide*, by Russell A. Perkins.

Writing and Editing

Particularly when writing books or newsletters, you'll need to be concerned about writing style and good grammar. "Writing is hard work," Poynter says, "it is an intellectual and emotional workout." He advises using action nouns and verbs and recommends studying newspaper writing as an example of placing words you want to emphasize at the beginning of a sentence. Help the reader draw a mental picture by appealing to their five senses. Dacyczyn says, "We create pictures for people, because money is the dullest, most boring subject there is. When you read my newsletter, you get a visual image immediately - that's deliberate." Be concise. This is essential in newsletters, where space is a premium, but also because it enhances readability.

Courses and books abound that teach you how to organize your material and refine your writing. Gabriele Lusser Rico's *Writing the Natural Way* emphasizes right-brain techniques such as clustering and language rhythm. *On Writing Well* by William Zinsser presents the principles of good writing as well as a discussion of various types of writing, such as science, business, sports and humor. These two are general

47

books on each end of the spectrum. Many good ones exist in between. In addition, you can find books directed to a specific topic such as travel writing or inspirational writing.

Newsletter and book publishers often rely on free-lance editors to polish the final writing and spot any "holes" or redundancies. To find a good editor, ask for referrals from associates, check the Yellow Pages, or call a professional association of freelance communicators.

Producing a Finished Product

The foremost technological advancement of benefit to self-publishers today is desktop publishing. With a computer, desktop publishing software and a laser printer, an independent business owner can produce printed materials that match the quality of bigger publishing houses.

Although Dacyczyn insists on continuing to publish "The Tightwad Gazette" using typewriter composition and manual cut and paste, even though she could now afford a desktop publishing system, she recommends that beginners take advantage of the new technology. She calculates that desktop publishing would save her only five hours a month, because her expert graphic design skills allow her to work quickly and efficiently. "That's not worth it for me," she says. "But with the average person getting in, desktop publishing is imperative because they probably don't have the skills."

Computer capabilities are continually improving, so specific purchase recommendations made here would quickly be obsolete. Some general advice, however, can be made. To start your computer purchase research, look at the two major systems available today: the IBM PC and its clones, and the Apple Macintosh line. With the release of Microsoft Windows, the PC begins to resemble the Macintosh in graphic capabilities. Likewise, more accounting and business management programs are being released for the Macintosh. The two systems are coming closer together in their abilities, but it would be worthwhile to explore the differences thoroughly. The Macintosh was designed for more graphic uses from the beginning, so much of its software is "hard-wired" in, making it typically easier to use than the PC for desktop publishing.

With either system, make sure you have an adequately sized hard drive and sufficient memory (RAM) to support the desktop publishing software you'll be using. A laser printer is a must, but a color version is optional, depending on your publication needs.

A scanner and a modem probably rank as desirables, not necessities, but if you plan to scan in illustrations rather than paste them up manually, or if you have other people sending you typeset files, this equipment could certainly be worthwhile.

For software, choose a page layout program and, if that program doesn't easily allow text editing, a separate word processing package. Also select a drawing or design program and consider an accounting package. If you're publishing a newsletter, you'll also need a good database to maintain your subscriber mailing list. Additional software depends on your needs. Bellotti, for example, uses a spreadsheet program to produce the statistical charts included in his books.

More details on actually producing your camera-ready pages can be found in any of the books on self-publishing.

The next step after preparing your final document is to print it. This is one of the most costly factors of book publishing and therefore worthy of your careful attention. Too-high printing costs can ruin the profitability of your endeavor. On her first book, Edwards and her husband hand-collated the pages in their living room to save $1,000. She was producing 1,000 books and her printing costs were already at $4,000. Knowing she had to charge four to five times the cost to make a profit, Edwards realized that spending an additional $1,000 meant raising the book's price from around $20 to $25, an amount she saw as too high to sell.

For each new project, you should get quotes from several printers. Send the request for quotes out when your manuscript is nearly complete so that you can supply the printers with the specifics of your project, such as the number of pages, paper stock, ink colors, binding method and size of the finished product. Williams provides details on the bidding process and a list of recommended printers in his book on desktop publishing. Each printer has a specialty, so you may not end up selecting the lowest bidder—especially if your project has unusual requirements such as foldouts, unique binding or a tight time schedule. Having a local printer isn't necessarily a consideration. Bellotti, for example, routinely uses a printer in Michigan. "I request quotes for each edition," he says, "but this printer always comes out best."

Edwards has her books produced in Minnesota, a region of the country known for leading-edge printing. She works with a printing broker who operates like a building contractor, going to various vendors for the best paper, cover, binding, etc.

If your entire publication is online, rather than in the form of physically pasted-up pages, you may be able to save time and money by finding a printer that will work directly from your floppy disk.

Getting Your Product Into the Customer's Hands

Distribution is the term used to describe that sometimes difficult task of getting your printed book or newsletter out of your closet and into the reader's hands.

"The hardest thing is getting into bookstores," Bellotti says. "I went around to the local stores and the book just sat there. It's hard to get into the chains." This is a cold fact of the publishing world. Like any retailer, bookstores have a limited amount of shelf space, which they must fill with titles they know will sell. This presents a problem for self-publishers, but not one that can't be overcome.

The first way to address the dilemma is to go around it by not pursuing bookstores as a distribution channel. Instead, focus on direct mail through carefully placed ads in newspapers and magazines, through mailings to potential customers, or both. Direct mail is the only effective means of distribution for most newsletters, newspapers and magazines. "High Country News," a newspaper about the West, sends a one-page letter and a reprint of a "Christian Science Monitor" article about their publication. An order card and return envelope complete their simple but effective solicitation.

Selling your product directly to the end user—rather

50

than through distributors—follows the advice a fellow member of the Minnesota Publishers Association once gave Edwards: the closer you can get to the end user, the better; you make more money. Edwards has found this to be true. "Bookstores don't buy my books," she says, "and actually, I'm much luckier (for it) because bookstores return what they don't sell and they often don't pay for six months." She says book distributors who supply bookstores want a discount up to 60 percent off the retail price and require her to pay the shipping." I might make a dollar or a dollar and a half a book on those orders."

Edwards' "create your own books" sell well in gift shops, but the shops also take a 50 percent discount and Edwards must pay her sales rep a 15 percent commission. "I have a foot in two industries," she says. The book industry involves printing, copyrights and an ISBN (International Standard Book Number); the gift industry requires Edwards to have independent sales reps all over the country. Her favorite method of distribution is direct mail. Her books are popular at wedding showers, for example, and the gift recipient uses the order form in the back of the book to buy more copies for friends.

If you're determined to see your book on the shelves of the bookstore chains, you might want to try approaching the store or book distributor after your book has been selling well over a period of time. Sales statistics can be very convincing to number-conscious distributors. Poynter lists the major distributors and their idiosyncracies in *The Self-Publishing Manual*.

Another alternative, if you're willing to give up the publishing end of a particular title, is to have a major publisher, who is well recognized by distributors and bookstores, publish your book. This isn't always easy, but it is possible. Bellotti uses several methods: advertisements in basketball and related publications such as "Sporting News Yearbook;" direct mail to people in the basketball business such as managers and coaches; an agent to contact publishers; and a membership in the Publishers Marketing Association. Every six months, the Association brings 50 books before a committee

51

of representatives from B. Dalton, Barnes & Noble, Baker & Taylor (one of the largest distributors) and others. To get to the committee, the book must meet certain parameters. Once it's there, committee members accept and agree to carry approximately one out of every three books presented.

Many independent publishers consider it important to have several distribution means to avoid the "all eggs in one basket" syndrome. Early on in her business, Edwards defined what channels of distribution she would use if her efforts with retail sales representatives didn't work out. She decided direct mail would be one avenue, so she went to the library, wrote down names and addresses of gift stores in major shopping areas and sent them extra book covers she had printed at the time of her press run, along with an order form.

Selling More Copies Through Promotion

Setting up channels of distribution is half the battle. Informing potential readers that the book or newsletter exists is the other half. Your promotion efforts include those you must do before your book is ready for distribution as well as after the copies arrive from the printer. You should write these into your publishing schedule so you don't miss important opportunities that are valuable at particular points in the life of your publication.

During the writing phase of your book, apply for an ISBN and SAN (Standard Address Number) through the R.R. Bowker company (see Poynter's book for details). The company also administers Advanced Book Information (ABI) service, which lists your book in "Books in Print" and several other directories. Being listed in such volumes gives you immediate publicity and credibility. While your book is being printed, you can write to book clubs, prepare mailing lists, send inquiries to reviewers, prepare ads, send book announcements to distributors and mail pre-publication offers.

When the book or newsletter is ready for distribution, a new phase of effort is required. It consists of speaking engagements, book signings, advertising and any other form of promotion you can think of. This is an area where you can be creative in finding promotion methods that match your style and comfort level. "Going to a store and showing store owners my books made me queasy to say the least," Edwards says, "but I could send a brochure."

Edwards says she didn't realize until after printing her first book how difficult it would be to sell. "I found out later that 95 percent of the business is the marketing." Edwards had observed how one author who published a Christmas book for women would talk to women's groups and then sell the book on the spot. "But what can you say about a blank cookbook?" Edwards says. "And speaking wasn't my thing. If you're a good speaker, it's a good way to sell a book."

Speaking tours appeal to many authors. It's a chance to travel, meet your readers and spread the work about your publication. For others, it's a necessary, but not thrilling, part of publishing. Dacyczyn, who hates traveling, has appeared on "The Donahue Show," "To Tell The Truth" and many other programs. In January she'll begin a 12-city speaking tour to promote her new book. "I'm really a homebody," she says. "I'm doing it because I'm employing lot of people. I tell them, 'I hope you appreciate this.'"

The radio and television talk shows came about after Dacyczyn sent out press releases to 14 local Maine newspapers. The newspapers ran stories and publicity mushroomed from there. Articles have appeared on the cover of the "Wall Street Journal" and in "Money" magazine, "Glamour" and numerous newspapers. On the biggest day after a "Parade" magazine article, her office was avalanched with 22 two-foot trays of mail. Prior to the news releases, Dacyczyn had tried giving out sample issues, advertising and dropping off the newsletter at various stores and offices. "I thought there would be this word of mouth thing," she says, "and it would spread like wildfire, but it didn't." Since the local newspaper stories, she hasn't had to look for publicity. "I think the main way to get subscribers is through the media. They're always looking for a good story. I haven't found anything else that works."

The key, Dacyczyn says, is to take advantage of the expert status awarded you once you're published. She cites a "Home Office Computing" article that says, regardless of the

53

type of business you're in, the way to get cheap advertising is to establish yourself as an expert, because the media are always looking for experts. If you are a dry cleaner, for example, you could become an expert in the care of clothing and write a book, teach a course or publish a newsletter.

Book reviews are another successful means of promotion. One month after reviews appeared in "Library Journal" and "Booklist," Bellotti received orders for more than 400 books. These are examples of pre-publication reviewers, sources of information for libraries and bookstores that want to stock your book before customers start asking for it. Magazines such as "Outside" and "The Atlantic" are examples of post-publication reviewers, sources for potential readers to learn about the book.

Order Fulfillment

Now the orders are coming in from distributors and individual customers and your job is to fill them. In the publishing industry, this is called "fulfillment." It includes storage, inventory, picking, packaging, shipping and invoicing. In the beginning, when the numbers are small, you may easily be able to carry out these activities in your home office. Later, it could become unmanageable without additional space and employees.

Bellotti enjoys doing every aspect of his business himself, including the packaging. "If it got to be too much, I could hire a fulfillment organization," he says. Edwards, on the other hand, quickly became bored with the routine aspects of business such as bill-paying and packing orders. She hired a neighbor to pack orders. "She loved it," Edwards says with a chuckle, "so I thought, why should I deprive her?" Edwards' office has evolved from a tiny room containing her typewriter, phone and book-packing supplies to a spacious area in the family's 150-year-old mansion in Georgia. "Sometimes it looks odd to have all this modern equipment sitting next to old wavy glass," she says, "but I feel like these things were invented just for me." She can fax orders to the Minnesota warehouse that ships her books and get the order out the following day. She found that equipment such as a postage meter, photocopier and auto dial telephone could seem expensive at first, but that it pays off. "The computer is incredible," she says. "I used to pay sales reps by hand. Now I just push a button called 'generate sales commissions' and out come 30 commission statements."

Dacyczyn, too, has taken outside measures to fulfill orders for "The Tightwad Gazette." Coping with the newsletter's rapid growth has been the most challenging aspect of her business, she says. The subscription list contained 1,500 entries before the "Parade" article and escalated to 50,000 within a month. Dacyczyn hired temporaries and made plans for expansion. "Every time we traded up," she says, "we didn't trade up high enough." Three months after purchasing a computer, she needed a bigger one, and yet a larger one three months later. The same problem occurred with office space. The front room in her house became unbearable with employees and machines. She built an attached office between the house and barn, but hadn't finished when she knew it wouldn't be big enough. Finally she bought a building, one with lots of expansion possibilities, where all the employees now work to fulfill orders and answer inquiries. Dacyczyn herself remains in her home office.

All this talk of big numbers, fulfillment warehouses and large offices should not necessarily be taken as advice to do likewise. An established need must come first. Dacyczyn warns that most businesses tend to have the reverse problem: investing too heavily too soon. She advises not to expect 100,000 subscribers in two years. A number between 5,000 and 20,000, depending on the subject and your ability to publish a newsletter, is more realistic. It is tricky to judge how to grow.

Secrets of Working from Home

Like any home business, independent publishing requires skill and imagination to run it well while children and spouse are afoot.

Diane Pfeifer, a successful self-publisher and a friend of

Edwards', married another home-based business person - a professional comedian - and had her first baby at age 40. She now sends her two-year-old to daycare ("school," as she calls it), discovering like most mothers that taking care of children while running a business is next to impossible. "Children need other children," Edwards says, "and you can't have them putting Play-Doh in your computer keys." Edwards says she was fortunate that her children were past the baby stage when she started her business. In fact, it was partly her daughter's requests that convinced her to publish a book. Already stimulated by a gift store owner's suggestion that she could sell an illustrated blank cookbook, Edwards started listening to her daughter from a different perspective. "She was 9 or 10 at the time and had a little interest in cooking. She would ask me, 'Before you die, would you write down these recipes?' It would be how to make yogurt popsicles or something. I thought, I bet people would like a book they could fill and pass down to their kids."

Edwards creatively involved her children in the business from the beginning. She made them "officers" and had them help with stapling and mailing, paying them for their efforts. (This was 10 years ago, when tax laws allowed business owners to pay their children and have them taxed at a lower rate.) To handle the problem of children answering the phone, she offered to pay the kids $1 for every book ordered when they took the call. They practiced it and Edwards let them at it. "They practically killed each other trying to get to the phone," she says. "One time I was gone out to the store and when I returned, my daughter was just about floating. She had taken an order for 140 books from a distributor. I had to pay her."

Dacyczyn started her business with four children. Her husband was retiring from the Navy, with the intention of staying home with the kids. He got involved full time with the business, however, and didn't realize that his goal had been sidetracked. In addition, Dacyczyn had to have someone full time at the house with the children. Eventually, they hired someone to replace him so he could get back home. Now with six kids (a set of twins arrived 15 months ago), Dacyczyn feels her situation is unique. Her husband loves being a full-time "househusband" and isn't looking for another job.

Prior to this ideal arrangement, however, Dacyczyn worked with the children running around her. "I managed by having the kids be very independent very young," she says. "We have a place in the pantry we call the 'peanut butter and jelly station' where they can get food at any moment so I don't have to get interrupted." She did some baby-proofing in the office - cartons with lids on, trash covers, X-acto knife storage and now, with toddlers 15 months old, a gate in front of the door. She does the latter particularly because she can become so engrossed in her work, she becomes unaware of her surroundings. "I'm very good at tuning them out," she says, "which means sometimes they can't get my attention when they need it. A kid can be drinking ink one foot away and I won't see it." Her assistant, a father himself, has expressed amazement at her ability to encourage the children to resolve their own problems.

Once You're Published

Being in print seems to confer expert status. You'll be asked to give speeches, autograph books and grant interviews. You may pursue additional income opportunities such as private consulting, public seminars or magazine articles. Bellotti's goals include videos, coaching clinics and consulting to basketball teams. One of Edwards' is publishing a baby book for another author.

All this activity, however, may not leave much time for new product development. This can be especially devastating if your true love is not running the business, but creating something new. Eventually, to keep a business thriving, you'll need additional products. If it's a newsletter, a new issue must be printed; if your genre is books, a new volume. Schedule time out of every day to work on the next project.

Parting Thoughts

"And hang in there," Edwards says. "People can pooh-

pooh your ideas so easily - especially your husband." Early on, she followed the advice of a "Success" magazine article on how to know if you have a good idea: tell some people (not your friends) about your product or service. If they exclaim, "I wish I'd thought of that," you're on to something. "Their positive response gave me assurance," Edwards says. "Plus, I had a burning feeling in my tummy that it would work."

Chapter 4
Opportunities in Educational Services

"Knowledge is only a name for our relationship with life," said Cornelius Hirschberg, a salesman who spent his leisure time pursuing knowledge and wrote a book about his hobby titled *The Priceless Gift*. Hirschberg periodically laid out a plan for several years of study, covering the areas of history, philosophy, literature, mathematics, art, music and science. In a discussion with Ronald Gross, author of *The Lifelong Learner*, Hirschberg said, "I always have lived, and always will live, my life as it can be lived at its best, with art, music, poetry, literature, science, philosophy and thought. I shall know the keener people of this world, think the keener thoughts, and taste the keener pleasures, as long as I can and as much as I can. That's the real practical use of self-education and self-culture."

While few of us are as disciplined and systematic as Hirschburg about education in our adult lives, most of us do pursue lifelong learning in one way or another. It might be a cooking class, a communication workshop, a time management seminar or a computer course. Our motivations are equally diverse: We may be looking for a better job, trying to stay mentally stimulated, exploring new career options, expanding our minds, seeking relationships with fellow enthusiasts or just having fun.

59

This interest in continuing education has created a tremendous market for people who love to teach and want to mold that activity into a business. From seminars to consulting to private tutoring, independent educators are making money selling information on topics they understand, often turning their avocation into a vocation.

What Does the Market Look Like?

The range of instruction outside of a traditional academic degree program is broad and varied, but can be broken down into two major categories: general public (also called open market or consumer market) and business and industry. General public education includes private instruction, after-school classes for children and small-group workshops, often provided through open universities. Nearly any topic you can think of is taught today, covering a wide range of subjects: arts and crafts, business, careers, communication, computers, cooking, dance, foreign language, music, personal finance, relationships, sports, yoga, martial arts and much more.

Within these categories, you might find individual course headings such as Beginning Power Volleyball, A Taste of Wine, How to Buy a Computer and Software, Papermaking as an Art Form, Starting Your Own Mail Order Business, Getting the Love You Want, and Cooking With a Wok.

Such classes are popular for eight different reasons, Bart Brodsky and Janet Geis explain in their book, *The Teaching Marketplace*. People sign up for courses to get personalized answers to specific questions, socialize and network with others who share similar interests, learn more effectively than they could on their own, get away from their day-to-day life as a vacation or retreat, obtain up-to-date information, meet prominent people or experts, explore feelings or ideas in a group, and/or validate their mastery of a skill or subject.

The business and industry market includes consulting, seminars, custom workshops and ongoing training. Companies hire consultants in every aspect of business, including marketing, finance, computer systems, manufacturing, business planning and management. Popular seminar topics include time management, public speaking, stress management and conflict resolution. Many organizations routinely arrange for skill upgrades for their employees, such as training on a new computer or a management course for a recently promoted supervisor.

Some professionals work solely in the business arena, others devote themselves to teaching individuals. Many combine the two. Brodsky and Geis quote one consultant as saying, "I spend 80 percent of my time working in the community, but I earn 80 percent of my money from corporate contracts. I enjoy community work more, but corporations really pay much better." Obviously, this isn't true for every independent educator. Your course content, personal interests and goals all have an effect on which market, or market combination, will work best for your business.

Narrowing Your Market

The large number of options can seem overwhelming as you begin to consider your own opportunities in this field. Should you give seminars to professional associations, offer private instruction to individuals, pursue corporate training contracts, hook up with an educational institution?

Chances are, you're starting from one of two positions. Either you are certain you want to teach, but haven't chosen a topic, or you know the subject area you want to focus on but aren't sure how to package it. If it's the former, look at what you love doing. Rick Shepard, who offers computer instruction and consultation on IBM-compatibles, says, "I found myself spending all my free time on the computer. It was an addiction I had, so I decided I better start making money at it." At the time, Shepard was in the construction business, but computers had been an avocation for a long time. While Shepard was growing up, his father was involved with computers at Johns-Hopkins. "So I learned programming at a young age," he says.

Programming skills aren't required to introduce someone to word processing or financial spreadsheets, of course. We often take our own skills and knowledge for granted, thinking

61

we're far from being a master in the subject. But a student who knows nothing about bicycles will see you as an expert as you explain how to repair a flat tire, clean the chain, or adjust the brakes.

As you search for the right topic area, consider your hobbies. Have you been knitting or crocheting specialty gifts all your life? Have you fallen in love with rock climbing? Do you have the best paleontological library this side of the Mississippi? You might also reflect on comments your friends and family make about you, such as, "How do you always manage to look so pulled together?" or "These photographs make me feel like I'm there." Or, "You're kidding! You made this from leftovers?!"

Of course, just teaching a two-hour "Impromptu Meals from the Refrigerator" class is a far cry from having a thriving business. Not to worry. One class, offered through an open university, for example, will give you a taste of the education business and let you test yourself, your audience, and your seminar topic. You'll discover whether you really enjoy teaching classes and if people are interested. And it can be a springboard for future ideas. For example, at the end of your session, send around a three-question evaluation form: What did you like about this class? What didn't you like? Which of the following topics would you be interested in (with a checklist)? You're off and running with material for your next course offerings.

Starting in this part-time, exploratory way has distinct benefits. Shepard began by taking out a small ad in the local paper offering computer instruction. He took on students slowly until he had enough to quit his job. This kept his expenses low and helped him build a client base that would lead to word-of-mouth advertising later. He warns not to rely on your business as a source of full-time income immediately. "Don't assume you're going to make any money in the first year," he says. "You might even lose."

Shepard advises, "Look at what you would be doing anyway," and make a business out of that. "It's better to love the work to begin with," he says. "Like any sole proprietorship, you work all the time for not as much money as your hourly rate makes it sounds like you're making. I make money because I have to make money. The bottom line is I love doing it."

Another area to consider in narrowing your market is your current employment. Sit down with your job description or a list of a typical week's activities, and identify areas that might be of interest to others. Your job title may be "Graphic Designer," but you probably also meet with clients, use a computer, work with a printing company and provide project cost estimates. These are all potential classroom topics, and presented with enough creativity and flair, they could all be interesting, worthwhile course offerings.

Some people find their favorite topic by drawing on their personal histories. Were you once a shy person? Diagnosed with a "terminal" illness? Assigned to work in a foreign country? Others in the same situation will appreciate your insights and experience. Any topic that requires a neophyte to gather information you've already accumulated through research or "the school of life" has strong potential.

How to Tell If Your Seminar Will Sell

It is possible, but unlikely, that a topic you are enamored of will not interest enough people to keep you prosperously employed as a home-based educator. You can minimize this possibility by first looking around to see which seminar topics are selling, then by broadening or narrowing your topic to make it appealing to more people.

A good place to start is your local bookstore. Have there been many books published on your topic? If not, perhaps that reflects a disinterest by the reading public (and readers are often seminar-goers). Or it could be an untapped area waiting for your entry. Newspapers list upcoming events and carry advertisements for seminars. Look for repeated seminar listings as the best indicators of a successful offering.

Public interest in topics varies over time and there are regional variations as well. A monthly newsletter, "Marketing Classes for Adults," is published by Learning Resources Network to monitor these trends. You can write or call for their current subscription rates at 1550 Hayes Drive, Manhattan,

Kansas 66502, (913) 539-5376.

You can make your topic more appealing by expanding it if it's a limited one, or narrowing it if it's a broad one. For example, if your topic is "how to promote your bed and breakfast," it would probably be better to expand it to "how to start a bed and breakfast." If you are an expert on time management, consider an entire line of targeted classes such as "time management for writers," "time management for mothers" or "time management for secretaries."

Often the best measure of whether a seminar will sell is to see what happens when you offer it. This is called test marketing, a term used to describe trying out a product or service on a small sampling of people to see if it will be successful. Large food manufacturers do it all the time, introducing their newest product to consumers in a select geographic area and gauging the response. The idea behind test marketing is to ensure your seminar will be a hit before you invest large amounts of money in promoting it. One of the best methods is to offer the class through an existing organization such as an open university. With a minimal fee for a carefully written seminar description in the school's catalog, you'll discover how many people register, who they are and what they thought of the class.

You could also provide the seminar free or at low cost to a local organization. By talking with participants after your presentation (or asking them to complete a brief evaluation), you will either hear something like, "That was great, I'd love to hear more," or an unenthusiastic but polite, "Thank you for coming." The latter indicates you have more work to do, either on your presenting skills or your topic. The former suggests you press onward.

Once you've chosen you're topic, you can decide whether it's appropriate for a consumer market, a business audience, or both. And your mind will be focused and open to creative ideas for packaging and promoting it.

Satisfying the General Public

"The largest market for independent classes is college-educated adults who are looking for leisure activities, practical information and personal growth," say Brodsky and Geis in "The Teaching Marketplace." To reach this market, you can rely on existing channels, such as community colleges, continuing education programs and adult schools or promote the class yourself. You might start by offering your seminar through an existing organization so you can rely on their promotion efforts, usually a catalog distributed to the community. Appearing in the catalog is also an implied endorsement that gives the potential student a good impression of your credentials. Other benefits include readily available classroom space and the ability to test your market without investing a large sum of money for your own promotion.

After experimenting a bit and deciding the teaching business is for you, the next logical step is to expand into self-promotion. Shepard finds that a small display ad in the classified "Instruction" section of his local newspaper has been a steady and reliable source of new clients. It is more to his liking than the classroom setting, too. "My edge is one-on-one instruction," he says. "I will do classes if I'm asked, but it's not my preference. I enjoy the interpersonal interaction." He has considered direct mail, but says it's too hard to narrow it down for his diverse group of clients, ranging from college students to secretaries. It turns out that word-of-mouth advertising has become Shepard's best source of clients. And it has him comfortably busy. He says he hesitates to do anything more because he wants to control his workload, believing that if you get too busy, the quality of your work inevitably declines.

One creative method of promotion is to market your classes as a joint venture with a retail store. Seek out the store that most closely matches your topic. Possibilities include retailers of bicycles, gourmet kitchen equipment, natural foods, books, sewing machines, camping equipment and computers. In bringing you in to speak, the store provides a service to its existing customers and probably attracts new ones. You will gain recognition and the potential for word-of-mouth advertising from audience members, as well as your fee, which varies from store to store.

Some instructors join together to create a weekend

event consisting of complementary seminars or workshops. A day on stress management may consist of a meditation workshop, a journal-writing class, a conflict-resolution session and a yoga class. Educators share the promotional costs and the proceeds.

Classes for children present an interesting opportunity. Parents are often eager to provide after-school activities for their children to avoid the "latchkey" phenomenon, that block of time between the end of the school day and the end of the adult workday. You'll need to arrange with schools or other facilities for classroom space and possibly student transportation.

Working with Business and Industry

An independent educator's work in business and industry can be varied and rewarding. Public speaking, private consulting and custom training are all possibilities. The demands, however, can be substantial. If you are a speaker, you must love talking before a group and your speaking skills must be top-notch. Private consulting requires expertise and experience that your clients are lacking. And custom training calls for a thorough knowledge of your subject as well as classroom teaching skills. Add to this the sales skills required to market yourself, and you are ready to approach the business market.

Money Talks

As intimidating as that may sound, however, many business owners have started out modestly and grown into their work. Gloria Golbert, for example, started speaking in public as a hobby. "Every organization I belonged to asked me to introduce the guest speaker," she says, "and I was always praised highly. Then volunteer organizations asked me to speak, then gradually professional organizations asked me to give programs." After a while, she says she thought, "Gee, I wonder if I could charge for this. (It took a long time; I'm a slow learner.) Very reluctantly and nervously, I started naming

66

fees. To my surprise, instead of 'forget it,' the response was, 'Oh, is that all?' " For a number of years, Golbert worked part time as a speaker. About five years ago she was faced with the difficult decision of leaving a good position to risk full-time self-employment. "It was a real risk, and I'm glad I took it," she says. "I now earn more than I did at my job, and I'm having more fun."

Public speaking now provides Golbert with 100 percent of her livelihood. She is hired by businesses, professional organizations, conferences, conventions and educational organizations to give seminars on communication, time management, public speaking, personnel, secretarial skills and stress management. She is occupied with speech-giving about two or two-and-a-half weeks each month, much of which involves travel. "It seems to be easier to get out-of-town engagements," she says. It's the old axiom: if you're from out of town, you must be an expert. "You have a lot more credibility than in your own backyard," she says.

Getting business clients required "a lot of self-marketing," Golbert says. She still spends a fair amount of time making cold-calls by telephone, although most of her business now comes through word of mouth and third-party referral. "I don't enjoy cold-calling, but I do it," she says. While Golbert will often follow up cold calls with mailings such as letters of commendation and brochures, she seldom uses direct mail per se. She finds it expensive and not a good return on investment. Recently she had a videotape made of herself giving a seminar. "I send that to interested people. It's the proof of the pudding."

When Golbert isn't speaking, she's recharging her batteries after the intensity of being on the road or preparing her materials. "I think people have the impression that you get one wonderful seminar and you never have to work on it again, you just give it again and again. But today, your information has to be so up to date. I'm constantly updating. If you have a statistic that's two or three years old someone in the audience will jump up and say, 'But aren't you familiar with the more recent research?' " Customizing is also important. A time management class for a computer firm may be different than one for a hospital staff. Although the time management basics are the same, giving industry-specific examples makes the seminar more interesting and helpful to the participants.

Larger companies, in particular, will often bring in speakers as part of an ongoing wellness program for their employees. And in their concern for productivity improvement, they will often reimburse employees for education fees involved in upgrading skills.

Consulting Know How

Consulting is another way of providing your expertise to businesses. As a consultant, you may get involved in research, advising, planning, evaluating and even training and supervising. Among other things, companies hire consultants to help them identify new markets, control pollution, implement drug and alcohol abuse programs, conduct feasibility studies and collect receivables.

There are a number of skills you'll need to be an outstanding consultant. These include the ability to get along with your clients, accurately diagnose problems and find appropriate solutions, which may involve technical expertise, communication skills, marketing and selling ability and management skills. Clients will be relying on your fresh perspective to allow you to troubleshoot their problems and come up with solutions. You will probably be asked to provide a written report of your findings. Finally, the client may ask for help in implementing your recommendations. For example, Shepard, the computer consultant, is currently designing a computer database for a church. He also customized a word processing program for a blind medical transcriptionist so that she could quickly enter information into standard medical forms on her computer. In one ear, she hears the computer screen speak to her through a speech synthesizer; in the other, she hears the physician's dictation.

You may start your consulting business with a certain amount of knowledge about your subject area. Once you are into the thick of things, however, it can be difficult to keep that information current. In our fast changing world, ideas and facts you accumulated five or even two years ago are probably out of date. Shepard keeps up with the latest changes by subscribing to several publications, including a CD-ROM subscription to Nautilus. He also relies on CompuServe's system of forums for answers to sticky problems. "It's an incredible resource," he says. The forums are based on specific hardware and software interests (WordPerfect, for example). "Some of the best people in the country get into these forums," Shepard says. "And you can get an answer within 24 hours. Robert O. Metzger, author of *Profitable Consulting*, refreshes himself by periodically returning to academia for a short time. He encounters bright, energetic students, reads, does meaningful research and writes. He says it helps him get rid of biases – "all the false logic and ill-perceived facts that build up like wax on a coffee table when you don't have enough time to read or be reflective."

Most consultants charge a per day (diem) rate, plus expenses, although other compensation methods, such as a monthly retainer or a fixed-price contract, are also common. Using the per diem method, Herman Holtz, author of *How to Succeed as an Independent Consultant*, advises a $500 per day minimum. He explains how that fee is required to achieve an annual salary of $50,000, and why you should consider it a reasonable rate. A written contract will help you get paid and give both you and your client a clear understanding of the work you are to perform.

Once you have the contract, it's important to keep good records in terms of the work you're performing and finances. "I keep a student log of what I did, what my impressions were, how much time I spent," Shepard says. "It's invaluable. For clients I bill on a monthly basis, I can justify the hours, and if a student comes back in a year and says, 'do you remember when we did this?' I may not remember, but I can look it up." Small consulting projects can lead to ongoing training opportunities. Pat Baker provides PC-based consulting, helps individuals select a computer system, and trains them in its use. "The original concept of my business (which he started with a partner) was to be a training organization. We found that it was too narrow a definition to attract enough business." Some months later, Baker's partner went back to a "real job" and Baker continued full time for nine more months. He expanded his services to include consulting and has now dropped back to part time, giving him time to work on a master's degree in computer information systems.

Baker says many small and large companies provide the services independent educators are trying to sell. Even computer retailers are offering training. To compete with the size and resources of a larger organization, he says, "you have to know your market really well. Nail down your target market before you begin trying." Baker believes you can be successful as a home-based trainer if have a high degree of planning. To add to your professionalism, consider joining the American Society for Training and Development (ASTD).

Preparing Your Class or Seminar

Whether working with the general public or professional organizations, you will need to carefully shape the content and presentation format of your seminar, workshop or training class. "The best seminar presenter sounds as if he is in love with his subject," says Allan Mulligan in *The Complete Guide To Developing And Marketing Your Own Seminar*. "His information is accurate, true and important, but he puts out just the right emphasis, the right pitch of voice, the right turn of a phrase, the right amount of detail. His comparisons and examples enlighten and excite you. You respond with enthusiasm, understanding and determination.... This means the speaker spoke not only from the heart, but from a highly researched, highly developed and refined text that has become part of him.... A presentation like this is a work of art. No one can do it without a lot of work."

Even if you are extremely familiar with your topic, do at least a small amount of research to add bright new facts and case examples to your presentation. Next, organize your information into an order that flows smoothly. Finally, look at the material from the perspective of delivery: where would it be good to pause, break into small groups, raise your voice or make a gesture? This three-step process is helpful even if your class is a hands-on workshop with little lecturing. If you are teaching a custom stenciling class, for example, you need to decide how much information to present—realizing, for example, that beginners would be overwhelmed with every detail of the process—and in what order.

Before you begin your research, spend some time thinking about your audience. Who are they? Why do they want to attend your seminar? How much background do they already have on the topic? What do they want to walk away with? This will help narrow your research efforts into areas that really matter to the participants.

Research can be done by reviewing existing materials such as magazines, books and computerized summaries at general or specialized libraries. Most trade associations also publish reports and other documents. Original material can be obtained by creating and distributing your own questionnaire or interviewing individuals on your topic. Questionnaires are typically used to get general demographic data – how many homeowners grocery shop more than twice a week, for example. Interviews can bring out more qualitative information, such as how mothers feel about taking their children to daycare. The research data you accumulate can be used to support your statements, draw conclusions or illustrate points. It can also lead you to new thoughts about your subject, making you a leader in your field.

After you gather your material, it's time to organize it. The topic itself often suggests an organizational method. If you are speaking about surviving divorce, for example, you might start with a discussion of the common symptoms people experience when ending a love relationship. This will immediately soothe your participants' fears that they are the only ones having trouble sleeping or doing their work. Then you can go on to the reasons for such symptoms, and techniques for moving beyond them. An art history class may be best if organized chronologically and a computer repair class might be organized around the component parts of the equipment.

Writing your presentation out as a full report is not just an exercise. It organizes your thoughts and allows you to capture in one place all the details of your research. You can use it to rehearse your speech in private and guide you along

71

when speaking in public. When you are actually speaking in front of a group, you won't read the report verbatim, but everything will be in front of you in case you forget key points or what you intend to cover next. It can also serve as a source of handout materials. Package it in its complete form to accompany a cassette recording of your talk, or reshape it into checklists, summaries or questionnaires.

And don't forget visual elements: graphs, diagrams or other images that might help participants remember or better understand your point. But don't use an illustration just because you think you have to. It should truly be a help to the audience. Multimedia devices such as slide projectors are clearly useful for a topic such as photography, but probably are not appropriate for "Cooking With a Wok."

After preparing the content of your course, you can turn your attention toward its presentation. Certainly a speaker on the subject of personality types needs to hone her public speaking skills to draw the audience in and keep them engaged. But even a yoga teacher should think about how the course will be delivered. The skills required in this arena can be broken into three categories: the environment you want to create for the students, your role and the way you will deliver your instruction.

Too few teachers think about the kind of experience they want to create for class participants. Is this a relaxing, settling time for students that could be encouraged through pleasant music and soft lighting as they enter the room? Or is your intention to inspire and stimulate students, leaving them with the energy to put what they learned into action? Golbert recommends a bit of investigation before speaking at a hotel or conference center. It may never occur to you to find out the color of the wall that will be behind you when you speak, but Golbert remembers a time when she was wearing a high-necked, sea-green dress in front of a sea-green wall. Audience members in the back of the room saw "a decapitated head" floating around in front of them. "I always ask for a room with no windows or with shades or drapes, because the brightness of the light can make me or the audience have to squint," Golbert says. "There's nothing worse than having participants gaze out the window at colorful umbrellas and people with drinks in hand." She also asks the facility to avoid booking events in immediately adjacent rooms, if possible – "You'll be going along fine, when the marching band starts rehearsing in the room next to you."

Reflecting on this first area will lead you to the next: your role in the event. Are you a group facilitator, allowing the participants to do most of the talking and learn from each other? Or are you an expert the student seeks for high-powered information they didn't have before? Your role will also help you decide how to dress for the occasion. If you are a consultant speaking to a chamber of commerce group, you will undoubtedly be dressed in your business best. Students in an after-hours class on computers may respect you more if you at least start with a professional image, even if you loosen up as the evening continues. Whatever the situation, never look more casually dressed than your participants, says Dr. Jeffrey Lant, author of *Money Talks: The Complete Guide to Creating a Profitable Workshop or Seminar in Any Field*. All this attention to personal appearance may seem unwarranted, but Lant says your first impression can hinge on it. You don't want participants to be distracted by how you're dressed or doubt what you have to say because you don't look the part.

Polishing your speaking skills is essential to make your delivery more effective and enjoyable. You can practice speaking on an amateur basis by joining Toastmasters. For specific techniques, listen to instructional audio tapes on the topic of public speaking. Think about both the language you will use (simple, precise, clear language takes work) and your tone of voice. Be conscious of your body – hands, stance, eye contact – and the speed of your presentation. Consider having your seminar videotaped, then look for glaring problems, moments that drag or parts that could simply be improved. Join the National Speakers Association for ongoing information about the profession.

Interacting with an audience is a skill in its own right. Before your presentation, think about how you will handle participant questions. Will you take questions during your lecture or only after? What will you do if a question seems out of place, hostile or not of general interest to the group? Recall speakers you admired and how they related to their audience.

Get regular and current tips on public speaking by subscribing to "Sharing Ideas," a bimonthly international news magazine. For subscription information, contact Royal Publishing, Inc., 18825 Hicrest Avenue, Box 1120, Glendora, CA 91740, (818) 335-8069.

More Promotion Ideas

The free or low-fee method of testing mentioned earlier can also be used as a means of promoting your business. "At the end of each engagement," says Golbert, "give a very powerful commercial message for yourself, such as 'I'm also available to speak at your next convention or business or professional association meeting.' Or, 'I specialize in conferences of this nature.' Follow this with 'Please take my literature. I look forward to hearing from all of you again.' " A variation on this technique, Golbert says, is to "give just enough information in your presentation so that people are just fascinated and dying to hear more, then say, 'Oh our time is up. I wish I could say more. But I am available for future programs.' "

Post flyers or distribute brochures at locations your participants might frequent, such as libraries, stores, community centers or schools. Telephone or mail brochures to current or past students, encouraging them to come to new class offerings. Start a regular newsletter, perhaps with other speakers who have topics that relate to yours.

Publicity – coverage by the media – can happen, but don't rely on it as your main source of promotion. In a small community, you may have success by simply calling the features editor of your local newspaper or the radio or TV talk show hosts to see if they would like to interview you. Lant recommends developing a basic promotional package (sometimes called a media kit) for approaching the media. It consists of a standard media release, a "problem solving process article" (a sampler of your expertise), a biographical narrative, a "context document" (a background piece on your subject area), a sample question list, a public service/calendar announcement and a photograph.

Keep track of the response rate to your various promotion efforts so you can evaluate which are the most successful.

Keeping Costs Down

Running a business out of your home is the first step in keeping costs low – your overhead can be nearly nonexistent. Baker started his business in a store front. When his partner left the company, Baker moved back into his house. "If I had it to do over again," he says, "I'd start out that way."

Independent educators also recommend not locking into classroom space unless you have a number of classes scheduled and can get a lower rate than when renting by the month. Otherwise, rent only what you need, when you need it. Occasionally, you will find someone who will donate space, but unless you are a non-profit or have a special connection, this is unlikely. The least expensive spaces are usually churches, libraries and community centers. Look for any building that is currently used for a limited number of hours each day, such as schools, warehouses or dance studios. Shepard uses his own home when necessary, but prefers to go to his client's location. If you expand your business, you may be able to bring on additional consultants as subcontractors, rather than employees. You'll be spared the overhead expense, and the consultant will be free to operate on an independent, part time basis. Check IRS regulations thoroughly, however, to be sure your subcontractor(s) won't be considered employees for tax witholding purposes.

Increasing Your Profits

Other than simply getting more contracts, increasing your income can be done in three ways: raising your fees; selling add-on products such as books, audiocassettes and newsletters; and marketing additional services to one-service customers.

"In the beginning I undercharged," says Golbert. "Now

I charge more until [the buyer] starts negotiating." She stays at that higher fee for awhile, then, over time, increases it by small increments. She also assesses the number of people in the audience who might be hiring her for additional programs, in which case she might charge less. Likewise, she may reduce her fee if the organization reproduces her handouts and workbooks. "It's also subjective," she says. "I consider how much I want to be at that particular place – there are some wonderful convention centers." If it's an undesirable location, she'll say, "If I'm going to be there for three days, they'll have to pay me considerably more."

Selling books or audiocassette tapes is a natural adjunct to your public speaking and consulting once you have mastered your presentation and know your market well. You have already done the research on your topic. Now it's just a question of repackaging it into another form. If you gave an informative, enjoyable talk, your audience should be eager to take home materials that will help them remember and apply what they learned. And, once you've published a book or cassette series, you can try to get it distributed through bookstores and other outlets such as catalogs.

Don't overlook the opportunity to sell other people's books and tapes that would be of interest to your audience. You can sell the books themselves at seminars, display a sample with an order form, or mail an advertisement and order form before or after the event. You may want to avoid stocking the books by having the manufacturer drop ship them to your participants. Selling third-party books and tapes is a particularly good tactic when you are first starting your business and don't yet have materials of your own. Your participants gain access to additional resources and you get a percentage of the sales receipts.

A participant is a valuable contact. You can maximize your profits by selling additional products and services such as a quarterly newsletter or a monthly audiocassette tape. Set these services up on a subscription basis and you will have a steady income stream as well as a contact list for marketing future seminars and services.

Many clients who hire you for one project will hire you

for additional work if you let it be known that you are available. Help a client select a computer, for example, and they might bring you in for customized training.

The concept behind increasing your income and profits is to maximize your knowledge, selling it again and again in a number of different ways and formats.

Making It Happen

Every business owner admits to challenges and difficulties, but continues because the benefits outweigh the disadvantages. "I like the control of setting my own hours," Golbert says. "And I can take a vacation or a religious holiday without having to explain myself."

She says self-discipline is a key ingredient. "It's too easy to say, 'Oh, I'll make some cold calls in an hour,' or do something else around the house." Financial self-discipline is required too, she says. "One month you eat steak, another bread and water. It's not a stable, steady income. No one is taking the money for taxes, so you have to mentally figure that in when you get a check." Insurance and benefits are your responsibility too. As a public speaker, Golbert sees a different group of people each day of the week and sometimes misses the teamwork, friendship and camaraderie that occur in a organization. She also finds long periods of time away from home tiresome, although she enjoys the travel. Golbert has given presentations in Australia and New Zealand, and has upcoming engagements in England and Scotland.

The bottom-line advice is simple. "Just go out and do it," Golbert says. "It's fun and exciting and a way to see the world. I enjoy it very much." Shepard agrees, "The lifestyle is great."

77

Chapter 5
Opportunities in Child Care Services

"I've always been involved with somebody's children. Teaching was just a natural progression. I get a real kick out of seeing kids doing something they've never done before. Like sitting down with them and teaching them about phonics, then all of sudden they read the word 'cow' and they say 'Oh, I did it!' "

Judy Eggleston is an example of what it takes to be a successful home-based day care provider. She loves children: teaching them, caring for them, helping them grow. She made the move from public school teaching to home day care in 1978 when her third child was born. The cost of a second car, better clothes for work, driving 20 miles and the additional child care just wasn't worth it anymore. "I've got to find something else," she said. "I decided to take my training as a teacher (kindergarten to second grade) and move on to something else."

Today Eggleston is president of the Family Childcare Association in her city. She has moved her business three times and operated it in three different states. Her home is filled with six full-time children, one before-and-after-school child and one after-school child, ranging in age from infancy to six years.

A Business With A Human Touch

For people who love children, starting a home-based day care service can seem a natural and enjoyable endeavor. Often it is an extension of raising your own children. "I liked taking care of children," Bonnie Holman says. "And I wanted to stay home with my daughter, who is now in the fourth grade. I

79

decided to try day care." The work involves choosing activities that carefully feed young minds, providing guidance and supplying generous amounts of love, with a dose of discipline for good measure. The joy of working with children, say many business owners, is greatly enhanced by seeing the delight of the parent, who knows his or her child is well cared for.

But a day care center is also a business. It requires record keeping, contracts, interviews, insurance and other legalities. As with any home-based business, keeping personal and professional lives separate is a challenge–particularly when a group of other people's children is in your home every day.

With these two aspects in mind – child care and business – you can begin to assess whether a day care business is right for you. First, look at your desire and ability to work with children. "This can be a very high stress business," Kathleen McCormick says. "Parenting is stressful in and of itself. Parenting other children can be too. You have to really examine your temperament and your resources, including the resources your family can provide, as well as those in your immediate surroundings or those a phone call away." McCormick started her business with the daughter of a teaching mother, who would care for the child herself in the summer months. It was a commitment McCormick felt she could handle.

If you lack experience in working with groups of children you might want to "borrow" some children and have them come in for a sample day. Or volunteer for a day (not just an afternoon) at another day care provider's home. You may discover you're not suited for the work at all or only want to do it part time, which is one option.

Holman carefully researched the day care business until she felt confident she could succeed. First, she purchased books on child care businesses and read them from cover to cover. Then she visited local child care establishments, both home day cares and centers. Even though her daughter had been in child care for several years, Holman didn't assume her knowledge was complete. "I was looking for fees, questions they asked parents on an initial interview, the ratio of children per caregiver and how their general day went – what they did and what time they had lunch," Holman says. "I wanted an overall picture. I wanted to check several places, and take the best things from each." This is also the method she used for setting her prices. She calculated the average of other providers' fees.

Interviewing day care providers, especially those in your geographic area, is an essential activity for determining what the business is like. If you go on to actually open a day care, these contacts become an invaluable support network. In McCormick's Minneapolis neighborhood, for example, the demand for child care is tremendous, so providers have little sense of competition. They welcome the opportunity to talk with newcomers, because they know a need exists and because they received help in starting up themselves. "There are six day cares in our neighborhood," McCormick says, "but we always encourage families to start one. We figure, the more the merrier!" The providers have formed a group that meets monthly. They go out for dinner, or have a trainer come in or simply exchange information.

Also look carefully at the area you live in to determine what kind of families make up the neighborhood. Are they "part-time families," i.e., those that have at least one parent working only part-time, or full-time families? What is their income level? This will help you decide if your goals match the needs of your community.

In addition to personal interviews, much information can be obtained through your local day care association. One trick in all of your research, Eggleston says, is that you must be smart enough to ask the question, "What are some things that my family is going to have to put up with?" She says some providers are so busy telling you about how to get into the business, they forget to talk about the drawbacks. And, like any business, drawbacks exist. For example, Eggleston says, often the husband of a potential day care provider will say, 'Sure honey, do anything you want to do.' "Then, when honey does whatever she wants to do, he is really bent out of shape because she's no longer free to come and go as he wants her to," Eggleston says. She suggests that you not start your business until your husband and family know as much as you do about

81

the business. They should understand what will be involved, what will be required of them, and what sacrifices are demanded by having children in your home every day. Everyone needs to agree that the sacrifices are worth it, she says. "Husband and sons can no longer run around in underwear and t-shirts," she says. "That's a sacrifice for them." They must know about it and be willing to comply.

Not everyone compiles their day care research and goals into a business plan, but it is a good idea, especially if you are leaving a full-time job. A plan can help you analyze the costs and benefits of starting a business and can force you to identify goals. "I didn't have to do a business plan," McCormick says, "because I wasn't driven by the economics, whereas a neighbor of mine went through the process because she was leaving a job. Now I do look at what make-up of families and children I need to procure X amount of money."

The Issue of Licensing

Starting a day care business involves complying with certain legalities required by the state and city where you live. Some of these regulations are applicable only to licensed providers; others affect all home-based day care businesses.

Licensing is how a government agency ensures that its requirements are being met by a day care provider. This can be helpful to parents looking for a provider, but is certainly no guarantee of good care. According to some estimates, only 10 percent of providers are licensed.

Holman is a prime example of a provider who has opted out of licensing, although she has fulfilled all of its requirements including continuing education and knowing CPR. She applied for a license immediately upon quitting her outside job, but because the agency was backlogged it took them two years to get to her name on the list. When they finally did contact Holman, she found their requirements for licensing included numerous meetings, all held during the day. By then Holman was already operating her day care business and couldn't attend the meetings. She tried discussing the problem with agency administrators, asking them to set up alternatives to the day-time meetings. When she met with icy resistance, she said "Forget it."

Because Holman is adamant about providing high-quality child care that meets safety regulations, she has not experienced problems attracting parents even though she operates without a license. She follows the regulations for child restraint and insurance when taking children in her vehicle, as well as in providing space and sleeping arrangements in her home. Red Cross certification in first aid and CPR for infants and children are a must, she says.

The benefits of being a licensed provider, in addition to attracting parents who are looking for the governmental seal of approval, are the opportunity to participate in food reimbursement and grant programs, networking possibilities and referrals. Even though McCormick started her business with just one child, she became licensed. "I did it for many reasons," she says, "including that I could participate in the food reimbursement program to licensed providers and obtain a certain level of insurance that could only be acquired by being licensed." She also receives many calls from potential clients as a result of being licensed.

In the majority of states, licensing is administered through social services, human services or welfare agencies. In some states, the health department is responsible for licensing, and in other states, regulation is through the children's services office. Day care regulations differ from state to state. In some states, Eggleston says, you simply register. In others, you must have a license. Many states have begun a fingerprint system, which Eggleston says is good protection for the children, but she believes it should be a requirement for anyone working with children, including teachers.

The specific rules of running a day care also vary from state to state and usually cover physical space requirements, age groups, group size, staff qualifications (including continuing education), and staff/child ratios. The state may require that toys be geared to the age group you care for, that pets be immunized and that you personally pass a physical examination. Pre-certification classes in child development and nutrition training are usually required, and in states that demand a periodic license renewal, additional workshops and courses specific to childcare must be completed before you can renew your license.

In addition, the health department typically has regulations about issues dealing with food and sanitation, and the fire department has codes for fire prevention and safety. You may need to install a fire extinguisher and an additional fire alarm, for example, or purchase gates to keep young ones out of dangerous areas. If you have children of your own, these may be things you have considered buying anyway. Local governments often have requirements that differ from the state's, so check carefully to ensure you are meeting both. Zoning ordinances may affect your ability to run a business from your home, assuming it is in a residential district.

Also check your homeowner's insurance policy to see if you are covered if an accident occurs with the children in your home or vehicle. You can usually get a rider on your policy to address these issues.

Setting Up The Environment

Preparing to care for children in your home can be a fairly easy and inexpensive task if you already have one or more children of your own. Basically, you'll need to prepare the surroundings and supplies for the children, and establish the space and methods for handling the business side of the work.

Most day care owners start with toys and other equipment used by their own children. A caveat applies here: your children should not be expected to share their personal toys with your day care clients. The day care must be separate from your childrens' rooms and personal belongings. This gives your children their own space and gives them the power to choose if they want to bring other children into it. Holman's day care clients eagerly await the arrival of her daughter at the end of the school day. Most often, the fourth-grader takes the younger children into her room, ardently teaching them new things and helping them. But in the 15 percent of the time that she's "perturbed" that someone's in her home, she is free to go to her room and close the door.

Eggleston bought a second television so that her own, older children could watch programs of their choice, some of which are inappropriate for pre-schoolers. McCormick bought extra duplicate toys because certain ages have a difficult time sharing.

Garage sales are perhaps the best place to purchase additional toys. Eggleston, who is on her third toy kitchen center, has found that buying quality equipment, such as Fisher Price toys, is well worth the extra cost. She also recommends buying from day care providers who are going out of business and from people with grown children who are ready to part with toys. McCormick takes advantage of Minneapolis grants to help with the cost of insurance, portable cribs, high chairs, outdoor equipment and other big purchases.

Of course, running a day care business is more than just caring for children. You will need to set aside an area in your home to do your bookkeeping, store client files and prepare contracts. "There is a lot of paperwork in this business," McCormick says, "especially if you are involved with a food reimbursement program and if you want to take advantage of tax deductions associated with having a home business." The latter is not a minor event, as most providers discover once they start tracking the expenses they considered too small to record. Replacing toys and purchasing groceries for children's meals are obvious expenses and should be recorded on the books. But don't overlook gas and car maintenance receipts if you take the children on outings; washer and dryer costs for blankets, sheets and towels the children use; cleaning supplies; utility charges; party favors; movie tickets; and pizza parlor receipts.

Two excellent books to help you with record keeping are available from Red Leaf Press, a division of the non-profit organization Resources for Child Care (RCC), which McCormick deems "a great advocate for day care providers." One book is "The Basic Guide to Family Day Care Recordkeeping." The other is "Family Day Care Tax Workbook," which is updated annually. Both volumes are by Tom Copeland, an attorney employed by RCC. Red Leaf Press also offers other helpful materials including "Sharing in the Caring," a packet of forms for establishing policies, writing contracts and other nuts-and-bolts activities; "Family Day Care Contracts and Policies," also by Tom Copeland; and, one of their most popular items among providers not inclined to paperwork – a calendar keeper, which helps you record emergency numbers, mileage, monthly expenses reports and food and attendance logs. It even suggests activities you can do with the children. Contact Red Leaf Press, at 450 North Syndicate, Suite 5, St. Paul, Minnesota 55104-4125; telephone: (800) 423-8309, fax (612) 645-0990.

Those who are uncomfortable with numbers, McCormick says, should find an accountant who has expertise in day care. Attend a workshop offered by the accountant or set up a personal appointment directly. This is a good suggestion even for the math literate because an accountant can help you set up your bookkeeping system and advise you on tax laws. A lawyer is another helpful professional to have in your service. He or she can review your contract and your insurance policies, helping you to prevent legal problems and avoid liability. Ask for referrals from other day care providers or your local bar association and try to find an attorney with experience in the day care field.

Doing Business

A key component in setting up a day care business is establishing policies: opening and closing times, late pick-ups, vacation, sick leave, sick children. Your position on some of these policies will be influenced by state requirements; others are entirely up to you.

Policies should be written into a formal contract, which is reviewed at the time of the initial interview and later signed by both you and the parents. Make sure the contract includes the amount you expect parents to pay for child care and when you expect them to pay. Holman recommends payment in advance to keep things simple and avoid hard feelings.

Eggleston's contract allows her to take five professional days a year without a loss in pay. This year, for the first time, she will be closed for two weeks at Christmas, following the lead of many day care businesses that close between Christmas and New Year's. She lets parents know well in advance. Holman does the same for her time away, and counts on her clients to inform her of their vacations as well.

McCormick always takes her summers off. "When I interview families they know I close the end of June and begin after Labor Day." Her clients agree and find alternatives. Some have seasonal employment themselves (tax accounting or teaching, for example). Others find child care for the summer and take vacations of their own. They might hire a high school student for the summer, which often costs less than paying McCormick.

Providers occasionally forget, or don't realize, that they have control over their daily and yearly schedules. Holman started her business with a weekly financial goal that she expected to meet with three full-time clients. When everyone she interviewed wanted part-time care, she changed her focus and now has a successful and flexible schedule. She cares for one child from 9 a.m. to 4 p.m. and another from 8 a.m. to 1:30 p.m., Monday through Friday. A third child stays from 8 a.m. to 1:30 p.m. one day a week. The parents of these children are working part-time or have other activities on a part-time basis. "I'm very flexible," Holman says. "I can take the children extra days or hours. Parents like that." It also allows Holman to be the back-up provider for three other children.

This year McCormick went to a four-day schedule rather than five. "I had more children coming back this fall than I could handle," she says. Previously, she catered to the part-time market. Now she has four full-time children. "I had to look at what I could do. There I was at 11 p.m. peeling my carrots for the next day. I thought if I had that one day a week to catch up – do my paperwork and run errands – I could make it. " She advises providers to set up arrangements that work for them. Her own child's day care provider worked only three days a week so she could complete her master's degree program.

The initial interview, where all of this is discussed, is important to parents and providers alike. (The assumption is that you have pre-screened potential clients over the telephone before inviting them into your home for an interview.) This is the time to be completely honest about your policies and goals. Parents who don't find a match won't hire you, but that also means you won't be constantly battling over agreements you couldn't make in the first place. Providers can be assured that parents who want what they offer will find them, usually through referrals.

The initial interview is also the time for you to get to know the parents. Many a provider has had regrets after accepting a child they liked, but who had parents she didn't. Prepare a list of questions before the interview that you feel will give an accurate picture of the parents' attitudes and beliefs. Helen McCrorey and Dolores McCrorey offer some sample questions in their book *The Business of Family Day Care*:

- What do you recommend as an effective means of discipline?
- Why are you considering in-home care rather than a center?
- What are your normal working hours?
- If the client is a single parent, will the absent parent be allowed to pick up the child?
- Do you foresee any problems with your child adjusting to a new environment?
- Does your child have any behavior problems I should be aware of?
- What are your child's security items (e.g., stuffed animal)?
- Do you allow your child to watch television if programs are screened and the time spent watching is limited?
- Are there any activities you do not recommend for your child?
- Any dietary concerns?
- Any health problems?
- Does your child prefer playing with others or being alone?
- How well does he amuse himself with toys, picture books, or puzzles?

You will probably think of other questions as well. The goal is to get a good understanding of the child and parents you would be taking on as clients. This information will also help you set your fees. The fee for a toddler who is toilet-trained, for example, will be different than the fee for an infant or a school-age child. The number of hours you care for the child will obviously also be a key element. Don't forget to factor in the number of meals you will provide, any specialized services and the cost of field trips, which will increase your insurance premiums. Many providers have special rates for the second and third child from one family. Because rates vary across the United States, check with your local day care association and other providers in your area to get a range of fees currently being charged. Eggleston's sister, for example, runs a day care in North Carolina, which has one of the lowest rates for childcare ($50/week). Eggleston's neighboring town of Boulder, Colorado, has one of the highest ($150/week for infants). If a family's situation changes, requiring more or unusual child care hours, for example, do not hesitate to renegotiate the fee and the contract.

Go over the contract and send it home with the parent, along with an application form that asks for medical information and emergency contact names. Both forms can be further discussed at the time of the follow-up interview, when the contract can be signed by both parties. What follows is usually a probationary period, a pre-determined block of time, ranging from 30 to 90 days, during which both you and the parents can decide if the arrangement is working. A probationary period allows either of you to gracefully end the relationship if for any reason it isn't satisfactory.

Getting Clients

The difficulty you will experience in obtaining clients will depend on your region of the country, area within a city and your own policies and fees. Many providers find that formal advertising is unnecessary or useful only in the beginning of their business. Holman advertised in the classified section of her city's newspaper when she started. Since then she has relied on word-of-mouth promotion. Likewise, whenever Eggleston moved to a new city, she placed an ad but discontinued it when she had enough new parents, thereafter relying on referrals from existing clients. "Being recommended by someone who is real satisfied is a tremendous way to get business," she says.

Recommendations are most likely to occur if you have

put effort into building and maintaining a good relationship with your clients. Parents want to know their child is special to you and that you are caring for the child as you would your own. They probably do not find it a completely stress-free experience to drop the child off in the morning and drive away. Show your concern for their situation by talking with them about the day's activities or their child's delightful antics the previous afternoon. Put up a bulletin board for day care families, where parents can post announcements. Or, invite parents to help out with holiday parties, field trips or other special activities. "Establish a good relationship with the children and with the parents," Holman says, "because if someone is going to take care of your child you want them to be polite and kind and considerate to you as well as your children."

McCormick, too, says word of mouth is her main source of new business, along with referrals from various public agencies and day care associations. She often gets calls from private referral agencies, those organizations that contract with larger businesses to coordinate employees' day care needs, asking if she has any openings. Being in the right neighborhood doesn't hurt either. "In South Minneapolis," she says, "people will pull you off the street when you're out walking and ask you if you provide childcare. My provider was across the street and two others were in the neighborhood, who became my mentors and supporters."

Free referral services can be a good source of business, but beware the referral service that demands a fee or a discount to put your name on the list. "I refuse to pay to get on a referral service," Eggleston says. "Day care services where I live are already $50 to $75 per week cheaper than a nearby community. When I was asked to give a discount to be on a referral list, I asked, "Why should I give your employees a discount? It's already cheaper if they use my services.' "

Company newsletters are another form of advertising. Larger companies usually publish a newsletter for their employees and may accept non-employee advertising for a nominal fee. You can also distribute brightly colored flyers to businesses that might have customers looking for day care.

Beauty salons are a good example. Talk with the business owner to see if she would be open to displaying your flyer. Or mount 3 by 5 cards on bulletin boards in laundromats, schools, grocery stores or any other business that encourages it.

The Daily Routine

Children need a varied schedule that allows time for rest, play, group activities and solo activities. Full-time care will include lunch (and maybe breakfast, depending on the hours you set), snack times, naps, and clean-up time. Don't forget to leave time for hand washing and tooth brushing and, if you have infants and toddlers, diaper changing and toilet training.

A schedule, rather than a completely unstructured day, helps you and the children. It provides a balance between activity and quiet times, something every human being needs each day. Planning also encourages you to spend some time thinking about the educational content of your day.

Among the activities you may want to schedule are work time, free play (when children can explore according to their own interests), circle time – group activities such as story-telling or singing, meal time, rest time, outdoor play, small group time (working closely with you on a particular activity or subject), clean-up time and nap time. Older children who no longer need naps can be encouraged in quiet activity during regular nap time.

Patricia Gallagher gives 25 sample activity plans (enough for a month) in her book, *Start Your Own At-Home Child Care Business*. The plans can be used as is or modified to meet your own schedule and the ages of children in your care. She includes activities ranging from "The ABC Song" to finger-painting to "name things that are yellow."

In planning activities, think about what your own child would like to do. A hobby or personal collection can be the topic for a circle time or small group activity. "There is a tremendous amount of resources for working with children," McCormick says. Tap these resources, from books to videotapes, when deciding what might be appropriate for your children. Also talk to other providers for new ideas and tips.

Getting out of the house can be refreshing for both you and the children. Holman regularly takes her children to the park. There the children expend physical energy, and Holman gets to talk with other mothers. Day care providers have taken field trips to museums, gone to an afternoon movie or had lunch at a pizza parlor. (Note: Make sure your insurance covers accidents that might occur while you are out.)

Clean-up times teach children the importance of putting away their toys and cleaning up their messes, and it is also a way to preserve your home for your family. "You have to guard against trashing the whole house," Eggleston says. "After lunch, I load the dishes and run the vacuum. I have the little kids pick up after themselves."

Many day care providers find their greatest challenge is coordinating caregiving with other tasks like doing the dishes. Do the cleaning and maintenance you must do to keep the environment pleasant, but remember that running the day care is your full-time job. Just as you wouldn't expect yourself to do the mending or write family letters at an employer's office, likewise don't expect to accomplish all of your personal tasks while the children are napping or otherwise engaged. Your responsibility, and what you are paid to do, is care for children.

If you need help in caring for the children, perhaps because you have an appointment you cannot reschedule, choose a caregiver wisely. You might know a friend or relative who would be qualified. Keep in mind that most states have regulations about who your substitute can be. He or she must be over 14, for example, and if under 18 can watch the children for no more than two hours. A teenager is a questionable choice in any case. "Having them take care of one child for a couple hours would be okay," Eggleston says, "but six are enough to challenge me. I wouldn't want to give that to a teenager." Eggleston says she can get people from several good groups, such as Take A Break, Inc., but it's an expensive alternative. Fees in her area are $30-40 just to use this service, plus $8 an hour for a certain number of children. On the rare occasion when Holman needs help, she brings in someone her families already know and trust.

Meeting Problems Head-on

Problems are certain to occur in your day care business. It may be difficult children, unreasonable requests from parents, broken contracts or missed payments. They are all situations that can be worked through, however, as witnessed by the experience of other providers. You can learn from their failures and successes, and do as much as possible to prevent the problems from occurring in the first place.

A common problem is parents who make unreasonable requests. You must simply know what you will and won't do, and be willing to say no. Often, a parent will call at the last minute, saying, "I need to run to the bank first, so I'll be by to pick up Cory at 5:45." Even though your closing time is 5:30, you meekly agree to this impingement on your time and your policy. The parent arrives at 5:50, not 5:45, and your family's dinner is now 20 minutes late. "They think you don't have a life," Eggleston says, "that you'll just be hanging around. I have learned to say, 'No, that won't work. You will need to pick her up by 5:30 at the latest.'" Eggleston asks parents to pick up their children as close to 5:00 as possible and tries to have everyone out by 5:30. "This is a more wholesome environment for a healthy marriage," she says. "You don't want the children challenging your marriage."

Other unusual requests may include special diets or cloth diapers instead of plastic. You must decide what is "unreasonable" for you. Eggleston will occasionally honor a cloth diaper request, but she was trained to clean a cloth diaper immediately, not drop it in a soaking pail. "It should be cleaned right away," she says, "and that's something I'm not going to do."

Occasionally, a child may become a problem, either individually or as a part of a group. The child may throw temper tantrums or start biting. Get the child under control as quickly as possible, protecting other children from attack. Then talk with the parents.

Changes in a family's economic status or the child's

93

entering first grade may cause the child to become difficult or rambunctious. These changes may mean the child no longer fits in with the group of children you care for. You and the child's parents must learn when it's time to let a child move on to a different provider. "Sometimes you have to be wise enough to know when to tell the parent they need a different setting," Eggleston says. "I had to let a couple of girls go recently. It's difficult when you try to run the older ones and younger ones together. The younger ones want to do what the older ones are doing and it just doesn't work out."

Although many home-based day care owners accept infants, it does require special effort and, occasionally, unique worries. Some years ago a day care child died in Eggleston's home from Sudden Infant Death Syndrome (SIDS). This upset her greatly, of course, and for a while she stopped taking infants. Then, after a couple begged her to take their baby, she reluctantly agreed. "You tend to hover," she says, "but I was always a person to try to overcome what I was afraid of. I went back to doing it. The little girl was a dream to keep." Later she accepted the 4-month-old brother of a boy she already cared for. "I was a little anxious," she said, "but I learned to ride it out. If I had had a screamer or a crier or a never-happy baby, I may have quit infant care and never gone back."

Caring for a sick child can be a particularly difficult problem. If the child becomes ill or injured while at your home, you must provide the child with whatever medical care he or she needs and, of course, contact the parents. Many states prohibit providers from admitting children who are obviously ill or have a contagious disease. If it is a minor illness, the decision is up to you. And if a parent asks you to give a child medicine, you must have their written permission to do so. Some states, such as California, require hospitals and other facilities to provide treatment only if you bring the child in with a parental authorization form. Have this form completed in advance and keep it readily available at all times.

Taking Care of Yourself

"Most people who leave (this business) are burned out,"

Eggleston says. "They say they need more adult contact. That's their own fault. You have to take responsibility for yourself, be involved in adult things. Take care of yourself and your family."

These are words of wisdom that every day care provider comes to appreciate sooner or later. Spending eight to ten hours every day with three to six children under the age of five takes its toll if you don't take precautionary measures. A combination of personal and professional activities usually provides the solution.

For yourself, get a perm once in awhile, Eggleston says, or a facial or enroll in an exercise class. She attends at least two monthly women's meetings, one business-related, the other an affiliation of her church. A year ago, she was offered a business trip to New York as part of the Save the Children program. Even if you are a homebody, as Holman admits she is, you will occasionally feel isolated. As a Mary Kay beauty consultant, she sees adults at least two evenings a week. She completes errands on the weekends, and in general feels a balance between her in-home and outside activities.

The telephone is McCormick's primary link to other people. She uses it to talk with friends and other day care providers and she tries to make the best use of her phone time by simultaneously preparing vegetables or tidying the house.

In addition to protecting yourself from burnout, you must protect your family too. "The house shouldn't always be a mess," Eggleston says, "or the laundry undone. And once in a while take each other out for dinner, saying, 'This is the fruit of my labor here.'" Maintaining a normal family life is easier if you have a separate space for the day care activities. In most homes, however, this is not the case. Because she uses her whole house for day care, McCormick finds it difficult to keep the area up to her standards. Her solution is to periodically hire someone to help clean.   Cleanliness and order, however, is only one aspect of preventing the business from infringing on your family. When Eggleston's older children were in high school, she often provided night-time child care and was unavailable for many of her children's extra-curricular events. They came to resent this a bit, although they realized that

95

without Eggleston's income-producing activities, they wouldn't have the money to enjoy certain activities and material goods. Eggleston heard them, though, and now goes out of her way to call them and even send them a little money, playfully saying, "I made this from babysitting." She also makes a concerted effort to attend her 14-year-old's football games and other activities.

Final Concerns

If you are considering a home-based day care, "really use the books that are available for reference," Holman says. "You don't have to follow them exactly, but read at least two books." They will provide you with details not discussed here and give you a broader understanding of what's involved in a day care business. Talk to local childcare providers and the day care association, too.

"Really look at yourself," Holman says, "and make sure you're able to deal with children effectively and kindly. Most importantly, don't go into it just for the money. Then the children won't get the care they deserve. And don't overwhelm yourself with too many kids."

Although Eggleston entered the business because she loved children, and not simply to make money, she's finding her income greater now than when she was teaching school. "Even when my youngest gets out of school," she says, "I probably won't go back to teaching public school. I may go back to school to get a master's to teach people how to do this. I would like to continue in this field, teach people how to do it well." A testament then, that there is much to learn about running a day care, and much joy to be gained from working with children.

Chapter 6
Opportunities in Computerized Research and Information Services

> *"The intellectual equipment needed for the job of*
> *the future is the ability to define problems, quickly*
> *assimilate relevant data, conceptualize and reorganize*
> *the information, make deductive and inductive leaps*
> *with it, ask hard questions about it, discuss findings*
> *with colleagues, work collaboratively to find solutions*
> *and then convince others."* — Robert B. Reich

While we are undoubtedly in the "Information Age," few people feel informed. Most feel overwhelmed instead. Herein lies the opportunity for the information specialist, the person who can help businesses and individual clients define exactly what they need to know, gather the data, analyze it, and put it to effective use.

The information services industry is in an interesting period in its development. It is a transition time involving old stereotypes, new technologies and a changing market. There are some very good opportunities for those who are willing to listen to the market and who are flexible enough to adapt and respond to changing market demand.

When personal computers and on-line services first became popular, small businesses started appearing across the country, offering "database search" capabilities. Many of those companies are now out of business. Providing a narrow service for an uneducated market proved difficult at best. "Starting a business to provide just database search is a killer," says Pat Wagner of Pattern Research. "By the time the Yellow Pages comes out, half of those businesses have a disconnected phone number."

A Changing Identity

Wagner, like most successful information service entrepreneurs today, has an expanded definition of the term "information broker." It is beginning to mean someone who finds and delivers, within any legal means, what his or her client wants to know. This broader scope includes data analysis, strategic planning, consulting, seminars, and, of course, the traditional on-line searching and document delivery.

"A lot of people running information businesses start with what they think the market wants. If the market doesn't want it, they fold," Wagner says. "We started with the service, responded to requests from customers and grew organically. We had to learn new skills and accommodate and change our vision to meet client needs."

Wagner, with her husband Leif Smith, divides her company's services into four main activities, all under the umbrella of Pattern Research: a national information service called Office for Open Network (Open Network for short), training workshops on issues related to communications and information, writing, and consulting.

This type of diversification and flexibility is what has made most of today's "infopreneurs" successful. They know their market and their own skills, and do not try to accomplish the impossible. They creatively identify a number of services that can keep their business diverse, interesting and viable.

Evaluating the Marketplace

Understanding the forces at work in your geographic locale is the initial step in painting a realistic picture of business opportunities and challenges.

First, evaluate the market for information services.

Clients will pay for information only if it will help them make more money or better decisions. An individual faced with a spouse's medical problem, for example, may want to make an informed decision about treatment based on what medical experts are saying. An attorney defending a client accused of a crime wants information that helps her win the case. A manufacturer considering an expansion into international markets will want market data and economic trends for each targeted country.

The best clients, then, are those who recognize the need for information and are willing and able to pay for it. Wagner cites statistics from a couple of years ago indicating that some 95 percent of the money spent on database services comes from the legal and financial communities, because that information is easy and worthwhile to computerize. Investment bankers, insurance companies, stock brokers, marketing firms, advertising agencies, public relations bureaus and attorneys are some of the most likely candidates for information services, say Sue Rugge and Alfred Glossbrenner, in their book *The Information Broker's Handbook*.

Even in a small town, or perhaps particularly so, these companies can benefit from computerized information. They may not know it, however. Educating the market is often a necessary part of the information business, one that frustrates and exhausts many information brokers. Even CompuServe, one of the leading on-line services, admits that 99 percent of its subscribers understand only 1 percent of its capabilities.

Ignorance can work against your business or play into your hand, however. It can force you to work harder and be more creative in your marketing campaign. Done wisely, however, educational efforts can establish you as an expert who quickly obtains key information that brings your clients success.

You will also want to evaluate the services of your city's public and university libraries, and the librarians' attitude toward information brokers. Libraries that offer fee-based information searching can consider you a competitor, and even those that don't may see you as such and avoiding referring patrons to you. This situation has arisen from a number of

99

factors, including a tight economy that forces public institutions to create additional sources of revenue, and private information brokers who abuse library services, asking librarians to do their work for them.

Both sides have legitimate points. "It's unethical to abuse a library employee's time and resources," says Jo Chanaud, a reference librarian at the Georgia Institute of Technology. Perhaps "abuse" is the word that needs to be mutually defined by both sectors. "People have a right to use the services of a public university or library," Geneson says. "Information brokers are just making a living. If you're unfamiliar with how to use a microfiche reader or a particular index, it's the librarian's job to teach you, whether you're a broker or any other kind of citizen out there."

Cassandra Geneson is an information broker turned private investigator, with ten years of experience providing database searching and document retrieval. Today she uses her research skills for her own clients and to help other investigators. After attending professional meetings across the country, Geneson found that library communities in Pittsburgh, New York, Chicago and Milwaukee, among others, do make referrals to private services. When librarians in these cities see a patron attempting an activity beyond the average person's everyday skills, such as writing a business plan, researching competitors, or researching a product, they will typically say, "Maybe you need a database search or some primary research done."

What if you find yourself in a city where the animosity between private and public information specialists is high? If you can't beat them, join them, say authors Rugge and Glossbrenner. They suggest using the library's fee-based service as a subcontractor to free your time for marketing and providing what the librarians can't, such as problem-solving and analysis.

Evaluating Yourself

Now that you know information brokering isn't just a quick way to make money and that you can't survive on database searches alone (Geneson says it takes hundreds of clients to support one researcher, because they don't need that many database searches), it's time to evaluate your own strengths and weaknesses.

Rugge and Glossbrenner list five essential qualities required to be a successful information broker: 1) intelligence, meaning being a quick assimilator, able to process a large amount of information in little time and having a good memory; 2) personality, meaning confidence, listening skills, eclecticism and perseverance; 3) education, not necessarily in the form of a degree, but at least the knowledge and skills that would normally come with that degree; 4) background and training, meaning a depth of understanding about something, e.g., hospital marketing; and 5) skills, including touch typing, computer proficiency and quick thinking during on-line searches.

If you're lacking in any of these skills, you should either acquire them or find a partner who can pick up your weak areas. Marketing and sales, for example, is an activity many researchers dread. But without it, your business can't exist, no matter how skilled you are at gathering and analyzing information. "People won't just come to your door," Wagner says. "You have to go out, to professional association meetings, client offices, local organizations."

"You have to really love what you're doing," says Evelyn Reid of Information Search Associates. You must be able to work with deadlines and income uncertainty. You must be good at keeping the lines of communication open with your client during the course of a project. "It's important to remember that you don't have to know everything," she says. "You just have to know how to find out about everything."

Getting Started

Pattern Research's core business – Open Network – was started in 1975 by Smith on $45. Smith, then a cab driver, drove for 30 days straight. He lived on the income, plus $15 from each of his first three customers, while starting the business. A friend who believed in Smith's work gave him a free room, and Smith relied on peanut butter and cereal for sustenance.

When Wagner joined him, she owned a publishing consulting firm, where she had learned the importance of educating clients, marketing and sales. Over the years she had talked to hundreds of people starting new businesses and found out what they had done wrong. Nevertheless, success for Wagner and Smith came slowly. "It took us about five years to not have to rely on other sources of income," Wagner says. She became an adjunct professor at Denver's Metropolitan State College; Smith did some programming and consulting. "We didn't do anything right. The only way we survived was to keep our overhead pathologically low. We didn't have kids, and we had the support of both sets of parents, who saw minor cash infusions as an investment in our futures."

Smith's background was in economics and philosophy. His vision was to be a philosopher-entrepreneur, selling his ideas to customers. Wagner came from the worlds of theater and journalism and sported an almost religious commitment to the marketplace of ideas. "Everything I've done in my life has had to do one way or another with keeping the marketplace open to all new ideas, making sure none are censored," she says.

This unique passion for learning inspired Wagner and Smith to fashion their business into a service that would give people the tools to present their ideas and get them accomplished. Their clients tend to be innovators, primarily small business owners but also entrepreneurial types within corporations. They come during a big change in their lives that requires new information – relocation, a new job, a non-profit start-up, a business expansion.

Reid had always enjoyed research. She did it for friends and for a doctor writing a book. She loved the milieu of a library, learning, the challenge of finding information, being creative. Four years ago, her C.P.A. husband had a client, a lawyer, who needed some research. Reid did the research and wrote a small report. When her husband told her he was billing his client for her time, Reid was incredulous. "You mean people get paid for doing this?!" she exclaimed.

She researched the industry, wrote a business plan and six months later incorporated. Her company, Information Search Associates, provides business research, consisting of on-line searching, manual searching, interviewing (personal or telephone), analysis, document retrieval and searching public records. Her Yellow Pages ad reads, "Information is Power. Primary & Secondary Research Services, National, International Business Intelligence."

Arjay Morgan, a Tampa-based writer, started the information services aspect of his business by following his nose. Through serendipity, he became a member of CompuServe's advisory board. (He had been a CompuServe subscriber and was a specialist in writing about high-tech subjects.) As he got to know more about the on-line service, he began to see that nearly anything could be found within its 600-800 sources, ranging from "Grolier's Encyclopedia" to "Mother Earth News." The trick was how to pull out the data without spending $500 when it could be had for $50.

After Morgan put together a deal with a private client, based on an hourly rate plus expenses, he began to see that his on-line search skills could be sold separately, apart from his writing expertise. Although he doesn't formally promote the business, his clients include small corporations, an ad agency and other writers. "I'll often get a call that's really a rumor check," Morgan says. "When I realized it was usually a stock market rumor the client was interested in, I called my stock broker, who told me there was an electronic service called "The Rumor Wire.""

Database searching contributes to Morgan's annual income, but he uses it mainly for himself rather than others. It has allowed him to become a more efficient and effective writer. For example, a trip to either the Tampa City Library or the library at the University of Southern Florida takes Morgan an entire afternoon with driving, parking and researching. Both are federal repositories, but invariably, he says, the government document you want is in the library you're not at. Now he saves time by going on-line and often finds "that one nugget needed to perk up an article." It's those extra details that eventually allow him to command higher

103

prices for his free-lance writing.

Providing Multiple Services

In Tampa, Morgan says, information brokers as such are few. They come up against STAC (Southern Technology Applications Center), a subsidized research service of the University of Southern Florida staffed by professional electronic librarians. (STAC is an incorporated organization affiliated with NASA and headquartered at the University of Florida in Gainesville, with affiliations throughout Florida and Texas.) There are, however, many private investigators in the area.

There will be more of a demand for informational services, Morgan believes, but the kind of information in demand becomes more and more esoteric. "It used to be enough to answer how many angels dance on the head of the pin," he says. "Now you have to find the number of black angels and the number of Oriental angels."

This combination of fee-based public services and a changing market demand requires the information broker to carve a niche that matches his or her skills.

Reid recently received her Master's of Social Science degree, with a certificate in international political economy. She believes the credential will be significant as she specializes in helping companies go international. One of her recent ongoing projects has involved textiles in Guatemala, Peru, El Salvador and Mexico. Reid has a variety of clients in Florida, Atlanta, Indiana and Chicago.

Wagner holds over 120 training workshops across the U.S., primarily in Colorado, but also in California, Oregon, Arizona and Alaska. She started her seminars on conflict management, improving communication in the workplace and entrepreneurial skills because those were the topics her clients requested. Wagner is also a columnist for two national magazines, and she and Smith provide consulting to businesses and organizations attempting to organize information. Their Open Network service allows subscribers to call, write or visit the Pattern Research office as often as they like, requesting contacts or resources that will help them in their own exploration. Wagner says this diversification is part of the secret to their success.

Wagner doesn't do database searches herself. Instead, she directs clients to the information they need—what documents they need to look in, where they need to search. Although she will refer clients to specialized librarians and information brokers, she often recommends that the client go to a professional association meeting. "Neophyte marketers think they can magically look in a database," she says. But it can't usually be found there." She says only a portion of the information people need is on a computer right now, which will always be true because of the expense of converting information and updating it. "If someone calls and says, 'I need a list of all the people in Denver who make over $50,000 a year, what database should I access?' I explain that it's not on a database because the information changes too fast and is too expensive."

She might start the client out instead with a more qualitative approach. For example, if someone wants to do research on starting a wellness center that integrates fitness and holistic health practices Wagner asks, "Would you like to talk to a few people that went bankrupt doing the same thing?" They always say yes.

Geneson uses her research background and training as a private investigator to quickly find information that she, other investigators and attorneys require. She is adept at searching court records, and knows what can be found in probate, bankruptcy and divorce files.

Some information brokers offer an electronic clipping service, regularly providing clients with current data on a particular topic. Others, like Katie Allegato, develop their own databases, then rent the lists to small businesses that want a smaller mailing list than is usually offered by large list brokers. She also maintains customer mailing lists for clients who don't have the time or equipment to do it themselves.

Tools for Information Brokers

The primary tool for the information broker is the

computer, regardless of the type of services offered. The computer is used for on-line searching, invoicing, list maintenance, statistical analysis and report generation, among other services. Deciding which computer to purchase is a choice based on the capabilities required to perform your services. Wagner, for example, maintains her mailing list of thousands of names on a Macintosh, with software designed by Smith. When they upgrade again, she says it will be to a Next computer because of its powerful tools. In five to ten years, it may be something else.

"We're more sophisticated in computer use than the average small business," Wagner says. "We look for patterns and ideas." She stresses a common mistake among information brokers: buying a DOS clone machine in order to save money, then trying to continually upgrade it.

Wagner and Smith change operating systems every five years. They say it can seem like a luxury to throw out everything and start over, but the prices are dropping so fast, it's worth it. "We don't do this just to be innovative," Wagner says. "You can't afford to own old machines, unless you love to tinker."

You will need a modem, of course, the faster the better, with good communications software. Reid has a dedicated line for her modem, one for her fax machine, another for her business, and yet another for her home, for a total of four lines. She also has a laser printer and a photocopier. It's best to start with a pared-down office – a computer, modem, printer and fax – until you get clients and are certain you want to stay in the business. Add new equipment and software over time. One way to keep costs low is to use shareware—a form of software that is provided for a small distribution or downloading fee on the agreement that if you keep and use the software you will comply with the publisher's registration request.

On-line searching requires subscriptions to various databases. Each of the 500 databases currently available requires you to learn a different "language" to access them, so you will want to research and carefully select the services you will use most. Wagner recently obtained an InterNet account, which she considers the very best of on-line services, allowing you to have dialogue with hundreds of bright people all over the world. Other popular services are DIALOG, NewsNet and NEXIS. While CompuServe is considered more of a consumer-oriented system, it is beginning to offer more hard-hitting business information. A directory of on-line services is published by Gale Research, Inc. Titled the *Directory of On-line Databases*, it is considered the bible in the field. For a catalog of Gale publications, including this directory, write to Gale Research, Inc., Book Tower, Detroit, Michigan 48226, or call (800)-877-4253.

In addition to on-line services, the library will be one of your primary tools. Make sure you are familiar with your library's resources, including microfiche and CD-ROM, and have your library research skills honed for maximum efficiency. Various reference books such as *Where to Go for What*, by Mara Miller can help you do so.

If you don't have the time to retrieve documents from the library yourself, or the money to hire a "runner," consider using the document delivery service offered by some database producers such as Predicasts, ISI (Sci Search and Social Science Search) or Compendex. Full service companies such as Dynamic Information, Infocus and Omnifacts can also be helpful.

For business owners who intend to offer a regular update of information to their clients, DIALOG database's electronic clipping service is an effective tool. For a fee, you can store your search request on the database and the company's computers will automatically run the search for you as new information arises. The results will be posted to your electronic mailbox. On your own computer, you can format the information and send it on to your client, with a bill that includes a mark-up on your DIALOG charges.

Information specialists need to regularly read professional journals such as "Information Today On-line," "Database" and "Database Searcher." Organizations, too, should be a part of your tool kit, including the Association of Independent Information Professionals (AIIP), which offers special member rates to on-line services. Wagner suggest attending professional meetings of all kinds, particularly those of your clients'

107

industries. Reid, for example, is a member of the Society of Competitor Intelligence Professionals and the World Trade Center's association. Be visible, Wagner says. Show you care, pick up the latest gossip, meet people, talk about the issues. You will end up sitting next to people you wouldn't normally have access to on a marketing basis.

You can meet other information brokers and discover the latest in information technology by attending one of the two trade shows in the industry: On-line/CD-Rom Conference (800) 248-8466 or National On-line Meeting (609) 654-6266.

And don't forget to read. Read voraciously and read eclectically. The "Wall Street Journal," for example, is part of Reid's daily diet. She also picks up the supplemental reading lists of a favorite professor's international business courses. The lists are compiled from a wide variety of sources and give her insights on the most current topics being discussed. Reading can be supplemented with hearty dialogues, both among your peers and with people on-line. You never know when one piece of information or chance conversation will lead to a breakthrough for your business.

Performing the Work

A typical day in the life of an information broker, say Rugge and Glossbrenner, goes something like this: scan the newspapers; sign on to your electronic mail services and collect mail, answering some letters immediately; check your appointment book; complete the marketing report you're writing for a client and get the FedEx package ready; take calls from clients and prospects; read business magazines at lunch; work on a Rotary Club speech; make business development calls, trying to book appointments; handle an immediate search request; write a proposal for a prospective client; send out documents; spend an hour on bookkeeping; do on-line searches after 6 p.m., when the rate is low; watch a television show you taped earlier; fall into bed exhausted.

Your job as a home-based information broker will include everything from calling a prospect to writing the final client report or delivering the search documents. You will need

108

to be a salesperson, an investigator, a listener, a thinker and a writer, usually all in one day. Wagner, for example, gets up at 5, reads the paper, sends faxes off to clients around the world so they can read her messages when they get to their offices, and completes a good deal of writing. While office hours for drop-in's are 8 a.m. to 6 p.m., clients can call until 10 p.m. Fortunately, Wagner is home-based, so she can provide such service. She can give free advice if it strikes her fancy, but will ask the inquirer to call back at 7 p.m. so she can do the dishes while they talk. Instead of going to restaurants for business lunches, which she feels is too expensive, too time-consuming, and often poor quality, she will invite clients to her house for cheese and crackers and fruit. Most people are relieved, she says. In nice weather, she puts chairs out on the lawn. In bad weather, she's spending her time serving her clients rather than commuting.

Actually executing an assignment starts with the reference interview, where you determine the client's needs. You can then return to your office to think through a preliminary research plan and attach costs to it, ending up with a project cost estimate you deliver to the client. Upon agreement and, preferably, a signed contract, you can begin the research. Carefully identifying where you hope to find the information, you can visit the library or search a database. If you are going on-line, it's important to identify, before signing on, the key words that will narrow your search quickly and accurately. Use the database's thesaurus, if it has one. Once you've found the on-line records you need, view them on your computer as needed and then print them, or ask the database publisher to print them for you (you will receive the printouts a few days later). Finally, compile the data into a report that matches the client's initial objectives and deliver it, along with your invoice.

Reid has found that one-third of a typical search is spent on the phone talking to trade reps or trade commissions. Another quarter is on-line effort. She has not yet found an efficient method of document retrieval, so she goes to the library herself or asks her part-time contractor in Washington, D.C., to obtain documents found at the National Library of Medicine in Bethesda, for example. She says telephone interviewing is becoming an increasing part of the business.

The key to performing the work efficiently, thoroughly and at a maximum profit, is to think a project through carefully before beginning any research efforts. The more accurately you define what it is you want and where you will find it, the less likely you will be to add up on-line charges groping through a database. Make it a general rule to not go on-line unless you absolutely must, because a database isn't always the most efficient tool for your search. You might be able to find the information at the library just as quickly, for free. If it's an expert you need to interview, first ask friends and associates for referrals, then scan magazine and newspaper articles for names. If you still come up empty-handed, go on-line and place an inquiry.

To stimulate your thinking about where information you want might exist, consult Alden Todd's *Finding Facts Fast*. As you gain experience at research and on-line searching, you will find short-cuts and time-savers that translate into money savers.

Marketing the Information Service Business

"Marketing" refers to the many activities involved in getting clients, including 1) defining your product or service; 2) identifying the most likely clients for what you're offering; 3) positioning your services in relation to other options available to your clients; 4) making your product or service conveniently available to your clients; 5) advertising and selling your product or service.

After completing the first two steps, which were discussed in detail earlier, you can consider positioning. As an information broker, you are competing with other options a client has, ranging from in-house computer analysis to foregoing the information completely. View your service from your client's perspective: what do they need that they can't accomplish themselves? Many physicians, for example, are new to computers and unaware of the information they could access on-line. If your background or interest is in the medical field, you could offer to do immediate searches to help in patient diagnosis and treatment plans or research papers.

If you are an effective marketer, you will make it your job to thoroughly understand the client, identify what they need most and define how the information you could gather might help them. Like Geneson, Wagner sees educating the market as one of the most challenging, and essential, parts of her business. Prospects and clients may not realize what you can provide to them or how they could use it.

Of course, some prospects may not be worth the effort to educate. Engineers, for example, typically think of themselves as already on the leading edge and believe they know everything they need to know, according to Rugge and Glossbrenner. Academics are on such a limited budget that it can be hard to serve them at a profit. You will want to target the types of organizations mentioned earlier for the best use of your marketing dollar.

Reaching and educating prospects can be done in a number of ways. Personal contacts are an obvious place to start. Ask each person you know or talk with to refer you to someone else. Follow up with your brochure and business card. Most information brokers have found that a blanket direct mail campaign is generally not a good method for selling your services. Instead, you should target your list carefully and send a personalized letter demonstrating what you can do for the prospect. Follow up with a phone call and try to get an appointment.

The more visible you are, the better your chances of getting business. Don't overlook public speaking, trade journal articles, television and radio talk shows, press releases and the Yellow Pages. Much of Wagner's and Smith's business has come through publicity. They have been written about in over 250 places, including *Megatrends*, *The Aquarian Conspiracy*, *Capitalism for Kids*, *The Independent Scholar's Handbook*, the "Washington Post," "Christian Science Monitor" and the "Wall Street Journal."

"Because I'm out there a lot," Wagner says, "people hear about me." In addition to her monthly columns, she was on a monthly radio show for three and a half years and was a talk show host for a year and a half. "We've found advertising next to useless," she says, "except for some direct mail for work-shops."

And then there's the method you cannot control and cannot predict but can do your best to encourage: word of mouth. "Clients love what we do," Wagner says. One said, "I told 20 people about you last month." That may not all turn into business, but it is 20 people who didn't know about her last month.

Wagner advises new businesses to hang in there. Potential clients have the attitude of, "Businesses like this come and go all the time; we'll wait and see if you're going to be around." There's a quality of client you won't get in the beginning, she warns, because they're suspicious.

Reid, on the other hand, has found some success in advertising, primarily in a local business journal. She also provides seminars through the World Trade Center. She advises that you know exactly what you want to do and for whom. Who is your target market? What do you want to do for them? Once she has a prospect, her marketing efforts continue with the reference interview, a formal term to define the meeting in which a client talks about their needs and objectives. For someone first starting out, Reid recommends that you hone your communication skills, both listening and talking, because an effective interview is both the basis for the sale and for the parameters of the project. If you misunderstand what your client intended, you may end up delivering (and paying for) unwanted data. You must also recognize when your target market is changing, she says, because client needs changes as do your own interests.

Geneson doesn't sell to the business market, but pursues private investigators at professional association meetings. "As far as I know, I'm the only investigator in the state of Colorado that knows how to do on-line searching," she says. "It's a valuable service to investigators. For example, if an attorney client has a personal injury case, he will want to know what the medical community is saying about the effects of certain drugs. The only way to get that is through a bibliographic search."

Pricing is an aspect of marketing few beginners are comfortable with. When you are involved in a business you love to do, Reid says, it seems unnatural to charge people to do it. She initially charged $35 an hour, knowing it was low. Then, about two years ago she was talking with an AAIP comrade, who, upon learning Reid's fees, said, "Oh, you're one of those!" Perplexed, Reid asked what she meant. The associate replied, "You're dragging down the entire profession." That wasn't Reid's intention, and it got her started thinking about professionalism, and how her fees reflected on that. She has since raised her fees, which are currently $85 an hour for analysis and reports. The average in the information business is $50-150 an hour. She charges a separate, per-article fee for documents, and passes on-line charges on to her clients.

Wagner and Smith want to keep their services open to the widest range of people, and still price them so as to make a decent living. They are adding products at several different price points ranging from $65 a year to $3,000 a day.

Working From Home

Most information specialists use their home as their main workspace and go to client offices for meetings. Wagner, however, welcomes clients to her home office. She and Smith once had a beautiful office in a Victorian townhouse on Denver's Capitol Hill for three years. A mistake, she says. They moved back to a house six years ago.

"We're trying to present a style of communicating with our clients that enhances their ability to build working relationships with people," she says. "They come into our neighborhood — we live in a wonderful neighborhood, a real neighborhood — and they see our wildflowers, our old trees, kids playing in front of the house, cats, and dogs. Even the most corporate people rarely say 'People won't take you seriously.' Instead they say, 'Wow, I wish I could do that.' Anyone who says you're not important because you aren't paying $1,200 a month (in business rent) is someone I don't really want as a client."

Wagner appreciates the lack of separation between her personal and professional lives, saying, "The same values I

hold in my personal life I try to practice in my professional life."
Providing "tools for explorers" is almost sacred work for Wagner.
"I love to learn," she says, "and I do, from all these people who
come to us – socialists, liberalists, multi-millionaires, community activists who are trying to accomplish something. They
ask me to help them, but to do that, they first have to teach me
what they know."

Words for the Wise

"If I were to start another business," Wagner says, "I
would do a very careful business plan that determined how
much money I needed to charge to pay my bills. Then I would
ask people, 'Would you pay this,' and ask for a letter that says
they would do it. People fool themselves." Wagner also
considers it essential to build a network outside of family and
friends. Otherwise you can get into what she calls the Hapless
Capitalist Syndrome, sitting around the kitchen table on a hot
night, drinking beer, hearing friends proclaim, "It's a great
idea! Do it!" but discovering that, to anyone except your mom,
it doesn't make sense. Build a team of people you can call on,
including your banker, she says. Call them for emotional help
and advice. You may not always hear what you want to hear,
but you won't be isolated from reality.

Chapter 7
Opportunities For Growing and Marketing Specialty Plants

Eighteen years ago, as she and her husband neared retirement, Lola Zimmerman took some extra herb plants from her garden and set them out in a wheelbarrow by the side of the road. She put up a price sign and left a jar for people to leave money and take change.

One thing led to another, and today, the Zimmerman's Herbfarm in Fall City, Washington, has a four-star restaurant, a gift shop, 17 different theme gardens, a school offering 250 classes a year and is the largest retail herb nursery in the country–growing some 639 different types of herbs. Early on, Lola's husband Bill had to "retire" from his job at Boeing in Seattle to help run the booming herb business.

After Win Franklin received his degree in environmental biology he got a job at the county health department. After 12 years he decided to take his retirement money and start a greenhouse business. He bought a used greenhouse and reconstructed it onto the side of his home.

Today, after seven seasons, Franklin's Windsong Farms has three greenhouses, totaling some 10,000 square feet. He supplies display annuals for public botanical gardens as well as supplying plants for several landscapers and elementary schools' spring plant sales.

When the oil business went belly up, unemployed geologist Theron Blazzard decided to grow tomatoes for a living. He bought a greenhouse and now, after five years, his backyard-operated Blazzard Farms can't keep up with the demand from local markets for his plump, tasty tomatoes.

Then there's the classic hippie-to-millionaire story of Mo Siegel, who in the 1960s began gathering wild herbs in the hills near his home. His herb-gathering business blossomed into the largest herbal tea company in the country – Celestial Seasonings – which was eventually sold to Kraft Foods.

Growing and marketing specialty plants is a business that people can literally grow into, whether they want a full-blown, full-time business or a part-time, supplementary source of income. In most cases, once a good market has been established, the small supplier has trouble keeping up with the demand. It all depends on where you want to go, some luck, and your ability to find and fill a specific niche.

The Big Picture

"Ornamental horticulture in the United States is a booming industry, and, as with any dynamic situation, there are lots of opportunities for enterprising individuals," Francis X. Jozwik, Ph.D. writes in his book, *How to Make Money Growing Plants, Trees & Flowers*. Jozwik has successfully operated a greenhouse and nursery business for more than 20 years. Part of the boom is due to lifestyle trends that include greening up our home environment and growing pesticide-free vegetables in our home gardens. Another part of this trend is the working couple with less time to spend in the garden—creating a market for garden and landscaping services (covered in a separate chapter).

Competition from the "big guys" isn't so much of a problem in horticulture, because the variability of plants and their need for constant care and diverse environments don't fit well into standardized growing methods employed by large corporations.

Although there are numerous large growers, Jozwik says that a little less than half of the live plants and cut flowers sold nationally are distributed through non-traditional outlets.

Unlike traditional field crops, specialty plants offer an opportunity for success with a comparatively small investment. "A person armed with little more than a few hundred dollars and the right knowledge can still start a profitable greenhouse or nursery. Contrast this with the hundreds of acres of high-priced land and expensive farm machinery needed to run a modest farm. An investment of one million dollars and more is commonly required for a traditional farm operation which supports a modern family in reasonable comfort."

Jozwik's book is an excellent source for detailed information on the plant business.

Practical Advice – How They Grew

Though it may appear so, none of the above businesses was an overnight success. Each grew gradually with a lot of cautious planning and hard work.

When Lola Zimmerman's roadside herb business started to boom, her husband Bill retired and built a small greenhouse for the herbs. The couple then converted an old garage into a store to sell some books and other items. What began as a casual retirement hobby and source of additional income bloomed into a full-time family business for the Zimmermans, their son and daughter-in-law and 20 to 50 employees, depending on the season.

Six years ago the Zimmerman's son and daughter-in-law joined the business and opened the restaurant, which began as a cooking class. Open April through January, the restaurant serves a set six-course luncheon and nine-course dinner specializing in seasonal, regional cooking distinctively flavored, of course, with the Herbfarm's herbs. The 30-seat restaurant–with seating by reservation only–has one booking day in spring and fall, and generally fills 75 percent of its seats through the season, keeping 25 percent open on a weekly basis.

Carey Van Dyke, the Zimmerman's daughter-in-law and Herbfarm business manager, says those who want to start their own herb business "better plan on being tied to the business. They better not be starting a business because they want to have the freedom of setting their own hours." Van Dyke says some of the challenges of running the Herbfarm are "financing – because it's so seasonal – and employee management, like any business. You're also subject to weather." The

117

most important thing for those considering the herb business, she says is "to love herbs and the romance of herbs."

The Herbfarm and its restaurant has been featured in "Food and Wine" and "Sunset" magazines. The theme gardens, which the public can tour for free, include a "fragrant flowers and herbs" garden, a "silver garden," of plants that all have silver or grey foliage, a thyme garden with many different types of thyme, a pioneer garden, with plants that the pioneers brought from the East to the West, and a Shakespeare garden with herbs specifically mentioned in Shakespeare's plays.

All this from an old wheelbarrow by the side of the road. "It wasn't something that I planned," Lola Zimmerman says, "It just happened."

Unlike the Zimmermans, most people don't "accidentally" launch such a successful business. Luck and timing were on their side. In the last decade, culinary herbs and herbal soaps, remedies and other products have captured the public interest.

Win Franklin of Windsong Farms says, "The big thing is starting small, trying to put out little capital to begin with and just slowly building on the business, in other words, you expand as the business expands." Franklin's first customer was a local florist who wanted unusual plants not available elsewhere. "The first year was a bit haphazard," Franklin says, "I continued to refine my horticultural knowledge by taking courses at a community college." As luck would have it, one of his instructors was from the Botanic Gardens and he asked Franklin if he was interested in growing some plants for the Botanic Gardens, which was also seeking unusual plants.

Franklin attributes part of the success of his business to doing all the work himself – including reconstructing used greenhouses – and says if he had had to hire out the work he would not be where he is today. He considers himself lucky in finding a used greenhouse to begin with.

"Make sure you have the capital. I have not expanded until I had the money to do it out of pocket – I've had no bank loans whatsoever – it's all been done out of pocket." Without payments on the greenhouse, he says if he loses a contract one year, the only thing lost is the income. "The main thing is not overspending. That's what puts people out of business, they grow too fast, too soon, they're overcapitalized."

Theron Blazzard says he jumped into his tomato-growing business with both feet and not a whole lot of preparation. If he had to do it over again, he says he would have first taken a small business course.

"It takes quite a bit of money and an awful lot of work." People who seriously want to go into business for themselves should, "Number one: take a small business course from either the chamber of commerce or some of the schools or private sources, so you know what you're getting into. You've got to get a market established – which is the number two item. You can't just start growing tomatoes and think you can go out and start peddling them everywhere – because it won't work. The big chains won't buy them; sometimes they won't even buy from small producers. It's a specialty type of market right now, at least for the small grower. You need to sit down and do it in a concise business manner or else you will surely fail."

Blazzard says it's important to have either the experience or enough of your own money to invest because, "Right now most bankers or people who loan money won't even talk to you if you don't have three to five years' experience." The best way to gain experience and learn the ins and outs of running a business is to work for someone else who's already running the same kind of business. "Go get a job in a greenhouse to learn how to do it." – that's the number three item, Blazzard says. Number four? ... "It wouldn't hurt to have a degree in horticulture."

STARTING OUT

Cities, counties and states have various regulations about businesses, including zoning. It's best to investigate these before you begin, so you're not in for any unpleasant surprises down the road.

The office of the Secretary of State, Department of Revenue and Taxation and the Department of Labor are all good places to start inquiring. Income and employment figures will also need to be reported to the Internal Revenue Service and to the Social Security Administration and Department of Labor.

With nurseries and greenhouses, it's necessary to have a permit for production and sales, and annual inspections may also be required. Some towns and counties charge a small business license fee. Also, check with your local health department for other applicable regulations.

Advice and information is also available from your local Chamber of Commerce.

Choosing a Specialty

There are two primary reasons for choosing any area of business: first, a strong and abiding interest in the subject matter; and second, the field must offer a reasonable chance of monetary success. "No one I know wants to spend their time doing something which holds no interest for them and no one I know wants to run a business which doesn't make any money," Jozwik writes.

So if you think you want to grow something for a business – part or full time – and you're convinced that you have a deep and abiding interest in growing and selling plants and that there's a good chance for a reasonable income, the next step is choosing an area of particular personal interest. Will it be seasonal bedding plants, a year-round crop of juicy, greenhouse tomatoes, cut flowers or herbs?

Fortunately, it doesn't have to be just one – although it can be. Several of these specializations can be combined in one operation. Below are some options:

- Greenhouse ornamentals for indoors and outdoors
- Ornamental nursery plants grown outdoors
- Ornamental perennial plants for landscaping
- Retail horticultural business
- Greenhouse vegetables, fresh fruit, and greens production for regular consumption
- Greenhouse herbs and unusual vegetables–fresh or dry–for consumption.
- Market gardens – outdoor production of fruit and vegetables,

including herbs and flowers
- Hydroponic growing of vegetables or flowers
- Herbs and medicinal plants production, outdoor culture for wholesale distributors, food markets or restaurants
- Seed production for specialty crops.
- Mail order growing for dormant herbaceous and woody landscape plants
- Outdoor and interior landscaping, including plant sales and installation
- Interior plant care for businesses or public installations
- Wildflower seed and plant production for specific climates
- Christmas tree production and sales, including Christmas items
- Horticultural therapy and learning services, for instance for special populations of physically or mentally impaired people or for normal learning and recreation
- Specialty businesses including mail-order sales of dehydrated produce
- "Pick your own" crops
- Cut flowers sold retail in shops or other markets, such as supermarkets, farmer's markets or private companies.

The second step after choosing a few areas of interest is determining which will make the most money with the least effort, and the third step is realistically evaluating which choice is best suited to your present life situation, including your local site and climate (if plants will be grown outdoors). Which specialty will work best, given your location, assets and temperament?

Marketing

In any business – home or otherwise – market research and marketing is as important a part of the equation as production. For people who love to do something and want to make a life out of it – whether it's growing flowers or writing stories – the marketing aspect is often overlooked. Marketing isn't more important than production, or vice versa, but both must function harmoniously for any business to succeed.

121

Because marketing is the abstract or intangible factor in the equation many people are more comfortable focusing on producing the product, which is the concrete and tangible factor. Unfortunately, this can be the road to failure for the home business. Though you may have the greatest product in the world, unless there's a carefully executed marketing plan to go along with the product the business is likely to be doomed to failure.

So, after deciding on a particular area, the next step is market research – where will you sell your product? Like Lola Zimmerman, you can start with a wheelbarrow by the side of the road – a casual way to test the market–but a marketing plan is essential for those whose main livelihood will come from the home business. As Theron Blazzard emphasizes, it's important to first figure out who will buy your tomatoes before you grow them. Most businesses that fail proceed in the reverse order.

Another alternative for people considering starting a horticultural business is to concentrate on marketing rather than on growing – in fact, you don't have to grow the product to have a successful horticultural business. Examples of this are retail flower shops or garden centers. Marketing operations are often more financially successful than growing operations.

The horticultural marketplace consists primarily of two areas: 1) mass markets of uniform plants, vegetables and flowers sold in volume, and 2) smaller, independent outlets of more unusual plants or produce sold with an emphasis on personal service and/or high quality.

Small-scale, home-based businesses are most likely to succeed in the second area, because they cannot compete in volume and price with mass producers.

What Is Marketing?

Richard Alan Miller, author of *The Potential of Herbs as a Cash Crop,* lists these fundamentals of any marketing plan:

1. Determining the needs and wants of the market. In other

words, what will sell in your area, and in what volume?.

2. Planning product availability. How much should you grow? How will you grow it? Will it be seasonal or year-round; grown outside or in a greenhouse? Can the product be stored (such as dried flowers, herbs or seeds)? How will you handle pricing, transportation and storage?

3. Effectively transferring the products to the consumer or buyer. How will you physically move the product?

4. Providing for product distribution. What system or systems of marketing should you use with your crop? Storage, transportation and processing are only part of this important aspect of marketing.

5. Providing for the appropriate functions to facilitate the entire marketing system.

There are two basic types of marketing to choose from: direct marketing and bulk marketing.

Direct (Retail) Marketing

Direct or retail marketing means selling your products to the consumer primarily through your own efforts. Advantages of direct marketing include increased profits (since there is no middleman) and opportunities for selling products that wouldn't attract commercial buyers – for example, gourmet markets where the emphasis is on high-quality, vine-ripened produce. In considering direct marketing, Miller says to ask yourself these questions:

1. What are the marketing requirements (consumer use, packaging, etc.) for your crops?
2. Is your focus on profit, a way of life, or some other value?
3. What are your expectations from direct marketing?
4. What are the alternatives?
5. Is direct marketing feasible with your crops?
6. Do you have a personality that lends itself to direct marketing – are you friendly and outgoing?
7. Do you enjoy meeting people and having them visit your farm/greenhouse?
8. Do you have the knowledge and experience to sell direct?
9. Can you produce what the public wants?

10. Is direct marketing in line with your personal goals and future operational plans?

Examples of direct marketing include roadside stands or markets, farmers markets, selling to local stores (herbs and spices to natural foods stores, for example), restaurants and specialty manufacturers, gift basket sales, and mail order sales.

In his book, *Backyard Cash Crops*, Craig Wallin lists 12 creative, direct-marketing ways to sell herbs:

1. Sell potted annual herbs in spring.
2. Wholesale your potted herb plants to florists, garden centers and supermarkets in the spring.
3. Sell hard-to-find herb seeds through mail-order ads in gardening magazines.
4. Combine wooden indoor window boxes with a "cook's assort ment" of culinary herbs.
5. Sell ornamental culinary herbs in small pots covered with florist's foil at Thanksgiving, Christmas, Valentines' Day, Easter and Mother's Day.
6. Supply your local pet stores with fresh catnip mice.
7. Rent a booth at the county or state fair to sell your herbs or herb products.
8. Retail your fresh-cut herbs at Farmer's markets, craft fairs and through local stores.
9. Retail dried culinary herbs such as savory, rosemary, sage, thyme and tarragon.
10. Talk to local food retailers about setting up a permanent herb rack to merchandise packets of dried herbs.
11. Retail herb teas and spice mixes, such as "bouquet garni," herb vinegars, jams and jellies.
12. Organize "Herb Parties" like Tupperware parties.

Bulk Marketing

Bulk marketing generally means wholesaling. A wholesaler maintains a rapid flow of merchandise through his warehouse to retail and institutional accounts. The wholesaler accomplishes this by offering a wide selection of merchandise, competitively priced. Wholesalers often furnish advice to help the retailer sell more goods as well.

As mentioned earlier, bulk or mass marketing and wholesaling are best left to large growers rather than smaller-scale home businesses because of the need for large volume and competitive prices. The home business person is usually far better off supplying high quality, unusual plants rather than uniform, mass-produced ones.

Business Planning

"Plan your work and work your plan," urges Richard Alan Miller, author of *The Potential of Herbs as a Cash Crop*. Creating a business plan requires such specific data as plant prices and outlets for buying them. Customer preferences are another crucial factor and can be hard to quantify. One possibility is to interview or survey potential customers. Visiting with your county extension office might help you to better understand your local market.

A business plan can be as simple and straightforward as the following one offered by Lee Sturdivant, who sells floral bouquet and fresh culinary herbs to local markets:
1. Find a place to sell your flowers and get the display and billing details settled.
2. Establish a small business, including some simple billing procedures.
3. Harvest, condition and arrange flowers.
4. Deliver bouquets to the store.
5. Check back to see how the flowers are doing.
6. Pick up any rejects.
   Start over with Step 3 again.

Remember that a store will be more likely to carry your plants, flowers or produce if they do not have to absorb the loss of those that don't sell. Sturdivant checks her flowers in the stores every day or so and removes the wilted ones. She gives the store 30 percent of the retail price and takes the loss on those that don't sell. Sturdivant's books, *Flowers for Sale: Growing and Marketing Cut Flowers* and *Profits from Your Backyard Herb Garden* are excellent resources for practical details on these businesses.

A more detailed business plan can include a timetable for accomplishing specific tasks with definite starting and completion dates. Sometimes, of course, it won't be possible to follow the timetable exactly. Some tasks will take more time than expected; others, less. The business plan is a management tool to help you organize everything, make sure actions proceed in a logical and orderly sequence and help you keep track of accomplishing your goals.

Accounting and Record Keeping

A simple way to keep track of expenses in the beginning is to open a separate bank account for the business and keep clear notes in the checkbook register. For peddling to stores and markets, buy an invoice book and use a new invoice for each delivery.

A common mistake people make is letting their personal assets mix with their business operation, Jozwik writes. "They let the business use their personal assets for free. The only way to see if a true business profit is being made is to charge the business for all materials and services you provide to it."

Production – Outdoors

The first step is determining what will grow on your particular site and in your particular climate. Order a copy of the U.S. Department of Agriculture's plant hardiness zone map (miscellaneous pub. No. 814). The zone numbers on this map will correspond to most nursery catalogs, indicating what is appropriate for your region.

There are various methods of outdoor growing, from traditional rows to "square foot gardening," to growing plants, shrubs or trees in containers. Outdoor growing can overlap with greenhouse production for some plants, which can be started indoors and then moved outdoors to mature.

Outdoor Growing Pros and Cons

Outdoor growing is where most plant production takes

126

place because it's more economical – an open field is less expensive to operate than a greenhouse.

Common nursery plants can be grown from seed, cuttings or more expensive starter plants from other growers. Although buying plants can save time from growing the plants from seed, and can also extend the range of plants offered, costs increase considerably.

Though an open field is less expensive to operate, outdoor plants are subject to more variables and threats (weather and pests, for example) than greenhouse plants. In fact, local climatic conditions and weather will be the primary consideration in choosing an outdoor crop as well as growing and harvesting it.

In *Backyard Cash Crops*, Craig Wallin offers the following "Ten Commandments for a Successful Plant Nursery" outdoors:

1. Pick your suppliers carefully to insure disease- and insect-free stock with a high survival rate.
2. Check to insure that the stock that you order will be hardy in your local area. Determine the "hardiness zone" before you order.
3. Match your planting stock to your planting site. For example, junipers need full sun, yews don't like wet feet, willows do.
4. Order transplants over seedlings when possible. Each time a plant is transplanted, the root system becomes denser and hardier. The extra expense will be repaid in superior growth and plant survival rate.
5. Plant early. By starting as soon as your land is thawed, the root system can "settle-in" before the new upper growth begins. Never allow roots to dry out when planting, and water regularly.
6. Allow room to grow. With adequate spacing, your stock will fill out evenly. No one wants a one-sided plant!
7. Cultivate and weed. This prevents weeds from choking out the lower growth on your plants and competing for available water and nutrients. Cultivating also reduces surface roots, making transplanting easier.

127

8. Use organic or slow-release fertilizers. The small extra expense will be amply repaid in higher profits when you sell your larger and healthier plants.

9. Prune often to remove dead growth and encourage new growth.

10. Check your plants often to catch insects or diseases before they get out of control.

What Should You Grow?

The range of possible crops is quite broad, depending, of course, on your particular local climate. Some of the more popular crops include flower bulbs, cut flowers, live flowers, culinary herbs, fragrant herbs, medicinal herbs, nut crops, landscaping plants, small fruits, specialty crops, tree crops, tree fruits and vegetables.

"Perennial plants are perhaps my first choice recommendation for those individuals who have a limited budget to begin a horticultural business," Jozwik writes. "Perennials can be started by almost anyone, anywhere. I favor marketing perennials primarily on the wholesale level for two main reasons. First, it simplifies the situation; you do not need to have a location suitable for retail activity and you do not need to staff it all the time. Secondly, since perennials are not generally a big volume seller, competition from larger growers is not usually severe. This situation allows you to make an adequate profit even when selling at wholesale." Jozwik says most garden centers and mass outlets will buy high-quality local perennials because they have a hard time finding them. Some popular perennials that germinate easily from seed include: Alyssum basket of gold, Achillea, Anthemis Kelway daisy, Armeria sea pinks, Aster alpine, Campanula Persian bellflower, Daily English, Delphinium Connecticut Yankee, Dianthus Brilliant, Gaillardia, Lupine, Poppy Iceland, Rudbeckia, Stachys lambs ear, Anacylus mat daisy, Aquileja columbine, Carnation grenadin, Coreopsis early sunrise, Daisy Shasta, Dianthus Sweet William, Digitalis foxglove, Geium Gypsophila pink creeping baby, Liatris, Linum blue flax, Myosotis blue, Poppy oriental, Pyrethrum painted daisy, Saliva blue, Veronica repens creeping and Viola.

There are many specialty crops people might never think of, for instance bamboo, bonsai, dried plants, ornamental grasses, specialty mushrooms, seeds and sprouts.

Besides the normal run of vegetables other choices might include such ethnic vegetables as:

Asian celery – similar to regular celery but with a stronger flavor and aroma.

Black radish – imported from Eastern Europe and the size of a turnip. Used as a garnish or in salads.

Borage – used in Europe for salad greens. Also has edible flowers.

Celeriac – a Northern European favorite eaten raw in salads or cooked like carrots or parsnips in soups and stews.

Chicory – this family includes endive and is now experiencing a surge of popularity as a "designer" vegetable. The fresh greens can be used in salads. The roots can be prepared like parsnips or dried and ground for a coffee substitute.

Cilantro – also called coriander, this plant is used in many dishes and the ground seed is a popular spice.

Daikon – a large, white radish used in Oriental dishes. Popular for stew, stir fries and pickling.

Eggplant – Thai and Japanese varieties.

Finnocchio – (also called Florence fennel) Used both cooked and raw in Italian cookery like celery.

Jicama – a Latin American vegetable eaten raw or cooked.

Lamb's lettuce – (also called Corn Salad) a winter salad green popular in Europe.

Salsify – from Europe, with a long taproot that is cooked like carrots or dried for a coffee substitute.

Yams – varieties that are popular in Africa, China, India and the Caribbean are different from those found in U.S. supermarkets, which are really types of sweet potatoes. Some varieties of yam can grow to 600 pounds!

Another unusual idea is growing plants that make natural insecticides. Recently, Oregon growers have been producing pyrethrum plants, a type of chrysanthemum. The daisylike flower heads contain a natural insecticide, called pyrethin, which is safe to use around animals. Previously, most pyrethin came from Africa, but droughts and lack of irrigation there have greatly reduced production.

Landscaping plants – trees and shrubs – grown in open fields or containers are yet another option.

Again, your choice will have to be based on local growing conditions, as well as personal preferences.

Production – Greenhouses

Greenhouse managers determine crop productivity by how many square feet a crop occupies for a specific period of time. For instance, current operational and structural expenses for a commercial greenhouse grower range from $.10-$.20 per square foot per week, according to Francis Jozwik. This amount does not include such materials as soil, seeds, starter plants and other costs. Therefore, a 2,000-square-foot commercial greenhouse (considered small by industry standards) would cost at least $200 to $400 per week to keep operational.

For a home greenhouse grower, however, the cost can be substantially lower, especially if a greenhouse is bought second-hand and reconstructed with your own labor on surplus land. Also, the commercial costs mentioned are for a greenhouse with paid employees. If you and your family operate the greenhouse, your costs will be much lower.

Most greenhouse growers start with bedding plants, such as flowers and vegetables, then expand to foliage and flowering house plants. The top three selling bedding plants are petunias, impatiens and tomatoes. After these come geraniums, peppers, marigolds, begonias and pansies.

Successful and easy-to-grow greenhouse crops include:

Bedding Plants: Ageratum, alyssum, aster, calendula, candytuft, cosmos, heliotrope, lobelia, marigold, pansy, petunia, phlox, portulaca (mossrose), snapdragons and zinnias.

Blooms: Amaryllis, crocus, cyclamen, daffodil, freesia, hyacinth, iris, narcissus and tulip.

Herbs: Basil, chives, dill, oriental garlic (garlic chives), marjoram, mint, oregano, parsley, rosemary, sage, savor, tarragon and thyme.

Houseplants: African violets, begonia, cactus, chrysanthemum, coleus, ferns, fuchsia, geranium, impatiens, ivy, jasmine, orchid, poinsettia, primula and spider plant.

Vegetables:

Cooler greenhouses (35-60 degrees): Beets, Chinese cabbage, carrots, endive, Chinese greens, kale, kohlrabi, lettuce, bunching onions, shallots, parsley, radish, spinach and Swiss chard.

Warmer greenhouses (60-90 degrees): All of the above, plus celery, eggplant, cantaloupe, peppers and tomatoes.

With ever-increasing heating costs, good solar design can save a lot of money on heating bills and also keep the greenhouse from overheating on sunny days. Insulating walls that don't receive direct sunlight can help, too, plus using some passive solar features such as rock in the greenhouse, which can absorb and store heat during the day.

Hydroponic Growing

"Bob Cheves, of Delray, West Virginia, got into hydroponics eight years ago when his seventh-grade daughter needed a science project. Since then, Bob has expanded to four 30-foot by 100-foot greenhouses producing cucumbers and lettuce," Craig Wallin writes in "Backyard Cash Crops." In one greenhouse, Cheves grows 20,000 cucumbers a year; in the other, 40,000 to 50,000 heads of bibb lettuce.

Hydroponics refers to growing plants in a water/nutrient solution instead of soil. One of the advantages of hydroponic growing is that a much larger crop can be produced in a much smaller space. For instance, one acre of a hydroponic crop can yield the equivalent of 20 to 30 acres of a conventional crop. Hydroponic crops are usually grown in greenhouses, so there's an extended growing season and more control over pests – enabling the grower to be less dependent on insecti-

131

cides. Good growers manage with only an occasional biological control.

Another advantage of hydroponics is reduced labor costs. Working the soil and weeding are eliminated. Plants are grown in lightweight aggregates such as peat or perlite with a nutrient solution circulating through it. Some popular hydroponic crops are lettuce, tomatoes and cucumbers. But other vegetables, herbs and flowers can also be successful hydroponic crops.

Other advantages of this method are that hydroponic crops are clean, uniform and flawless, which makes them appealing to both produce buyers and consumers.

A projected return for hydroponic lettuce from a typical 30 by 124 foot greenhouse is $57,000, with a profit after expenses of $43,000. For hydroponic tomatoes in the same sized greenhouse, the projected return would be $28,000 with a profit after expenses of $21,000, according to Crop King, Inc., a Medina, Ohio, company offering complete packages for new growers, including greenhouses, equipment, supplies, training programs and systems for small-scale growers.

Leaf crops provide the best return for commercial growers, the most profitable being leaf lettuce, bibb lettuce, endive and spinach because they are easier to grow than tomatoes, cucumbers and peppers. Their harvest cycle can also provide a year-round crop—and therefore, a year-round income.

Container Growing

More and more nurseries are using containers for growing because of several advantages over field growing:

1. The number of plants per acre can be much greater.
2. Container-grown plants can be sold year-round, regardless of the weather.
3. Container-grown plants can be grown faster because the soil can be blended to suite a particular plant.
4. Container growing is ideal for varieties that are difficult to transplant, such a pyracantha.
5. Saleable plants will be ready for market sooner.

132

Equipment

Unlike a big farm operation, a small grower can start out with a minimal investment in equipment: your own backyard, a few packets of seeds and some simple garden tools. It can be as grand or simple as you like. But again, the advice from those who are successful is to begin on a small scale and grow as the business grows.

Second-hand materials keep costs down, so consider buying used containers, greenhouses, refrigerators (for cut flowers) and tools.

On the business side – "Our first purchase, after getting a go-ahead from our market, was a rubber stamp. In this country, it's usually just that one little step that can put anyone in business," writes Lee Sturdivant in *Flowers for Sale: Growing and Marketing Cut Flowers*, an excellent and entertaining source of information. "The only major piece of equipment we felt we needed for the flower sale business was a refrigerator to store the cut flowers in before taking them to market." But Sturdivant says she knows successful flower and bouquet sellers who don't even own a refrigerator.

Other Outlets for Learning

Operating a greenhouse, nursery or small-scale farm, obviously entails many technical details and growing instructions that can't be covered here for each type of crop or plant. Classes, county extension agents, trade shows, conferences, seminars, newsletters, professional publications and other growers are good sources of information for the beginner, as well as enabling the established grower to stay on top of the latest crops, innovations, supplies and techniques.

Financial Assistance

For those needing financial help getting started, remember that the most important advice is to start small, not overextending yourself financially. Any new business is a risk,

133

and it's better not to borrow and go into debt if you can avoid it.

Friends and relatives are the most common source of start-up funds for small business people. But if you do borrow from friends or family, it's important to be businesslike and prepare a written agreement so there are no misunderstandings about the terms of the loan.

Banks and commercial lenders are another source of start-up funds, but because of the past savings and loan scandals there's no more "easy money." Banks will require collateral and a demonstrated ability to repay the loan. Banks and commercial lenders will also require a well-thought out business plan and will sometimes offer assistance in preparing one. An alternative that can work well for a horticultural business is a home improvement loan, which can be used for a recreational greenhouse. The structure must meet certain criteria. You can also check governmental agencies for small business grants. This type of financial aid does not have to be repaid and is available for some disadvantaged individuals and population groups or those in economically depressed areas.

Supplier credit is another possible way to finance your start-up business. Although it will vary from supplier to supplier, the best way to obtain credit will be to prepare a credit history and supply references from banks and other sources.

Finally, you may be able to borrow against life insurance policies or personal retirement programs.

Final Thoughts

Growing and marketing your own plants can offer a lifestyle that's low-key and relaxing, in touch with nature and the seasons, close to home and family, growth-oriented and pleasant. But it's not all just smelling the flowers and savoring the good life. Remember that the business side is just as important as the greenery–for the business to flower and bear fruit. The key here is in nurturing a profitable business, not just a pleasant pastime.

Chapter 8
Opportunities in Writing and Editing Services

Most of us envision the free-lance writer like Ernest Hemingway tucked behind a typewriter in a Key West mansion, surrounded by palm trees, cats and fascinating people and dashing off novels for great amounts of money in between jaunts to exotic, faraway places.

Actually, though, most of the writing and editing that needs doing doesn't involve novels or even magazine articles. And unless you are wildly successful, talented and lucky, you'll find that most of the writing you'll get paid well for is rather lackluster and mundane—and sometimes, downright boring. So it's important to ask yourself if you really enjoy writing for writing's sake—even if the subject isn't enthralling. What you'd like to write about and what people need written—and will pay you to write—are often two very different things.

The good news is that there's plenty to write about. Thanks to the miracles of technology, whole new fields have opened up and been created that didn't even exist 10 years ago, and for the industrious and flexible writer/editor, the sky's the limit as far as both income and options.

Most of what needs to be written is basic, practical, nuts-and-bolts material such as annual reports, newsletters, manuals, resumes and promotional material like brochures and new product descriptions. Writing is just like any other type of work, and when you come right down to it, it's not very glamorous, despite its popular image. Most of it is done alone and with a fair amount of struggle. Researching, interviewing, organizing material and marketing are probably 75 percent of the work free-lance writers do — which leads to another aspect of a writing or editing business.

There are a number of other branches of writing/editing work that can be part of your repertoire as a writer/editor. These other related services, for which many may be better suited — and better paid — will be discussed below.

Basic Requirements

First of all, you must be able to produce clear, understandable writing and have proven skills and experience. Free-lancing and providing writing and editing services is not a home-based business for those who have not already developed sound writing skills and excellent grammar. One needn't write the prose of angels, but one must be able to write clearly, accurately, quickly and concisely—and hopefully with a dash of inspiration.

Most free-lance writers are escapees from the staffs of newspapers and magazines or advertising and public relations firms—or all of the above. These people have the greatest advantage because, first of all, they have developed the necessary skills, and secondly—just as important—they know what editors or advertisers want. Thirdly, these people have also developed a network of editors, writers and public relations and advertising account executives with whom they have proven track records that will earn them more work or referrals.

English teachers are also strong candidates for writing and editing services for obvious reasons, though they might lack the market knowledge. Others who freelance may have been corporate or government in-house staff writers or editors, whose creativity and writing talent is drowning in the mire of bureaucratic jargon and politics and crying out to be set free. Although this type of experience isn't good preparation for the demands of the commercial writing market, it can give one good basic writing and editing skills, a high level of accuracy and perhaps even a specialization.

Those who are already working in one of the above fields have the great advantage of testing the free-lance waters

136

slowly—with the security of a regular income and benefits. A word of advice: Don't quit your well-paying job until you've got some regular assignments and clients.

Products Vs. Services

There are two broad distinctions to be made in writing: selling written "products" such as articles, plays, scripts, short stories and books, or selling your services as a writer. The first is generally the dream; the second, most often the reality.

Literature–the Great American Novel or the essay or article that changes history–generally falls under the "products" category. Such literary products are usually initiated by the writer. Nevertheless, it's not impossible to produce a classic while hired to do a job. After all, some of Bach's and Mozart's best musical work came while they were commissioned as court musicians.

Still, there aren't too many classic annual reports, newsletters or press releases. That's not to say that many writers can't satisfy their creative urge and clever pen by writing a CEO's speech when half the company has to be laid off, or a newsletter article about an exciting, new scientific discovery or invention that could change our lives. Creativity and challenge exist wherever you find them.

Many freelance writers do some of each category, perhaps bringing home the bacon with their writing services, while satisfying their creative dream by working on a novel or writing an occasional magazine article.

Products and Perfect Examples

Katherine Lance admits she is lucky. She has built a successful career based on magazine articles and books. Since 1976, when she began freelancing, she has written more than 30 books, one a 1985 best seller titled, *The Set Point Diet*. But nowhere in that book will you find her name. She ghostwrote it for General Foods, whose nutritionist–Dr. Gilbert Leveillie–got the credit.

"I don't mind ghosting at this point because I've got my

name on so many books. I want to see my name on a check more than on a jacket cover," she says. With "The Set Point Diet," she says, "All I did was write the theoretical stuff and the chapters about, 'Oh you've got to try this diet, it's the most wonderful thing in the world.' They were just basically looking for a writer who could take the information and put it together. They chose me, I think, because I had done several diet articles for "Family Circle" and "Ladies Home Journal."

She got the assignment for the book through a writing organization, the American Society of Journalists and Authors (ASJA), Inc. from their "Dial-A-Writer" referral service. This service links up established, qualified writers with clients who need work done. ASJA has more than 800 members internationally, and for those writers who qualify for membership, it's an excellent resource. For more information, contact the ASJA at 1501 Broadway, Suite 302, New York, NY 10036; telephone (212) 997-0947.

Lance's beginnings as a writer were also fortuitous. After college, where she majored in premed until she realized she was "bad in math," she was a secretary to a soap opera writer and then graduated into writing soaps. Next, she worked for a few years at Scholastic Magazines in New York City as an editor and a writer. While at Scholastic she started jogging. "This was way back in '73 when nobody jogged, and I thought, 'God, this is really wonderful, people ought to know about it. I think I'll write an article.' Anyway, I started writing about jogging, and it just happened to be the beginning of the jogging boom, and that's how I got into freelancing. Suddenly I was in demand and the women's magazines were assigning me to write for them, and when they saw I did a good job with exercise they started inviting me to write about diet, and I just kept learning about more and more things. Pretty soon I was making more money freelancing than I was working part-time." Eventually, she quit her job at Scholastic but continued to freelance for them "for years."

Around the same time, 1976, she also wrote "Running for Health and Beauty," which was the first mass market book on jogging. "It was before Jim Fixx's book on running—Jim Fixx interviewed me for his book—I'm mentioned in the acknowledge-

138

ments. But his timing was better than mine, because his became a real megahit and he became very rich and I didn't."

But her running book still sold a half million copies and subsidized her career for a few lean years. Lance says the magazine articles and best seller—even though her name wasn't on it—were a real high point in her career because they gave her a lot of credibility.

Her first magazine work was with top magazines: "Family Circle, Parade, Ladies Home Journal," and she says at the time she didn't realize what a big deal that was. Despite her initial and continuing success, she says she eventually gave up writing magazine articles "because it was such a hassle. You had to do so much research and so much work for something that ends up being two pages in a magazine, I figure that if I'm going to do this much research, I'm going to write a book. Magazine writing does pay well, and someone starting out should aim at it." Regional publications are easier, she says, as are some specialty publications.

Surprisingly, she notes, "I have never sold a magazine article that I originated—and I've originated a lot of them and sent out a lot of queries. Nobody's ever bought one that I've come up with. I've done all of them because I've been asked to do them. And yet I've sold almost every book I've proposed—so I guess I'm good at book proposals and bad at magazine proposals."

Lance currently lives in Tucson, having moved back to her hometown after 20 years in New York City. She is now so well established that she can live anywhere. Technology has made it a lot easier too, she says, with faxes and modems: "The electronic cottage is a reality." She says that even though she has done well, she still doesn't make that much money and would find it difficult financially to continue to live in New York, whereas she can have a comfortable middle-class life in Tucson.

Lance describes herself as a writer of fiction and nonfiction for children and adults—books and occasional articles. "I find books easier than articles. I got started in the health and fitness field and I still do quite a lot of that, but I branched out into medicine and diet and I'm possibly going to be doing a veterinary medicine book–natural healing for your pet. I'm getting ready to ghostwrite a book for a Chicago cardiologist on alternative healing for heart disease. I've got a children's mainstream novel coming out in the spring and I just recently finished a series of nine children's horror stories–nobody dies. So it's sort of all over the map. I think that most people who aren't Stephen King, who aren't rich and famous, sort of have to have several specialties. I think it's really hard if you've just got one thing to make your total living as a freelancer. A lot of the people I know who have only one specialty are married and have a spouse helping out."

Claire Walter has been a full-time, free-lance writer since 1975 and makes her living primarily from magazine articles and books. She specializes in skiing and regional and general travel. She's the western editor for Skiing magazine, with contributing–not staff–editor status. She says she does a lot of the "one ski piece a year" or "one summer travel to ski resorts of the Rockies" pieces that non-ski publications run. She writes for city, state and regional magazines, plus in-flight and trade magazines. She has also done six and a half books.

She visits some of the world's top ski resorts and vacation destinations. It's truly a dream profession, but Walter makes no bones about the fact that it's a business like any other. Such dream jobs don't happen overnight: "I've kept pretty specialized for 25 years," she says. Before freelancing, she worked in New York City as a magazine editor, public relations writer and account executive, specializing in skiing. She was eventually hired by one of her clients, Swissair, where during the recession of the mid-70s, she was laid off. Thus began her career as a freelance writer.

Despite the glamour, it's still a lot of hard work: "Nobody would take a vacation like some of the travels that I've done," she says. "Nobody would go to five ski areas in six days, driving through the night in between various things like stopping and checking out the hotels, looking at the snow-making pumphouse and air compressor–people don't do that on their vacations. They're the kinds of things that you have to do to have a solid background in your field–it's not vacationlike. I constantly interview strangers on chair lifts and cafeteria lines and just all over the place. I try to find out what skiers are doing, where they're from, where they like to ski, what they like/hate about the sport.

"I really try to keep up with it. I try very hard to spend time with ordinary civilian skiers who are paying full freight for this and for whom it's a special treat, because it's very easy to get jaded."

Specializing has given her the edge in her work: "I know a lot about skiing, and the ski industry and about the Rocky Mountains, so I can write pretty efficiently. I have comprehensive files, I can get answers to any questions I have with a phone call or two. I don't have to start over with everything. I always joke that I am a travel writer who doesn't travel. I don't get paid for being on the road, I don't get paid for anything other than the words that I run through my computer, and therefore I've got to make that really efficient.

Walter moved to Colorado three years ago from the New York City area to be "closer to the stories." Like Lance, she is well established and can live where she wants.

An Imperfect World

Besides talent, both Lance and Walter had the important advantage of being in the right place—New York City—and establishing strong connections through their salaried jobs before cutting loose. But that's not to say that you shouldn't try regardless of where you live if that's your dream. Both have managed a combination of pursuing their publishing dreams, while providing "writing services"—including Lance's best seller—in their chosen field.

But for most people, without any connections or experience, "Magazine writing as it's generally approached is more of a sport than an occupation," writes Nancy Edmonds Hanson in her book, *How You can make $25,000 a Year Writing (No Matter Where You Live)*. Her enjoyable and informative book is a must for anyone seriously embarking on the freelance road.

"To enter the field as a hunter in search of game requires the sure hand of a marksman, the stoic patience to stalk a canny deer ten miles through icy drizzle, and blind faith that the trophy of a lifetime will be yours if you prove yourself stouthearted," she writes.

"The sportsman's vision of the magazine game has vivid appeal to nine-to-fivers, representing as it does a break from their tame climate-controlled work lives.... As a test of stamina and savvy, hunter-style magazine writing ranks near the top. The prospect of a trophy-sized byline in a handsome periodical can make many a day slogging through the mud seem worthwhile. Yet even the pros can come back empty-handed. The success of yesterday's hunt never guarantees tomorrow's.

"Great sport," she writes, "But can a writer live decently by sport alone? When your bank balance hangs on connecting with the target most every time, you can no longer afford too many long shots. But that need not rule out writing for magazines as part of your freelance strategy."

Hanson says the trick is to "give up hunting and think like a farmer." To "plant a seed in fertile ground, tend your field and the chances are good that you'll reap your reward when the time is right." That fertile ground is less competitive publications such as specialty and regional publications.

Hanson names two key principles that make life as a successful freelance writer possible anywhere in the country (–she did it in North Dakota). "One is that you must be as creative in the kinds of jobs you'll ferret out and tackle as you are in the 'serious' creative writing you've produced in the past. The second principle is that freelance writing is a business. Not a calling. Not a lifetime date with the Muse. Not some kind of sacred quest that's somehow cleaner and more noble than the jobs you've held in the past (depending on just what those jobs amounted to). Nor is it a permanent respite from the pressures of employment which you now lament as roadblocks to the flow of your creative juice.

"Your bottom line can be survival, if you habitually choose only easy targets, or considerably better if you intend to soar. You are selling your time, your unique background and insights, and — yes — your precious daily ration of inspiration in return for a living and a lifestyle that offers returns like no other."

Writing Services

Getting down to the nuts and bolts, there are two main categories for which to write and provide writing-related services: individuals and organizations.

Individuals need correspondence, dissertations, resumes, book manuscripts, theses, term papers, speeches and magazine/journal articles. Such individuals might be students, doctors, lawyers, politicians or other business people and professionals.

Organizations need writers to produce manuals of all types, speeches, reports, training materials, abstracts, specifications, newsletters, magazine/journal articles, book manuscripts, brochures, sales letters, releases, briefing papers, bid packages, annual reports, case histories, scripts, correspondence, proposals, catalog sheets, direct-mail packages, indexes, product descriptions, employee communications materials, fliers, invoice stuffers, advertising copy, story boards, critiques and an almost endless list of other written materials.

The types of organizations that require these writing services include marketing, public relations, management, engineering, training/education, audiovisual, political, fund raising, radio/TV, medicine/health, food/diet, careers, small business, government and military affairs, advertising, direct mail, publishing, manufacturing.

Major Markets

"The five major markets for freelance commercial writers are corporations, advertising agencies, public relations agencies, graphic design studios, and audio-visual producers," Robert Bly says in his book, *Secrets of a Freelance Writer: How to Make $85,000 a Year.* Corporations and ad agencies are the biggest and probably account for 90 percent of the work assigned in this field, he says.

The way to make $85,000 a year as a freelancer, Bly writes, is to do commercial writing. Commercial writing is writing that may be used by a client to motivate, educate, inform or persuade. Most commercial writing is designed to sell or help sell some product or service.

He lists three important factors that help a writer to succeed in commercial writing:

1. A new attitude: Don't look down your nose at commercial writing. "There can be great joy, dignity and pride in being a successful commercial writer ... not to mention more opportunities and better pay. I am proud of consistently earning a six-figure income year after year in a profession where most full-time writers are scrambling to make the rent payment each month."

2. Dedication: "You must treat the work you do for your clients with respect–not contempt. If you can really muster no enthusiasm for writing an annual report or a corporate brochure or sales letter, your lack of enthusiasm will show in your writing."

3. Sales ability: "Whether you're writing copy for an ad agency, or the Great American Novel for the Great American Publisher, you have to sell your work in order to live. Fortunately, selling is an easily acquired skill and it can be great fun, too. I know some writers who say they enjoy the selling part of this business almost as much as the writing."

Writing is not just Writing: Related Services

A general list of the tasks often involved in many writing projects will include:

- Writing, including research, permissions, releases (where necessary)
- Editing (general and copy editing)
- Composition/typesetting of galleys and/or pages
- Proofreading and corrections
- Preparing layouts, roughs, comprehensives
- Copyfitting
- Illustrating
- Makeup of page mechanicals
- Production (duplicating/printing and binding)
- Word processing
- Desktop publishing

But along with these, there's another whole realm of related tasks in which many writers become involved: consulting, publication design, organizing writing projects, conducting research, leading programs and in-house teams, editing and critiquing, planning and implementing production, recommending and finding a printer.

Other Job Qualifications: Are You Right for a Home-Based Writing Business?

Given that you've already mastered the skill of good, clear writing, here are some other major factors to consider. Do you have the personality and temperament for the free-lance life?

The U.S. Department of Commerce offers the following list of some basic questions with which to test your true interest and suitability for the freelance writing and editing business:
- Do you get a kick out of independence?
- Do you genuinely like working with people? (after all, writing is a service business, pure and simple)
- Do you thrive on responsibility?
- Can you accept the inevitability of good and bad breaks and take them in stride?
- Do you generally learn from your mistakes?
- Are you able to juggle myriad projects and details all at once?
- Do you manage your time efficiently?

The second item could be misleading. Though it's true that you have to communicate and relate well to people for interviewing and marketing, most of a writer's work is done alone. Some gregarious types find the solitude of the free-lance life too isolating and lonely. If the thought of a day home alone–just you and your computer–fills you with a sense of dread and imprisonment, perhaps a home-based writing or editing business isn't for you.

Another issue is whether you can live with the stress of not knowing where your next dollar is coming from. Will you be able to pay your bills if your work assignments are down for a month, or even several months?

145

Equipment

It almost goes without saying that anyone starting a writing and editing service must have a computer, printer and, of course, telephone. Also essential are a good dictionary, spell-checking software and filing system. A tape recorder, modem, fax and copier make things easier, too, but might not be required immediately. They can be purchased as your income grows.

Computer software is a consideration, depending upon the work you'll do. The more common word-processing programs will make it easier to send and exchange work with individuals and organizations.

Temperament is Important

"I've always wanted to be a writer—ever since I was a little kid," Katherine Lance says. "I'm really well-suited temperamentally to being a writer. I like to be alone. I don't work well with others—as they used to put on my report card. I don't like having to be somewhere—it used to drive me crazy when I had a job. It was like being in jail—I had to be there." She says it annoyed her that so much time is wasted in offices: "People are drinking coffee and they're schmoozing. If I'm working I want to work, and if I'm not working I want to be comfortable and stretch out on the bed and read or something. So I think a lot of it is a matter of temperament. I think temperament is probably more important than talent for somebody being a freelancer working at home. A lot of people think how do you have the discipline to work, and I think, discipline? —don't be silly. How do YOU have the discipline to get up every morning and put on regular clothes and go somewhere?"

Lance says she has several friends who quit their editing jobs or whatever to freelance and couldn't take it. "They went nuts—they needed the contact or structure or something. I think that most published writers don't freelance full-time. I think that full-time freelancers are in the minority and it's

146

because of the temperament thing. You've got to be willing not to have any money for a while and not to know for sure where your next money's coming from and that's really hard for some people–and hard for me, actually."

Specializing

Both Lance and Walter are specialists, which as Walter says saves you from having to start all over again with each new project and can build you a reputation in your field — so they're calling you for work and not vice versa.

Another way to specialize is to work for one or more regular clients. "I do a lot of work for one organization — an association of financial planners," says Bruce Most, a writer who has changed his main focus from national magazine articles and books to local business assignments. "I edit a quarterly journal they put out; I'm technically the managing editor of it. I copyedit everything that goes into the journal, see it through production and am involved in getting articles, and helping out the review process for all these articles, it's a peer review journal and technical publication."

In addition, he says he does other types of writing for the same organization. "I write some monthly columns on financial planning that go out primarily to consumer publications — newspapers and magazines — and miscellaneous writing jobs like press releases and articles." He says this work probably takes up two-thirds of his time.

"So in some ways, my work is a bit more unusual compared with many freelancers in that I have a single large client — which provides a lot of stability for me. I still have the benefits of being on my own. I am still flexible in my schedule and can take on other projects. From a financial standpoint it does give me a lot of stability because I can count on at least a regular minimum amount of money to come in the door from the journal and the columns I write consistently every month."

Beyond that, he says, it varies. He does work with local public relations firms, for instance, doing brochures for various clients. "I've ghosted magazine articles for people, ghosted a book for a man here in town, who eventually went on to self-

147

publish the book. In the last five or six years, I've primarily done a lot of local work. I still occasionally will do magazine articles on my own. I don't have much time actually for that. In my early years I did a lot of magazine work. It got to be a bit of a struggle from a financial standpoint."

Although Most, like Lance, wrote for top magazines, he says it was difficult to keep an even flow of work. "I always joke with people that I was successful but poor, because I published in national publications — Parade, TV Guide, Science Digest, Popular Mechanics, Popular Science, several of the airline magazines — but I just found it difficult to do the volume that you need to do as a magazine writer. And it's not a great paying job. There's a relatively small number of magazines that really pay decently, to begin with — when you figure out the number of hours you put into a given article, let alone the number of hours you put into getting assignments. I even had a pretty decent percentage rate of query letters that eventually turned into articles. The fact is that the majority of them still fail."

He says at one point he did go looking for a regular job, but the job market was tight and he continued to freelance. He spotted his current situation with the financial planning association in the want ads. "They were looking for someone to edit the journal. I had never been an editor per se, but they were impressed because I had all these magazine credits ... and knew I could write. I had no background in financial planning." Most has been freelancing since 1970 — essentially his entire adult life. He says he always wanted to write and didn't want to get trapped into the security of a regular job that would prevent him from writing. He has written and sold a few novels, has an agent and is currently working on another novel. "From a pure pleasure standpoint novels would be first. Next, I enjoy doing magazines, then comes corporate writing. I certainly don't foresee going to work for someone on a regular basis," he says, but "local writing pays better and pays faster."

Getting Started and Finding a Niche

Herman Holtz writes in his book *How to Start and Run a Writing & Editing Business*, that finding a niche is one of the keys to success. The way to begin is to ask yourself the following questions:

- In which subject areas am I most knowledgeable or most expert?
- With which subject areas am I most comfortable?
- What kinds of products do I prefer to produce?
- With what kinds of clients do I wish to work?
- Do I prefer to sell writing services or written products?
  And, getting more specific, ask yourself:
- What three specific subjects do I know the most about?
- What in my educational and experiential background might be translated into subject matter for writing?
- What three things interest me most? (Hobbies? Favorite reading?)
- How much do I like working directly with people? All the time? Sometimes? From a distance? Not at all?
- Do I want a full-time or part-time writing/editorial business?
- What resources do I have available? (Money, equipment, know- how?)
- How important is image to me? For example, will my self-esteem be intact if I make money writing for trade journals?
- How much risk am I willing to take? (Am I a crapshooter or a blackjack player?)
- Do I prefer a proven type of writing or am I willing to take my chances in the more artistic/creative field?

Finally, Holtz says, "ask yourself what is perhaps the most important question of all: How serious am I about being a working writer? What if I find it rarely romantic, often sheer drudgery, and always hard work?"

The Business End

"It's not a business you go into to make money, at the same time, a lot of writers don't treat writing as a business, which is often a mistake," Bruce Most says. "The faster you gain the business skills and efficiency, the more money you'll make."

What to Charge

"I've always tried to work things out on an hourly basis," Most says. "You have to break it down, work in overhead and what you are really making an hour. Writers are terrible in negotiating for money and demanding better pay. We tend to put up with a lot of crap and seem to underrate our services. You get into writing for the love of writing so why pay for that? The love sort of overwhelms the business side. You just allow yourself to be taken advantage of. Writers are creative types and not by nature good negotiators and good business people. There are exceptions to that, but that's one reason we hire agents to do book contracts and so forth. That's their job: to sit across the table from the editor and barter for a bigger fee. We tend to get caught up in the project and the writing and we just don't demand what we should demand. It's one reason why we always find ourselves underpaid."

The other factor, Most says, is that everyone thinks that he or she can write. Unlike being a brain surgeon or a lawyer, almost everybody can write — but not necessarily well.

"They'd never think twice about hiring a lawyer and paying over $100 an hour, but they'll balk at paying a writer $30 or $40 an hour. They think somehow you're supposed to just do it out of the kindness of your heart — for $10 an hour."

Part of the problem, he adds, is perpetuated by writers themselves. They have a tendency to give away their writing just to see their name in print.

In his book, *Secrets of a Freelance Writer: How to Make $85,000 a Year*, Robert Bly names four factors that determine what you should charge for your writing/editing services:
1. Your status — whether you are a beginner or a pro 2. The going rate for your type of service (what the market will bear). 3. The competition — and what they are charging. 4. Financial need — how badly you need the business.

So figure out a liveable hourly rate and go for it. If you know how long it will take you to do a certain project and what's involved, you can bid by the project. If you don't, bid by the hour. You can usually negotiate a price. It's better to ask for too much and come down, than, for instance, to bid $500 for a project and find out your client was willing and expecting to pay $1,000. Here's where networking with other writers and/ or belonging to a writers' organization can really help. Find out what others are charging for the same service.

Marketing: How to Find Work

One of the real challenges and stumbling blocks of freelancing is the need to market continuously. It's easy to get involved in one project without setting up the next one.

Looking for clients can be done by various methods. One great way to start is word of mouth. Holtz recommends phoning all your friends and acquaintances and asking them to recommend you to others. Give free lectures and seminars. Mail out brochures, sales letters and literature to see who responds. Talk to people at association meetings, conventions and elsewhere, exchanging cards, handing out your brochures and collecting names and phone numbers. One of the most important contacts is your former employer — keep in touch with and solicit business from former employers. Many freelancers get their start with assignments this way.

Words of Warning

Randy Welch is a business writer, who also teaches business communications at the University of Phoenix. He came to writing with a bachelor's and master's degree in history. He worked as a reporter on a newspaper for a year and then became the editor of various smaller newspapers. He now does brochures, speeches, press releases, video scripts and other projects for corporations and various companies and has been freelancing since 1982.

He recalls a quote from actress Mercedes Ruehl, who won an Academy Award for the best supporting actress in 1992. Ruehl was interviewed by one of Welch's newspaper staff reporters. Talking about acting and trying to make it as an actress, she said, "There aren't really that many actors in New York that really knock your socks off. It isn't all that brutal. But on the other hand, it's so competitive, and everybody wants to do it, that you really shouldn't do it unless you have to."

"That sentence, when I first read it 12-13 years ago or so struck me forcibly as clearly applying to writing," Welch says. "It's a hard way to make a living, and don't do it unless you have to" — meaning that people should pursue freelance writing as a career only if it's the only thing that will satisfy them.

Welch further cautions: "Don't think, 'Gee, I want to write a novel or I want to write great fiction or nonfiction and the way to do it is to be a freelance writer.' It may well be the way to do it is to keep on with the job you've got, if that will allow you to carve out time. Or if that gives you the expertise to do the nonfiction or whatever it is you want to do. But being a freelance writer doesn't necessarily give you that time .... you spend so much time writing articles just to make a living and doing other stuff you have to do like finding the right insurance program and the right computer and everything else. I don't think you have any more creative writing time per week, per month, than people in a lot of other jobs who come to writing before or after work with a fresh mind that hasn't been doing writing all day."

Final Thoughts

"Many people who go into writing do so because they really love it," says Bruce Most. "I chose to be a free-lance writer because I like the life of being a free-lance writer. I like writing. I like being on my own. I like the flexibility."

Katherine Lance also concludes, "I consider myself really, really lucky. I don't know many people who really like what they do. I love being a writer. I love the freedom. And to anyone who's interested, I'd say to go for it!"

Chapter 9
Opportunities in Cleaning Services

Larry Peters is legally blind and Kitty, his spouse, is partially deaf. But together, this trim and youthful-looking couple form a crack cleaning team — so much so that their local Sears store has hired them as regulars. The Peters clean Sears six days a week and get the job done in two hours from 6 to 8 a.m. — half the time that it would take most people. The Peters have perfected their cleaning techniques to the point that it's an efficient art of teamwork based on experience and know-how. "We're good. We don't have to worry about the competition," Larry says. Nobody can do as good a job as we do."

They began cleaning as a couple about three years ago, "in between normal jobs," Kitty says. Larry, 43, roughnecked on an oil rig and later got a degree in computer programming, but says he has been cleaning on and off for about 20 years. Floors are Larry's specialty: "I can get a floor to shine without buffing it — though it looks like it's been buffed," he says. His 50 percent vision loss doesn't stop him from doing a great job, "I can feel the dirt," he says.

Kitty was raised in the south, where, she says, "South-ern women were taught one thing in life: how to be a housewife — that's it, cleaning house, cooking, sewing and all those little homemaking things." Kitty, now in her mid-forties, was also trained as a computer programmer and worked in a District Attorney's office and for the army. She started moonlighting as a house cleaner, in addition to working a daytime job, while she was single-handedly raising her three children — which she did alone for 19 years. Her first job was for an aunt, and then others began to come along. Her income from cleaning was so good she eventually quit her regular job.

The Peters prefer the freedom the cleaning business offers versus a nine-to-five job. "How many people can make $140 by noon and go home for the rest of the day?" Kitty says. "We have earned that money, though. We do a good job. The people are pleased — we're happy, they're happy. We like what we do."

"The American dream is to be self employed," Larry says. "There's no boss looking over your shoulder."

A Dramatic Career Change

Cari Hornbein worked for 10 years as a city planner before she started cleaning houses. She says going from white collar to blue can be both a relief and a shock. For Hornbein, cleaning is an interim job, which is allowing her flexibility and a good income while she goes back to school for a second B.A. — this time in landscape design and construction.

When her work situation as a city planner became too stressful, due to an ongoing conflict with a boss, she started considering other work. She had some friends with a house-cleaning service who were leaving the state and she decided to quit her job and take over their business.

Self-Esteem and Personal Growth

"Some of the stuff that came up going from a professional position to doing housecleaning was 'where is my sense of self-esteem coming from and my sense of self-worth?' I went through a period where I really felt horrible," she says, but she feels that a large part of this came from the negative situation she had been dealing with in her former position. She says she spent some time struggling with the question, "How do I make myself feel good about what I am and what I'm doing?' I realized I was using my (old) job in a lot of ways to build up that esteem and it wasn't really real."

Of her transition, she says, "It's been a good time for me in that I've been able to realize that I'm a good person just for

154

who I am and not for the kind of job that I do."

"The other thing I felt really relieved from was that I didn't have to be a bitch anymore. I've been a planner for 10 years and I've had a lot of responsibility." Dealing with developers, she found, "you have to draw a real hard line with a lot of the people in that kind of a profession. I found that it was developing a lot of negativity in me and anger. I'd come home from work and I'd be really tired and drained because I would be fighting people all day long. I don't want to fight people in the kind of work that I do. I want to do good things for people. So that's what I focused on — even as mundane as it sounds — doing good house cleaning for people because it's something that they really appreciate. As trite as it might sound, it would make me feel really good when a client would say, 'The house looks really good.'

"I think in our country there's such a push to be something that people — once they stop and think about it — maybe don't really want to be. We're such a driven society. We feel like we have to become something." Both her father and step-mother were doctors, and though she wasn't directly pressured to be a white collar professional, she always felt that she should be. She says it was helpful for her to take that time — the transition of leaving her old profession and trying something new — to look at the big picture. "I certainly had different ideas about what I wanted to get out of being a city planner than what's happening now. I wanted to be an advocate for the environment, but I haven't, I've basically enabled developers to do what they want to do."

Hornbein has been cleaning houses for less than a year, but plans to continue while she goes back to school part time. She cleans about 18 hours a week and now has the time she's always wanted to devote to one of her great loves — playing the violin. She also has time to do volunteer work and attend classes and workshops.

Getting Started

It doesn't take much, investment-wise, to get started in the house-cleaning business, says Katy Carnes of Seattle, who

155

has been doing house cleaning for 12 years. Basically, all you need is a telephone and a reliable means of transportation — be it your own car or a regular bus.

Some people begin to find clients by word of mouth. Others try a regular ad in the local newspaper or Yellow Pages. An answering service or beeper is a good idea so you don't lose new business. Try to return calls as soon as possible. Business cards add a professional touch and help people reach you or pass your name on to others easily.

You may also want to consider bonding–to make clients feel more confident about your trustworthiness. Liability insurance to cover damage and breakage is a good idea. Occasional accidents, like scratching a window or dripping the wrong type of cleaner on a hardwood floor or furniture can require costly repairs. Rates for liability insurance vary depending upon the volume of your business.

Who Needs It? Targeting Clients

Cleaning services fall into two main categories: residential and commercial. Residential jobs can range from tiny efficiency apartments to sprawling mansions. Commercial clients can range from retail stores or small offices to banks, restaurants or huge factories.

Residential

With the ever-increasing number of two-income households, the need for residential cleaning services keeps growing. Working people are increasingly willing to pay for the luxury of time they would otherwise spend on housecleaning — and will pay well for a job well done. Residential cleaning breaks down into one-time jobs and regular housecleaning or maid services.

Besides the two-career family, others who need cleaning assistance include single parents, busy mothers trying to juggle family, a career and possibly continuing education, two-career couples, the elderly, the disabled, new or expectant mothers, property managers and rental property owners, and individuals wanting spring or fall cleaning.

Commercial

There's a whole range of commercial accounts, each with its own specifications:
• Small offices such as insurance, law and escrow offices often need trash removal, dusting, vacuuming, restroom cleaning and window cleaning. These are the easiest of all commercial accounts to clean and generally pay quite well.
• Large offices require the same cleaning services, but, of course, on a larger scale.
• Medical offices, such as doctors' and dentists' offices and medical buildings, have similar requirements but take more time and care because of the higher requirements for sanitation. However, medical offices often pay more than other offices of the same size.
• Banks and savings and loans usually have one large lobby area and several smaller offices, which makes them easier to clean than office buildings of the same size. Large carpeted or tiled areas can be vacuumed or dust mopped rapidly.
• Restaurants and bars are the hardest places to clean because of the grease generated from cooking and the difficult hours available for cleaning them: 11 to midnight or before 6 or 7 a.m. is not unusual. As a result, restaurants and bars are often looking for good cleaning services because of the frequent turnover they experience. Restaurant maintenance, though difficult, offers beginners a good opportunity to build up a lot of business in a short period of time and support you while you're looking for other accounts.
• Small retail stores, such as hair salons, convenience stores, pharmacies and gift shops usually look for top-quality floor and window care. Dusting and general cleaning are usually done by employees.
• Large retail stores require highly technical floor maintenance that requires considerable experience and a large investment in specialized equipment (including automatic scrubbers and buffers). Not recommended for beginners.
• Property management companies handle the maintenance

of properties such as commercial buildings and arrange such services as window cleaning and general cleaning. They are a good source of work because they are constantly seeking reliable services.

• Industrial accounts such as huge factories or plants often need only to be swept and have a few offices and restrooms that need regular cleaning. They tend to be dirtier and dustier than professional offices, for obvious reasons.

• Government buildings — local, state and federal, including libraries, post offices and municipal buildings — are usually required to contract with the lowest bidder. Expect lots of paperwork if you go after government contracts. They are good accounts for beginners who have the patience, but because they accept the lowest bid, they are often not very profitable.

• Condominium and residential developments can include clubhouses, community recreation centers, swimming pools and tennis courts. It's usually necessary to go through a homeowners' association or property management firm or committee, but these accounts can be a great source of additional work with individual homeowners.

• Real estate firms are frequently looking for cleaning of business space, rentals, model homes and new construction clean-ups. Good work can result in many referrals.

• Subcontracting for other cleaning contractors is a good way for beginners to gain valuable experience. Many cleaning services hire subcontractors for both commercial and residential clients. Look for these opportunities in the "Help Wanted" section of the newspaper classified ads.

Equipment

Most clients furnish all the cleaning supplies. "All they're getting is our time — that's what they're paying for," Larry Peters says. But some cleaners like the Peters prefer to use their own equipment. Kitty and Larry Peters have their own top-of-the-line, self-propelled Kirby ("I have arthritis," Kitty notes). Their Kirby can be easily converted to shampoo carpets and even paint. Though it was expensive initially, "It makes us money," Larry says. They also use a Dirt Devil for the hard-to-reach places.

In starting a commercial cleaning business, it's best to find a local janitorial supplier to deal with. The word local is important, because the supplier can also provide on-the-spot advice and recommend particular products for different types of jobs — plus service your equipment when needed.

Janitorial suppliers sell to the general public as well as institutions and contractors. Frequently, those in the cleaning business will receive a discount, so be sure to ask.

Other outlets for equipment include national suppliers with mail order catalogs.

Services Offered and Rates

Before venturing into residential cleaning or buying any equipment for a commercial cleaning business, it's important to first determine what services you will offer.

Residential Cleaning Services

Besides such regular basic cleaning "packages," including vacuuming, dusting, floor cleaning, scrubbing bathrooms and wiping down kitchen cabinets, there are added options of:

• oven and refrigerator cleaning
• window washing
• floor waxing
• garage and patio cleaning
• fireplace cleaning
• carpet shampooing
• trash removal
• painting and minor repairs

Most residential cleaners avoid such time-consuming tasks as dish washing, doing the laundry, running errands, child care or picking up toys.

Commercial Cleaning Services

Services required for commercial accounts vary considerably, depending upon the type of business it is. See the section on commercial accounts for specific information.

Hourly Rates

How much you should charge depends on the type of work involved, what part of the country you're in, and many other factors. By calling around in your area you can quickly get a feel for local rates.

Cari Hornbein charges $12-$15 an hour, depending on the work. She charges the higher amount for housework that includes light cooking and childcare.

Molly Maid, Inc. charges $17.50 an hour for one cleaner.

Magic Jeannie, an environmental cleaner, charges $15 an hour.

The Peters, working as a couple, charge $20 an hour for general cleaning, but will occasionally do a flat bid on a one-time job.

Should you charge by the hour or by the job? Larry Peters advises: If you don't know what you're getting into, charge by the hour. But if you know exactly what needs to be done and how long it will take you to do it, charge by the job. Experience is the primary way to learn about the way to bid on a job.

Specialties: Green Cleaners, Chimney Sweeps and Carpet Specialists

Green Cleaners

A new niche that's rapidly developing is for "green cleaners" — those who use environmentally safe products. For people with allergies or in communities with a high sense of environmental awareness, such as university towns, using non-toxic, environmentally safe products is a smart move. Such a service also provides an opportunity to educate people

160

about environmentally safe cleaners.

Almost anything can be cleaned with baking soda, salt, vinegar and ammonia and various combinations thereof for the old-fashioned natural approach, and now there is a mind-boggling assortment of new "green" products on the market.

Jeannie Morrison started a "green cleaning" business called "Magic Jeannie" two and a half years ago out of her home. Now she's making $150,000 a year, has 10 full-time employees and has had to move out of her home and into a store front to accommodate the growing business. She supplies all the equipment and cleaning solutions and says her clients include both people with allergies and those who are simply environmentally concerned. Her rates are competitive with regular cleaners: $15 an hour. She charges the same for commercial cleaning — which is a little higher than most commercial cleaners — because she believes in paying her employees well. One commercial client hires Magic Jeannie to do the detail work after other cleaners do the heavier cleaning. Having never done cleaning before, she started the business after a head injury from an automobile accident made it difficult for her to do other types of work. She began using environmentally safe products because she's concerned about protecting the environment herself, and "The last thing I want to do is spray something awful into my face and breath it all day." She uses a combination of commercial environmental products and old-fashioned solutions made from vinegar and baking soda. "We use a lot of vinegar and water on floors, and it's the only thing that will clean windows and mirrors in smokers' homes." The "Creamy Cleaner" cleanser she uses is made from ground chalk.

Chimney Sweeps

With more than five million woodstoves and 25 million fireplaces in use in the United States, chimney sweeps can stay busy in many areas of the country. Woodburning leaves creosote deposits in chimneys, which harden and build up. If not removed, creosote can pose a serious fire danger.

Chimney sweeping is a low-overhead business with good income potential: professionals can make upwards of $400 a

161

day. Along with the cleaning service, chimney sweeps can provide clients with information on woodburning stoves and fire safety.

Chimney sweeps can do especially well with condominium or townhouse association contracts, doing annual inspections and cleanings on dozens of adjoining units.

A Rome, Georgia, franchise called Thee Chimney Sweep, Inc. supplies everything needed to start such a business, including about two dozen tools, plus accessories, safety equipment, a manual and even a top hat. The only additional purchase required is a ladder. All of the other equipment fits into a car, so it's not even necessary to have a van or truck. Thee Chimney Sweep, Inc., has been in existence since 1976 and offers a 14-day training session in Calhoun, Georgia. The company also has brochures and questionnaires to help you determine if this type of work is right for you.

Some of the skills taught in the training session are damper removal, smoke shelf cleaning, equipment set-up, cleaning from below the chimney and from the roof. The franchise also teaches how to maintain equipment for maximum performance and longevity. This particular franchise costs $8,500, with an estimated additional $3,500 in start up costs and $250 monthly operational expenses.

A less expensive way to learn the ropes and find out if you like this type of work would be to work for an established chimney sweep in your area for a while.

Window Cleaning

So you don't do windows? Maybe you should — window cleaners can earn upwards of $25 an hour according to Judy Seval, author of "How to Start a Window Cleaning Business." Seval's book covers everything from how to clean slimy slug trails and burnt-on barbecue spatters from windows to how to sell your window-cleaning business, should you decide to call it quits.

Seval lists some of the criteria that influenced her to start her Puget Sound, Washington, window cleaning business—named "I Can See Clearly Now":
• Independence and flexibility

- Work that provides good exercise
- Outdoor work
- A people-oriented job
- A low investment
- An income sufficient for a modest standard of living

The window-cleaning business met her criteria beautifully. "Because I was the boss, I could take time off in the middle of the day — or any time for that matter — for lunch or coffee with a friend. It was not uncommon to work 10 or 11 months a year and spend the winter months traveling to the sun."

"I found that the window cleaning business was great for staying in good physical shape. It involves a lot of arm movement, walking, bending and lifting. I never had such muscles!" An added bonus, she says, is that she lost her fear of heights.

"Being outside on this beautiful island, enjoying the clean fresh air and breathtaking views was a delight," she says.

"I enjoy people, and this business enabled me to meet people with a wide variety of interests and make many good friends."

And what about income? "This is a business that can be started with as little as $25. Because the business is a 'service' there is no inventory to keep track of, and no uniform to wear. The lack of overhead and inventory can make this business a very lucrative one. Because people are reluctant to wash their own windows, they are willing to pay well for the service." She says she was able to achieve results that the average person, lacking the technique, skill and equipment, could not, and it took only about a month to build up speed.

Carpet Cleaning

Kanda Taylor started a one-woman carpet-cleaning business after running her own residential cleaning service for about eight years.

"I was getting real frustrated and burnt out with all the paperwork that was involved and the record keeping and the supervising." She says she started the cleaning business before the industry really took off and her growth rate was

163

"phenomenal."

"A (carpet-cleaning) business opportunity came up and I decided to go with it. I also got to the point where I wasn't willing to put in the 50-60 hours a week. I had other priorities. That's why I really get a lot of satisfaction out of where I'm at in terms of my business—because it allows me the time that I want for those other priorities in my life." As a single parent, she wanted to spend more time with her daughter and home, and did not want to work evenings and weekends — often a requirement with commercial cleaning.

As for equipment, she uses a truck-mounted unit. Truck-mounted units can cost about $4,500 used or $9,000-$20,000 new. Another advantage is not having to lug the heavy equipment into the house. "Portable units are a waste of money and a waste of people's time. I firmly believe that when you do a job right, it takes the right equipment and the right attitude." She describes the right attitude as, "being willing to do a good job and not just go in and do it for the money. I do it for the satisfaction of knowing that I did the best that can be done at what I do."

Taylor charges by the square foot. "I feel that's the most fair method, across the board." Of the coupon deals that offer amazingly low rates per room, she says, "You get exactly what you pay for those — I know the horror stories. The coupon deal gets them in the door, by the time they walk out the door, they've added on moving furniture, or spot cleaners that cost extra and it's about five times what you thought it would be with the coupon." She charges $1.50 a stair. A lot of the coupon deals charge $2 a stair, which really adds on to the initial bargain.

With an average of 400-500 consistent clients, Taylor does an average of 20-30 jobs a month during the busy season (May-July). Residential clients have their carpets cleaned on the average of every 12-18 months.

Carpet cleaning is a seasonal business. The busiest time of year is May through July. August is slow because many people are on vacation before school starts. Business picks up again from September through December, remaining fairly consistent. January through March are fairly slow and she averages about 10-15 jobs per month then. "In wintertime you do a lot of flood jobs from broken pipes, and this is when Yellow Pages advertising can pay off big time." Weather is a consideration with a truck-mounted unit, because below-freezing temperatures can cause pipes and hoses to freeze.

Her advertising is mainly by word of mouth and her reputation is based on doing a great job. She even calls back a week later to make sure the client is satisfied with the work.

Child Care and Cooking

Though most residential cleaners avoid these services, they can be an added specialty for those who enjoy them. For example, Cari Hornbein does some light cooking and child care for some of her clients and says she enjoys children and being personally involved with the families. She charges about $3 an hour more for these added services.

Being Professional

As with any service business, professionalism is the key to satisfied clients and steady, repeat business. Here are some tips:
• Let clients know when supplies are running out.
• Take pride in your work and do a good job.
• Make sure expectations are clear on both sides.
• Follow up. Use a checklist.
• For those starting a cleaning service with employees or subcontractors, do the work yourself at least in the beginning to understand what it takes to do the job well.
• Look good. Maintain a neat and clean appearance. Dress professionally when estimating jobs — some people wear business suits to do estimates. Some cleaners arrive at the client's home in fashionable clothing, and then change to do the actual work.
• Keep an open mind and communicate with subcontractors and clients about problems as they arise.
• Send reminder cards for such seasonal services as carpet or window cleaning. It's a much better approach than pestering people with phone calls.

165

Problems and Hazards of the Work

Kanda Taylor was frustrated when her cleaning service employees misused her expensive equipment despite the training she gave them. Equipment breakdowns are to be expected and are both frustrating and an added expense. Make sure you invest in good equipment from the start to minimize breakdowns — which also means downtime for the business.

People considering cleaning work need to be in good physical condition. Those with bad backs should not even consider it.

How do you know if you want to do this type of work? "If people enjoy cleaning their own house, and they want to make money — but you've got to really like doing it," Kitty emphasizes. "It's not just the cleaning job. How clean you get it and how fast you get it done is the secret," Larry stresses. Speed comes with time and practice, as with any other skill.

A difficulty with frequent, regular clients and doing the job yourself is that it's hard to take time off. "We can't leave our people hanging," Kitty says. The Peters haven't been able to find any other people who will do the job to their standards and satisfaction.

Health Considerations

Because of concerns about AIDS and other transmittable diseases, wearing heavy-duty gloves is a must for cleaning public rest rooms. "Our hands are always cut up," Larry Peters says, so they always take this extra precaution.

Again, people with such chronic physical problems as a bad back should consider some other type of work. When using certain types of hazardous cleaning chemicals you should always wear a face mask. Kanda Taylor occasionally wears a mask when using some of the carpet cleaning chemicals she uses.

The Next Step: SubContracting vs. Employees

At some point, most people who clean for a living get

tired of it and need a break — perhaps permanently. That's where employees or subcontractors come in.

This is where a whole new set of skills comes into play: people skills. Managing and organizing and being able to listen to and communicate with people becomes extremely important at this point. Training is part of this next step, too. Reading books and taking classes and workshops on management skills is a good idea. Local bookstores and community colleges are good sources for information on these topics. A common experience of those who take a lot of pride in their work is that it's hard to find good help, or even help that can consistently do the job to your satisfaction.

With employees it's necessary to pay FICA and withhold other taxes, whereas subcontractors are responsible for reporting their own income and paying their own taxes. Subcontractors are usually part time and have other sources of income. Technically they have their own business license and need to have their own bonding — which can vary from state to state. It's extremely important to understand IRS regulations regarding the difference between subcontractors and employees, an area the IRS has been vigorously enforcing in recent years. Guidelines are available from your local IRS office.

A personal bond often covers a certain number of employees. The number of people covered in an employer's bond can vary with different bonding companies. Katy Carne says her bond (in Washington state) covers up to five people.

Purchasing Another Contractor's Account

In this case, you are not buying a business, but only the cleaning contracts, either residential or commercial. The price is generally based on the amount of the monthly billing. Accounts are sold on an average of three to five times the monthly billing, but can be from two to eight times the gross monthly income. With this type of arrangement, it's possible to pay for the accounts over a period of months rather than all at once in the beginning. This extended payment involves less risk and allows your income to accrue from the account to help

167

pay for the initial cost.

Franchises: Pros and Cons

Why consider a franchise, since home-based cleaning services can be readily started from scratch? According to "Franchises You Can Run From Home," by Lynie Arden, "There are now more than 3,000 franchises doing more than $600 billion worth of business each year, and there are also about 13 million home-based businesses in the United States. The lower cost of running a home-based business combined with the strong support system of a franchise creates a scenario for success that is hard to beat."

Store-front franchises can cost hundreds of thousands of dollars to start, whereas home-based franchises cost as little as $5,000 and rarely more than $50,000 to start.

Home-based franchises have become more common with the national switch from a product-oriented national economic base to a service-oriented one. The advantages of a franchise include security, training, marketing power, ongoing support, and a proven method of doing business. Having an organization to contact neutralizes the isolation effect of working at home. Some franchises even offer company financing to purchase the franchise and can help the buyer manipulate their personal resources to their best advantage.

Franchises also offer a technological advantage, supplying fax machines, computers, copiers and other electronic equipment to insure a more efficiently run business. According to Arden, home-based franchises can produce a profit within only three months, whereas independent businesses often take one to three years to become really profitable.

Carpet cleaning franchises such as Coit can bring in six figures a year, according to Kanda Taylor, who prefers to operate her own one-woman independent carpet cleaning business. But, she says, with a franchise, Co-op advertising is an advantage and "there's a lot of potential to make money in this business. You have to decide if you're going to be in it for the long haul or make the quick money and get out."

168

Disadvantages of franchises

The tradeoff for the security and greater visibility of a franchise is a loss of independence — the freedom to do it your own way. With franchises, it's often necessary to follow company procedures in all matters, big and small. You will also have to pay a royalty on your earnings to the franchisor. Like an independent business, franchise owners still must work on their own and have the self-discipline to do so.

Questions To Ask Yourself

For those considering a franchise, the book *Franchises You can Run From Home*, will be helpful. The author recommends asking the following questions:

1. Do I have the necessary background to succeed in this field?
2. Do I have the start-up capital for this business venture?
3. Am I financially prepared to operate this franchise until it turns a profit?
4. Am I genuinely enthusiastic about this business or industry?
5. Are the franchise and royalty fees in line with the potential profits and sales?
6. Is there a proven market for the service or product being offered? Does it have local demand?
7. Can I sell, trade or convert my franchise if I desire?
8. Is this a business opportunity that I want to pursue?

Amazing Success Stories

"I was a hospital administrator, working in support services, and I wanted to do something that gave me greater flexibility, greater income and earlier retirement," George Voss of Ann Arbor, Michigan, says. Voss now runs the country's largest Molly Maid franchise with 26 employees, grossing $600,000 annually — only three years after he bought the franchise.

Voss says that demographically his area isn't even that good because the gross income of clients is around $37,000 a year, versus higher income areas like Fairfax, Virginia, where the average is about $90,000. Voss is married, "approaching 40

— rapidly" and has three children aged 5, 7 and 10. He says he chose the franchise route so he could retire earlier than age 60, which was his only choice as a hospital administrator.

"If I can net $125,000 to $150,000 a year, it's going to make the value of the business approximately $350,000 or $400,000. And that gives me the opportunity to back out my time and start working, instead of 40, maybe 32 or 25 hours a week and delegating to a manager or two, and then partially retire close to 40 and easily be out by 50. And, so far it's been working. The numbers have exceeded my expectation."

Molly Maids is one of the largest and fastest-growing franchised maid services in the world. Today there are almost 400 franchises operating in the United States, Canada, France, Great Britain, Norway, Sweden and West Germany. Molly Maids was started in 1978 by Adrienne Stringer, a registered nurse who couldn't find a good maid service for her own home. So she started her own company, modeling it after English-style maids. Her teams wear crisp blue and white uniforms, are bonded and insured and arrive at clients' homes in Molly Maid cars with all supplies and equipment.

Molly Maids offers its franchisees a national group insurance program, a national group automobile leasing program, cooperative advertising benefits and Yellow Pages advertising subsidies. They also can assist with outside financing to help prospective franchise buyers. An initial training program takes place at the Ann Arbor, Michigan, company headquarters and travel expenses for two are included in the franchise fee, which is currently $16,900.

Marketing and Advertising

Many residential and commercial cleaners find it sufficient to run a regular ad in their local paper. Yellow Pages advertising can also work well, especially for specialized and seasonal services like carpet cleaning and chimney sweeping.

Some established cleaners like Kanda Taylor advertise primarily by word of mouth from satisfied customers. Business cards lend a professional touch and make it easier for clients to pass on your name to others.

"You do have to consider your marketing — that's either an inherent skill ... or a learned one that takes a big investment of time, researching and deciding where you're going to fit into the market," Kanda Taylor says. You also need to identify your goals and make a plan to achieve them.

Although Taylor bought an established business with a built-in clientele, she says "I got into it when the market and economy was really ready to fall apart and the previous owner had gone through a real burn-out and wasn't doing quite what he should have with his clients and was overcharging a lot of them. So I had to do some rebuilding."

The best advertising can be satisfied clients who refer you to others. "The main thing for me is doing the best job that I can do and being willing to put the time and effort into that to provide a quality service for my clients. Every job I do, I make a call back to that client to make sure that they're happy. If they're not, I jump on it right away to make it right. That's kind of my niche," Taylor says.

She thinks that people too often don't take enough care with their clients, "Once they make their money, they're gone," and that what distinguishes her in the business is "a different attitude. I'm more interested in having that client call me back year after year than making my money once and not worrying about whether they're happy or not."

Bookkeeping

It's best to keep daily records for any business, and the main requirement is that they are accurate and include all income, expenses and deductions. Record keeping also provides a way to monitor your business on a daily basis, helping you to understand the positive and negative flow of money. One of the first steps is to set up a separate business checking account, so business expenses don't get mixed up with personal expenses.

Taxes

Self-employed individuals need to make estimates of

171

yearly income tax and send it to the IRS in four quarterly installments due April 15th, June 15th, September 15th and January 15th.

Form 1040-ES, available at any IRS office or from a tax preparer, is required. After paying estimated taxes, it's still necessary to file your income tax return on the regular Form 1040 (not 1040-A or 1040 EZ) at year's end. It's important to keep accurate records of all business-related expenses and to document each expense with some written form of proof, such as a cash receipt, canceled check, mileage record, sales slip or petty cash voucher.

Self-employed people have many business expense tax deductions that employees do not. The IRS defines these deductions as something both "ordinary and necessary." An ordinary expense is one that is common and accepted in your field of business, trade or profession. A necessary expense is one that is helpful and appropriate for your trade, business or profession

Some business expenses commonly deducted by cleaning businesses are payroll, equipment (depreciation), janitorial supplies, equipment rental, telephone, postage, uniforms, interest, consultants, bonding, tax preparation, bookkeeping service, collection expenses, conventions, car wash, electricity, trash service, legal expenses, answering service, secretarial service, laundry and cleaning, trade magazines, travel, publications, rent, stationery, copying, books, employer taxes, office supplies, advertising, post office box, key duplication, business taxes, printing, repairs, automobile expense, professional fees, bank service charges, business licenses, sales commissions, business credit card fees, educational expenses, fire insurance, fees for services, liability insurance, payments to subcontractors, dues to business associations, meals and entertainment (80% deductible), Workmen's Compensation, office furniture (depreciation), permits, reference books, sales tax, utilities, and casualty losses.

   ...And that's not all. A complete list of business expenses that can be deducted is available in IRS Publication #535, "Business Expenses."

Conclusion

Many of the people doing cleaning services emphasize that they could make more money if they wanted to. But many said they enjoyed living more simply and having more free time to pursue personal interests. It's nice to know that the opportunity is there to get some extra cash when you need it, but that you can live well on your own terms, without killing yourself.

"You go through major frustrations," Kanda Taylor says. "There are times where I've gone through a lot of equipment and a lot of equipment problems and you end up dumping a lot of money, and I think I just want a normal job like everyone else. But the majority of the time I wouldn't trade it for anything."

Chapter 10
Opportunities in Lawn and Garden Services

From mowing lawns on weekends to a full-service land-scaping business, a lawn and garden service is one of those home-based businesses that can grow to whatever size of business you'd like – and you can grow along with it in knowledge, skills and income.

The Grass Can Always be Greener

It's the type of business that can be done part time for extra cash or full-time as a primary source of income. The hours are flexible and there's the freedom and satisfaction of working for yourself. Part of the attraction of the work is being physically active, staying in good shape and working outdoors – instead of being cooped up in some stuffy office, stuck behind a desk. As the business grows, some of the physical labor can be delegated to employees – usually a welcome step at some point in this physically demanding business.

With the ever-increasing number of working couples, fewer people are willing to spend their precious free time caring for lawns. Those who opt to pay for a lawn and garden service range from wealthy estate owners to working couples, busy singles, retired people, single parents and businesses.

According to some estimates, there are about 20,000 square miles of home lawns in the United States – enough to cover the states of Delaware, Massachusetts, New Jersey and Rhode Island. There's plenty of work on the home front – and probably right in your own neighborhood – for those willing to do quality work with a touch of business savvy.

175

Some of the businesses that need lawn and garden services are apartment buildings, offices, stores, shopping centers, restaurants and motels. For those who really want to expand and grow into a larger contracting business, bigger clients would include golf courses, business parks, schools, cemeteries, parks and municipal areas. For these larger grounds, however, it's necessary to make a substantial investment in costly high-speed mowers and other expensive equipment. And usually, country club golf courses, municipalities and large office and apartment complexes have their own full-time, in-house maintenance people.

Most people who are attracted to lawn and garden services enjoy physical labor and working outdoors with plants and gardens. Although it doesn't require great physical strength, a basic level of health, physical fitness and stamina is required. Those with chronic health problems such as back pain or severe allergies should obviously avoid this type of work. Though services can be limited to the basic physical labor of mowing and trimming, the more you know about lawn and garden care, the more clients will appreciate you and your services, and the broader your business horizons can be.

Types of Services

Among the various services offered by lawn and garden companies are mowing, edging, flower and shrub planting (extensive design and planting is usually done by a landscaper), fertilizing, clean-up, weed and insect control, aerating, power raking, lawn renovations, tree and shrub pruning and sprinkler installation and maintenance. Many lawn and garden services switch to snow removal in winter. Some tree trimmers deliver firewood in the off season.

Getting Started - Skills and Knowledge Required

The type of service or specialty you choose will determine the amount of knowledge and training you'll need. For instance, if all you want to do is mow lawns, you can probably start immediately. But, for additional lawn care, including

176

fertilizing, weed and pest control and such other services as aeration, tree trimming and landscaping, greater expertise is obviously required – and, in some cases, licensing is also required.

Most people who choose lawn and garden care have either grown up around the business or have a natural inclination toward it and, as self-taught landscaper John Spaulding says, "Just paid attention." Those who offer landscaping services sometimes have degrees ranging from horticulture or landscape design and maintenance to landscape architecture. Horticulture degrees tend toward an active hands-on approach, where the person is out in the field and doing the digging and planting. Landscape architects tend to be more office-bound and involved with the design end of the field. Typically a landscape architect has gone through four or more years of college and is licensed. Many states have a stringent testing and licensing process for landscape architects, but other states have no such licensing requirements and permit virtually anyone to call themselves a landscape architect, regardless of education or experience.

As John Spaulding illustrates, it's not necessary to have a horticulture or landscape architecture degree to make money in landscape management. After graduating from Michigan State University with a degree in social science, he worked for a garden center for two years, then a nursery for two more years. Next, he spent a year working for a greenhouse doing all the propagation and caring for indoor plants. He then joined a landscape management company, where he ultimately became a co-owner. He says he has also gone to a lot of seminars and read extensively. "I learned through long-term observation of plant material in different locations, in response to different weather conditions. I just know the area and I know what does well where, and why something isn't doing well based on the cultural end of it such as soil, weather conditions, things like that." Spaulding says he has always been an "outdoor kind of person."

For those who have the interest, but perhaps not the experience, local university extension services often offer horticultural courses as do other schools and community

177

colleges. The public library is always a good source of information. And, like Spaulding, an excellent way to gain the practical knowledge and skills – and get paid for it – is to work for someone else who is established in the business. Working part-time on weekends, evenings or holidays can provide a taste of the business before burning current employment bridges and giving up a regular income and benefits.

Another option is to buy a franchise from a company such as Lawn Doctor. A sizable investment is required, but the company then provides all the training, equipment, support and business information you need. According to Ed Reid, Lawn Doctor's national franchise sales director, "Ninety-eight percent of the people that we have awarded franchises to didn't know a bloody thing about lawn care before joining us. And, 90 percent of the people that own Lawn Doctor franchises had never been in an entrepreneurial role before." Franchises will be discussed in greater detail below.

Basic Beginnings

Eleven years ago Dan and Julie Brown began Prolawn Maintenance. "We started off with a little Toyota (pickup) and a small trailer, and Dan just had one big mower (walk-behind, self-propelled), a weed whip, a fertilizer spreader, an edger, a sprayer – those were the basics. Over time we have now accumulated four or five big 52-inch walk-behind mowers and lots of equipment," Julie says. For the last seven years, Dan has had one employee to help out; Julie has always handled the company's bookkeeping. Prolawn does "weekly package deals" from April to November that include mowing, trimming, fertilizing, pruning, flower planting, general maintenance and some sprinkler work, primarily for commercial clients. During the winter months, Prolawn does snow removal for some of these same clients. "In the summer we have 55 to 60 properties, in the winter – snow removal – we probably only have 10 at the most just because that's all that two men can do." All of the snow removal clients are also landscape clients, she says. Some of their bigger clients are the local Target store and a large office park.

Joe Reichert says he started his one-man landscaping business, "Garden Renovations" four years ago with a truck and an assortment of hand tools. "Bigger stuff, you can rent," he says, referring to rototillers, chain saws, jack hammers and trenchers for jobs like irrigations systems. Reichert, who has a degree in horticulture, does a broad spectrum of landscaping, but says, "My little niche is going into established yards that either haven't been kept up for a long time or keeping up the basic stuff already there or it's completely fallen apart and I re-do it – whatever might need to be done. So I do a little bit of everything: re-establish lawns, do a lot of plantings, tree and shrub trimming, pruning. I work with stone, do patios and walls, including retaining walls." He does his own designs after talking to homeowners to see what they would like. Reichert has been doing this type of work for 12-15 years for other companies or municipalities. He says at first you can pick up tools as you need them – even while on the job.

Karen and Marty Johnson opted for a Lawn Doctor franchise in 1983. They bought a second franchise in a nearby town in 1986 and at this writing are in the process of buying a third local Lawn Doctor franchise. Marty worked previously as a machinist. After paying the franchise fee, they received all the training and equipment they needed except for a van, which is either purchased by the franchisee independently or leased from Lawn Doctor. Lawn Doctor does fertilizing, weed, insect and disease control, plus aeration – but no mowing.

"The thing that we have over most of the other big companies is that we are local," Karen says. "Since my husband and I own and operate the company ourselves, our customers have access to the owner – which they like."

Basic Equipment

For general lawn care, the most commonly used tools are a lawn mower, hedge trimmer, edger, fertilizer spreader, rake, broom, trash cans, heavy plastic bags or tarp for removing debris, a whipstick or scythe for tall weeds, an axe, hand saw and chain saw for tree limbs. Also for trees you'll need a 14-foot, free-standing ladder, hand snippers and long-handled loppers.

For those who decide to start with or expand to larger areas, a 28- to 30-inch riding mower is recommended.

A truck is essential, once the business takes hold. A one-ton pickup, dump truck or flatbed with a hoist underneath the body will allow you to haul sod, topsoil or trees and unload debris easily.

For those starting out and not ready to make the investment, a trailer and hitch can suffice—and used ones can often be found in the classified ads. Choose a good-sized, sturdy trailer with large tires; smaller trailers often don't hold up well, and if you eventually invest in a truck, a too-small trailer may not be compatible. Trailers should have sides that are at least two feet high.

Both the pickup truck and trailer should have a hinged ramp or strong wood or metal planks for loading and unloading equipment. Various ropes, chains and load binders will be needed to secure the equipment. A tool box secured to a truck bed will help keep smaller tools organized and handy.

Equipment Tips

Depending upon what type of service you'd like to start, your basic equipment can range from hand tools to a truck and trailer full of equipment. Although some clients can provide a lawn mower, it's generally preferable and more professional to have your own reliable equipment that you know will do the job in a given amount of time. Many teenagers, however, have gotten their start in the business going door to door to mow lawns with no equipment. Below are some guidelines for purchasing equipment:

• Buy the highest quality equipment you can afford when purchasing mowers, shears, clippers and other tools. They will pay off in the end by outlasting the cheaper ones.

• Do comparison shopping to get the best price. If possible, ask other lawn and garden service companies or individuals for recommendations on brand names and types of equipment. Check "Consumer Reports" for the highest ratings on performance and reliability.

• Buy locally so if you have problems, it can be repaired quickly and easily. Make sure the store carries replacement parts, so precious work time isn't lost while waiting for mail-ordered parts.

• Chose simple equipment without too many options that can break. For lawn mowers, 20-inch rotary mowers are popular because they can fit into most spaces on residential or business properties. Larger mowers can be awkward and too large for the smaller nooks and crannies. When purchasing a mower be sure to pick up some extra blades.

Finding Clients: Marketing, Promotion and Advertising

Where do you get your first clients? There are numerous approaches as the following examples show:

• Dan Brown first got started finding clients by driving around, inquiring about new construction or other properties with lawns and following up with phone calls.

• Joe Reichert sporadically runs a newspaper ad for his landscaping services and depends upon referrals and repeat customers.

• Franchise owners Karen and Marty Johnson were provided with a list of prospective clients with names, addresses and phone numbers in their locale.

• Robin Pedrotti, who runs an aeration service in the San Diego area, distributes flyers, brochures and signs and puts a lot of energy into innovative promotion.

Pedrotti also suggests distributing literature at garden shops, door-to-door, or on car windows – "You can do this at shopping centers, grocery stores, hardware centers, etc. Don't put them on windshields. People get irritated about that. Instead tuck them between the glass and the car frame on the passenger side, facing the driver. Go to golf courses and put flyers on cars there, particularly if your flyer emphasizes 'Golf course green' lawns. There are lots of older people there who would love to have grass that looks like that."

For promotion, Pedrotti even suggests T-shirt give-aways with the name and logo of your company on it. Business cards are handy to give to potential or steady customers, plus

181

a few extra for referrals.

Pedrotti's book, *Lawn Aeration: Turn Hard Soil into Cold Cash*, is a good resource for starting almost any lawn- and garden-related business. Although its focus is on aeration, its general information on business procedures, administration, bidding jobs and selling and promoting your service applies to most service businesses.

Safety Precautions

When working with power mowers and weed trimmers or trimming tree limbs with saws, it's easy to get hurt. The following precautions should be taken:

• Wear protective clothing and gear. Many lawn and garden care professionals recommend wearing high-top, steel-toed boots year-round. Never wear tennis shoes or sandals when mowing. Wear a hat for sun and heat protection; a helmet is recommended for tree trimming. Heavy trousers offer better leg protection against flying objects than shorts.

• Wear safety glasses that are shatterproof— especially when working with rotary mowers, edgers or chain saws. Mowers and edgers can hurl rocks and broken glass at high speed.

• Wear headphones or ear plugs when operating loud machines like mowers, chainsaws, etc. Ear damage can result from continued exposure to such noise.

• Never use your hand to untangle or unclog a stalled mower. Many people have lost fingers or even limbs that way. Once blades are freed from an obstruction they can still turn even though the engine is off. After releasing the clutch and turning off the engine, use a trowel or stick to free badly clogged blades.

• Beware of harmful chemicals. Wear a mask and gloves for fertilizer and pesticide application. Over time, even small amounts can cause serious health problems. Don't use chemicals when they're not necessary and when they are necessary try using only spot applications.

• Drink plenty of liquids to avoid dehydration and heat exhaustion – obviously, this is especially important in warmer climates and weather.

• Use appropriate equipment for the job. Don't tackle a yard full of tall weeds with an inadequate mower. You can wreck your equipment as well as your back.

What to Charge

According to Kent Lugbill, who has run Green Mountain Services for 12 years, the average price for mowing an average-sized lawn is $15 to $35. The price depends on whether the grass clippings are bagged or left on the lawn (it's preferable to leave them on the lawn to help return nitrogen to the soil) and whether fertilization and/or aeration is done.

Julie Brown of Prolawn says a ballpark figure for monthly mowing and lawn care for a residential lawn is around $75 per month. It's up to you and your client whether they want to pay per mow, per month or per season for care.

It's hard to know what to charge when you're just starting out in a business. Robin Pedrotti offers some general guidelines based on his experience aerating lawns in Southern California. He has the following progressive plans – applicable to any business – for what to charge as you gain experience, speed and expertise:

• Plan A: the low end of the pricing scale. It's what I call the "Market Share" plan and what I consider to be the minimum you should charge. It's a reasonable place to start in this business. The priority is getting a strong share of the market in the first place and building a customer base. You won't get rich. But you will penetrate the market, make decent money and position yourself for big dollars in the future because you will have established that strong customer base.

• Plan B: the profitable level of the pricing scale. It's what I charge for most jobs now. I call it the "Profit Share" plan and it will make you good money. It's a good price level to jump to when you are feeling comfortable with the quality of the job you are doing, when you are comfortable that new customers will keep coming in, and when you realize the advice you are giving your customers is getting pretty good as your turf knowledge increases.

• Plan C: the big profits level of the pricing scale; what I call the "HiProfit Share" plan. Whether you can charge this will depend on your market and the answer to the question: What are people willing to pay? It's appropriate when you know you are doing the best aeration job in town and when your value as a turf expert makes you worth the price. Unless you've found a bonanza, you have to be careful not to price too many people out of the market. But know that the price you are charging is still reasonable. You are doing quality work. You should be paid well for it.

"The key in setting your price is that you want to hit both ends of the market," Pedrotti continues. "You want the customer who is very price conscious, and also the customer who will spend whatever it takes to make his lawn lush and green. The profit of this business is in volume and in appealing to everyone considering an aeration." This can be applied to other lawn services as well.

Specializing

Lawn Aeration

Lawn Aeration is a good-paying specialty, but requires a sizable start-up cost – namely the price of an aerating machine. Lawn aeration basically involves poking holes in a lawn with a special machine. A good lawn aerator mechanically removes small cores of earth and grass. This helps relieve soil compaction that occurs from traffic, watering or weather and allows the lawn's root system to better absorb water and nutrients from the soil, building a stronger root system and healthier turf.

Robin Pedrotti, author of "Lawn Aeration: Turn Hard Soil into Cold Cash," put himself through college aerating lawns on weekends, and after graduating with a degree in speech communications, continued to make more money aerating lawns part time than at his regular job at Xerox. Now a professional financial officer (broker), he has cut back to only one day a week, doing only a few jobs, yet he still makes $800 a month aerating. "Without much effort you can make $1,000 in extra income part time on weekends without disrupting your normal life," Pedrotti says. "You can make $35,000, $40,000, $50,000 a year doing it full time and only working eight months out of the year. You can make $10,000, $15,000, $20,000 a year as an all-out summer job if you're working your way through high school or college. And I know that's true because I've done it. It's great for teachers, firemen or anyone who has a flexible job schedule," Pedrotti says.

It's not a get-rich-quick scheme, he stresses. "This is a business. It is going to cost you $6,500 to buy the tools, equipment and supplies that it takes to start this business."

"Don't buy cheap" is his main advice for purchasing an aerator. Even though he got his start in the business with a small $1,100 aerator, he says the machine didn't deliver the fantastic lawns he promised customers. After testing several machines over five years there's only one he recommends, the Ryan Lawnaire 28, which costs about $4,500. In his book, he discusses in detail the advantages of this machine and the pros and cons of other brands and types of machines.

For those who are strapped financially, he says it is possible to start a bare-bones aeration business with only a truck (or a car and trailer) and $500. He is currently working on a guide for those who want to begin aerating with rental equipment. "It would be a temporary situation—you could build up your business from there until you earn enough to buy your own machine." The $500 includes items like a broom ($20 instead of a $350 air blower), a $30 spreader instead of an $80 one and a $100 a day rental fee for the aerating machine instead of $4,500 to buy one. Also included in the $500 is a telephone answering machine and other smaller items.

Another consideration is the work itself. The self-propelled aerator weighs about 350 pounds, so being able to heft this piece of equipment around a yard and up onto the truck requires some strength. "The real difficulty with the machine as far as where size comes into play is moving the machine around the lawn and making turns with it," Pedrotti says. A medium-sized woman could do it. If you weigh 100 pounds or so you're probably not going to like this, whether you're a man or woman."

Pedrotti's price ranges, based on the plans he mentions above and on national and local (Southern California) averages, for residential aerating of a front lawn up to 2,000 square feet are

- Plan A   Market Share $32.50
- Plan B   Profit Share $37.50
- Plan C   HiProfit Share $40.00

For "super-small lawns" he charges $22.50. He says the average front lawn takes about 15-20 minutes to aerate.

For larger lawns or estates of 7,500, 15,000 square feet and one acre, his pricing is as follows:

- Plan A   Market Share $85, $135, $400
- Plan B   Profit Share $95, $150, $500
- Plan C   HiProfit Share $110, $175, $600

"Keep in mind that it is critical to do a quality job at a quality price that cannot be beaten by a competitor," he writes.

The Natural Approach

In the last six years or so, both large and small lawn-care companies have begun to offer organic programs and environmentally safe systems. Such services have been popping up in the Yellow Pages alongside the others. Even the big chemical-applying lawn service companies are changing their names – but not necessarily their approach – to sound more environmentally responsible. And it's no wonder.

Research has shown that popular residential pesticides such as diazinon and 2,4-D (a major component of Agent Orange) kill birds and cause cancer in dogs. In 1987 diazinon was banned from golf courses after it killed 800 geese on a New York golf course. It is still legal for home lawns, however, and more than six million pounds of it are used annually in the United States. There have also been documented human deaths from allergic reactions to pesticides and fungicides used on home lawns and golf courses.

Many of the chemicals we've been using on our lawns for decades are just beginning to show some serious, long-term health effects. "Of the 36 most commonly used lawn pesticides, 13 can cause cancer, 14 can cause birth defects, 11 can have reproductive effects, 21 can damage the nervous system, 15 can injure the liver or kidneys and 30 are sensitizers or irritants," says Jay Feldman, executive director of the Washington, D.C.-based National Coalition Against Misuse of Pesticides.

Many people who offer lawn and garden services no longer want to risk constant exposure to questionable chemicals and are using them sparingly or have switched to "natural" or "organic" lawn care. Those offering environmentally safe lawn care are doing some of the following things:
• Mixing different grass varieties for improved disease resistance.
• Using fertilizers from animal manure instead of chemicals.
• Aerating and thatching to create healthy root systems and turf, rather than just dumping on fungicides and pesticides.
• Using only spot applications of chemicals, when they must be used, rather than dousing the whole lawn. This generally works only for residential and smaller commercial applications because it is more time and labor intensive.
• Xeriscaping or using ground covers rather than grass in difficult areas or replacing lawns altogether with native plants, grasses and/or wildflower mixes. Xeriscaping is a type of landscaping that uses native or drought-resistant plants in arid areas. Since the native plants have evolved to grow in these areas, they require less overall care and are resistant to insects, disease and climate fluctuations.

Other innovative approaches – actually old-time, home-made recipes – include:
• Using vinegar to kill weeds.
• Pouring a small amount of vegetable oil on the soil after pulling weeds to discourage re-growth by sealing the tap root.
• Using a mixture of orange peel and hydrogen peroxide as an insecticide/fungicide on lawns. It works well on soft-bodied bugs and moisture-loving fungi by simply drying them up. A good reference book on this subject is *Rodale's Chemical-Free Yard & Garden*, published by Rodale Press, Emmaus Pennsylvania. This book advises on natural insect, disease and weed

187

control; soil rejuvenation for higher yields, problem solving for 125 different types of plants, an in-depth guide to non-toxic products and a month-by-month garden care calendar. *Common-Sense Pest Control*, published by The Taunton Press in Newtown, Connecticut contains the "least-toxic solutions for your home, garden, pets and community."

The Franchise Option

Lawn Doctor has been in business for over 25 years and is the national franchise leader in automated lawn care. Lawn Doctor has approximately 300 franchisees in 32 states. "We don't cut grass, and we don't do windows," quips Ed Reid, Lawn Doctor's national franchise sales director. "We do weeding and feeding and then we have a custom care format for our people once they have built a base of business of seeding, core aeration and tree and shrub. We have been ranked nine years in a row in our category as the number 1 franchise in lawn care in "Entrepreneur" magazine. We are in the top 80 franchises for women in U.S., and have roughly 34 women running Lawn Doctors. We're in the top 50 franchises in "Black Enterprises" magazine of minority owned franchises in the country."

Lawn Doctor was started by Anthony Giordano, a former New Jersey hardware store owner, who started offering lawn-care clinics on Sunday mornings for customers. Giordano would advise people on various fertilizers, weed and insect killers and design custom programs for their lawns. Eventually, the customers wanted Giordano to come and apply the chemicals, too.

Robert Magda, an engineer friend of Giordano's, created a special machine that could be calibrated to distribute several different chemicals simultaneously on a lawn. This "Turf Tamer" is Lawn Doctor's main piece of equipment and claim to fame and success in the industry. The Turf Tamer can cover 1,000 feet per minute putting down four different types of material on the lawn simultaneously. Lawn Doctor uses granular or dry fertilizer rather than the big chemical tank trucks some other companies use.

The cost of a franchise is $25,500 with an additional

$5,000 in working capital required. The franchise owner has to pay a royalty of 10 percent of their gross income. An owner can expect to earn 20 to 35 percent of their gross sales. The national average gross income for franchise owners is $100,000 to $400,000 annually.

Included in the franchise package is $18,000 of tangible assets and goods, a down payment of $1,090 to the lease of the Turf Tamer, as well as hotel, food and training costs, including transportation for two people. The two-week training session takes place in Matawan, New Jersey. Financing (up to $10,000) is available for qualified people for five years at 12 percent interest.

Franchise Pros and Cons

Franchise owner Karen Johnson says one of the things she likes about Lawn Doctor is that franchisees don't have to purchase fertilizer or other chemicals from the company. They can buy them locally and shop for the best price. Lawn Doctor now also offers a non-chemical fertilizer – made from a by-product of paper – for customers who prefer it. Franchise owners can use their own vans or rent one through the company.

Johnson says that, although the royalty payment some-times seems like a lot, she's feels it's worth paying for the logo – the unforgettable big, green thumb – and the national reputation. "The royalty checks can get to be a lot, but what we get in return for paying them is constant – the name, like McDonald's, is worth a lot of money." An additional advertis-ing fund pays for various kinds of advertising, including TV – "great exposure that we could never afford otherwise." The additional advertising fee is usually less than 5 percent of gross income.

"When a person joins Lawn Doctor and is awarded a franchise a dealer development team stays with them on a very concentrated basis for two years. We have found that the most important part of putting a person in business is the first year – they're scared, they're frightened, and it's so important to provide that kind of support system," franchise director Reid says.

There are also state-wide meetings with other franchise owners. Johnson says she finds these meetings very helpful for discussing different approaches and/or problems.

Another great advantage she says, is having the company as a resource. "The agronomists are always testing new products and developing new equipment all the time," she says. "We can call them first instead of wasting time or money."

For information about Lawn Doctor franchises, call 1-800- 631-5660, which is the Matawan, N.J. headquarters.

Other Specialties

Tree Trimming, sprinkler repair and rototilling are some other lawn and garden specialties requiring varying degrees of skill and knowledge. There's more to trimming trees than cutting off dead branches. Cutting in certain places can help strengthen the tree. Depending upon the area of the country, a tree-trimming service can switch to a firewood or snow removal business in the winter months. Do some research at your public library, call a county extension service for courses and information, or work with an established tree trimmer to get the experience you need.

Kent Lugbill of Green Mountain Services includes tree trimming among his services. He says he generally charges a flat rate for removing a tree, for instance $200. An hourly rate, he says "kind of scares people." He says getting rid of the debris is getting to be a real problem. The transfer station he uses charges $14 a load, "and they don't like the stumps." So, when bidding a job, tree trimmers also have to figure in removal of the debris and trips to the dump. "Tree work costs more than garden work because it's more dangerous and involved. If you drop a tree on somebody's house or garage they tend to be upset. It's also more stressful because there's always a chance of getting hurt."

Lubgill also does some sprinkler repair and installation, which he says is a bit tricky to learn. "There are no books or classes on it and very little formal training. There's no certification and no real standard ways of doing things. It's not like plumbing or electrical work – there are almost no laws regulating it. It's basically something that people just learn by doing. Hopefully, they have somebody who knows something showing them how to do things. Suppliers can help some, too."

Lugbill says some of the sprinkler installation must be done by a licensed plumber, but "once you're past the vacuum breaker, anybody can do it legally. Installation of sprinkler systems tends to be not always well done."

Those with less specific skills can still start out and make a living doing basic yard work, raking, moving, garden rototilling and general maintenance.

Legalities and Accounting

Depending upon the services you offer, some states require licensing and bonding. The U.S. Department of Agriculture is the place to start for your own state's licensing regulations in the lawn-care industry. Simple bookkeeping is usually all that's required, but you'll need to check with the Internal Revenue Service for self-employment tax and Social Security procedures.

Tips

Be professional. "Don't look fly by night," says landscaper Joe Reichert. "Open a business account, have the business name printed on your checks – that's also good for discounts at nurseries, etc. Have business cards printed and put a sign on your truck."

"It's really helpful to start out slowly," Julie Brown of Prolawn says. "Dan didn't give up his full-time job immediately. He worked a year or two doing things on weekends. The equipment is important – getting the right kind of equipment – and a cash reserve is important to buy good equipment. Our truck and trailers were always used, but we've always bought new equipment and tools." It helps to have the warranty on equipment. When the Browns began their business, a bookkeeper friend helped Julie set up the books, which she said was quite simple. Other tips offered by Brown and others are:

• Be organized. Figure on spending some time to send out bills and keep on top of all the other office work once the business gets going. It really helps to have a partner or spouse to handle the office work and phone calls. When that's not possible, a pager can help you stay on top of customer calls and not lose them.

• Choose clients carefully. The Browns have found it easier to work with commercial people than homeowners. "Homeowners tend to be older and they're out there all the time every week, demanding extra things, and creating interruptions. Because they're there, they tend to be more picky and demanding – and often want to chat," which is hard on a busy schedule. If a potential client appears to be overly demanding or difficult, it may be better in the long run to let him/her go in the beginning.

• Provide good customer service and a friendly "yard-side manner." "It's amazing how often people call, whether there's something going wrong or they need this or that and how much time Dan spends on the phone when he gets home returning his phone calls. I think his personality is very important and beneficial to how well our business has done," Julie Brown says. "It's one thing to be able to do a good job out there physically, but I think you have to have some of those PR traits to make it work. It's just amazing how important that is. I think that's what got him a lot of his work initially. I think people liked him and they obviously liked the work and so they keep using him. That's definitely a biggy. You can't just look at it as the work end of it. You've got to kind of have the whole picture to make it work."

• Get contracts with clients. Try to get contracts to insure a steady and continued flow of work – two-year contracts, if possible. Decide on a price before the work is done and get it in writing. That way neither party has any unpleasant or unpaid-for surprises or expectations.

Disadvantages

Like any type of work, there are pluses and minuses with the lawn and garden service business. Some of the minuses mentioned are "You have to do all the books. You have to keep focused to keep the business going," Reichert says.

"You have to be committed – it's your business, and it can be hard around the holidays," Julie Brown says. In winter, their business switches to snow removal. "If there's a snowstorm on Thanksgiving or Christmas, Dan's out plowing snow. You have to have that commitment because you're responsible for doing those jobs, so you just sacrifice the freedom to say we're going to take the day off." Like any form of self-employment, there's the element of uncertainty and insecurity about income. "We retain about 90 percent of our clients," Brown says. "But sometimes lose clients to other bidders. You're not always guaranteed to have the same clients, Brown says. "We try to get people to sign for more than a year instead of just one season – we've always tried to get two-year agreements – but many people prefer to go from year to year." She says they start sending notices to old clients in February every year, but sometimes it's close to April 1 before they know who their clients will be.

Lawn and garden services are seasonal in most places – with the exception of Hawaii and Florida – so you'll have to plan for the slack period. Many people switch to another service such as snow removal. Others take time for vacation, travel and other pursuits. The seasonal nature of the work can be a disadvantage for some and an advantage for others.

Rewards

"There are more advantages than disadvantages," Julie Brown concludes after 11 years in the lawn and garden business. Some of the greatest advantages she and others name are "being your own boss, and having something that's your own." She also says they couldn't have made as much money as they've made working for someone else. In the slack season the Browns are also able to enjoy their two children and family life more fully along with other activities. "It was scary at first, but I'm glad we decided to do it."

Lawn and garden services are not for those who want to make a quick and easy buck. This business is for those who take satisfaction in an honest day's work and pride in a job well done. There's a certain aesthetic, nurturing quality to the work. Improving a client's surroundings by keeping a lawn and garden lush, green and healthy provides a visible and tangible reward. Add to this the client's expressed pleasure in having this pleasant work or home environment, and you have rewarding work that keeps on growing.

Chapter 11
Opportunities in Gift Baskets

In the early 80's a few people found they could make a very good living putting together gift baskets for individuals and businesses (who give them to employees or clients). Over the years the popularity of these gifts–and the opportunties for gift basket services–has steadily increased.

A Tisket, a Tasket: An Income in a Basket

Check the Yellow Pages in any fair-sized town today and you'll find listings of gift basket companies that create personalized baskets for any occasion and even ship out of state. In addition to all the holiday baskets, the theme possibilities are endless: boredom baskets with card games and puzzles for people convalescing in hospitals; romance baskets with champagne, glasses and romantic tapes; British tea garden baskets with cups and saucers, teas, scones and jams; earth baskets filled with environmental products.

The gift basket business ranges from the small, part-time "hobby-business" operated from one's dining room table or garage to a full-scale warehouse operation with a showroom and dozens of employees, including "account executives" who scout out corporations for new clients. It's an attractive business for new mothers who want to work at home to be with their babies or those who enjoy assembling creative "care packages" to send to friends and relatives – and want to expand it into a business. Most gift basket business proprietors are women, but that's not to say the creative, male homebody or househusband wouldn't enjoy the basket business as well. Other reasons for starting a gift basket operation arise from discovering a niche in a particular market or geographical area. One California property manager, for example, saw a need for gift baskets for new tenants and left the real estate field to start her own gift basket business, which she now manages full time.

Personalizing Professionally

Generally, those who start gift basket businesses are attracted to the fun and creative aspect of it. What could be nicer than assembling a hand-picked assortment of clever or delicious personalized presents or gourmet snacks. It's like a Christmas stocking. Though anyone can learn to assemble an attractive basket of treats, it takes a certain creative flair and artistic bent to enjoy the work and keep coming up with new ideas and styles (though trade catalogues and magazines now offer plenty of ideas).

Shopping enthusiasts will enjoy perusing the wide selection of items from distributors' catalogs or at local wholesale merchandise marts. Some of the perks of the business, once it is established, are invitations to trade shows worldwide to sample chocolate, gourmet food and wine. One recently wed couple who run "The Basket Case," a large and successful gift basket company in Washington, D.C., spent their honeymoon in France tasting cheeses.

Creating a beautiful gift basket for a satisfied customer offers both tangible and intangible rewards: the product itself and the happy buyer and receiver. But, like other home businesses, once the orders start rolling in, the business and organizational aspect can overshadow the fun and creativity for those who aren't prepared.

Personal Histories

Carol Onderdonk is a clinical social worker with a private practice who also operates "Personally Yours," a gift basket business in Boulder, Colorado. She specializes in baskets with Colorado and Southwestern themes. After moving to Colorado in 1989 she met a woman in a networking group who owned a Colorado gift basket business and "thought it would

196

be wonderful to send Colorado gifts back to my friends back in New York. I went to see her little basket shop in her home and thought, 'Oh, boy, wouldn't this be fun?' About three months later, I discovered that the business was for sale and I bought it – after much soul searching and fear and trepidation."

Starting the business in October, she says she somehow made it through her first Christmas. The following Christmas, she received an order for 1,500 $25 baskets from the local hospital and hired employees to help. She says she wouldn't hire employees again because of all of the paperwork and taxes involved. When she needs extra help around holidays now, she hires temporary people who will earn less than $600, thus avoiding the tax complications. Currently she has about 200 regular clients and divides her time between gift baskets and her social work practice.

In her Colorado gift baskets, Onderdonk packs hand-made candy from chocolate companies and such other locally made goodies as almond toffee, hot fudge brownie mix, jellies, popcorn and soup mixes. "From Boulder, there's Celestial Seasonings Tea and Allegro Coffee, and we have a wonderful nut-butter company here," she says. In the Southwestern baskets she packs chili jellies and mustards, pinyon-caramel sauce, salsas, moles (a tangy mexican sauce for meat and main dishes), posole soup mix, pinyon nut cookie mix – all kinds of southwestern specialties.

Onderdonk will make any type of basket a customer requests, including items such as candies, cookies, crackers, desert toppings, flavored oils and vinegars, pasta and pasta sauces, cheeses and sausages. She orders the items from distributors and the Denver Merchandise Mart. For the Colorado products, she says, "You kind of have to scout out. There's no one rep that represents just Colorado things. So, you kind of have to go around the state – which is wonderful fun."

Some of her clients are travel agents, real estate agents and the local hospital, which orders up to five baskets a week to congratulate, honor and acknowledge each department in the hospital, she says. For travel agents and real estate, she includes their own promotional materials "like mugs, business cards, note pads, key chains or pens." Onderdonk charges

197

anywhere from $12 to $200 for a basket, with an average price of $25-$30. About 60 percent of her clients are corporate; 40 percent are individuals.

Cheryl Wright was a senior merchandise manager with JC Penney, had a degree in marketing and distribution and had taught business and marketing at area colleges in Orange County, California. But when her first baby was born, she says, "I had no desire to go back out to work." When her business partner suggested the gift basket business she says she "felt that was something good to do from home and still sort of be working a bit.... Plus, I've always been real creative and kind of crafty. We basically almost stumbled upon the idea – and nobody was doing it around the area." So, three years ago they started Robin's Nest Baskets in Wright's garage, where they still operate it.

"You really have to have that work area. You have to have a whole room to devote to it, you can't just do it in the kitchen–like on the kitchen table," she says. Wright lives in Corona, California, which is on the outskirts of Riverside. Since it's close to the Orange County line, she says, "We border on a lot of real affluent areas, as well, and there's nobody (making gift baskets) in that area either, so it seemed to work out real well."

She started out on a small scale, by word of mouth and gradually built her business. Now with 10 or 12 corporate clients she feels she is still building her business gradually. She experimented with retail shops but said that was a dismal failure, because the shops' mark up made the baskets too expensive, and as a result they didn't sell. She has found that, like Onderdonk, her best clients are corporate ones. Her corporate clients, for instance insurance companies, send the baskets to their brokers at Christmas time as a way of thanking them.

Wright's gift baskets fall into every category: gourmet foods, baby baskets, wedding baskets, golf baskets – which she says are a big item since they also operate an office in Palm Springs – and even bereavement baskets. The gourmet food baskets contain crackers, coffees, teas, cheese, pastas, cakes; the specialty theme baskets contain small gifts like baby rattles and toys or golf trinkets. The bereavement basket contains coffees, teas, a mug with a nice saying or a pretty picture and a spiritual book with some poems.

Wright's business is listed in the National Directory of Gourmet Basket Retailers – sort of like Teleflora – which she says is a great advantage and resource. (The address is given below.) Through this service she sends baskets for local clients with friends, relatives or business acquaintances in other states and receives similar referral business from other states for her area.

Bonnie Barry started The Basket Case in 1986 in her Silver Spring, Maryland, home. She was the property manager, mentioned earlier, who saw a need for gift baskets for new tenants. By 1991, the business had outgrown its home base plus an additional rented storage area, and Barry moved the whole operation to a 4,000-square-foot warehouse, where she still manages it. She currently has six full-time employees, in addition to herself, and about 600 corporate clients. During the holidays she employs as many as 50 people and has up to 18 incoming phone lines. At these busy times she calls upon temporary service companies for help answering phones. After the first couple years of delivering the baskets herself she switched to a courier service, which does all deliveries.

Early on she focused on corporate clients and soon realized that she couldn't operate the business via an answering machine. "Bonnie has built her business strictly from the quality of merchandise and the service with which the merchandise gets there – from the phone to the delivery person, it's 'service, service, service,'" says Lyle Bush, The Basket Case's vice president of operations (who also recently became Bonnie's spouse). Barry agrees, saying people with message machines that say "Sorry we can't take your call, we're out on delivery," are going to lose corporate clients, who don't have time to wait or call back. "If you're not there, they're going to go to someone else." The Basket Case services the entire Washington, D.C. metropolitan area.

Compared to the other two businesses mentioned earlier, Barry's is much higher volume. It is no longer the laid-back, part-time, one-person home-based business with the

199

proprietor making the deliveries herself. But it shows where a home-based business can lead. She says in the Washington area there's a big network of businesses thanking other businesses and lawyers thanking other lawyers for help on a case. Businesses also send gift baskets for apologies: for instance, roofing companies send baskets to make amends when the roofers track dirt into a customer's house.

Because of the volume of the business, Barry has greater purchasing power and can get greater discounts. Around the holidays she buys a half a tractor-trailer load of cheesecakes – over 2,000 cheesecakes. Barry's baskets range in price up to $150, with an average of $43. During the non-holiday season, The Basket Case delivers about 18 baskets a day. During the holiday period, hundreds of baskets are delivered daily. Barry says it's been really tough building and running the business – and still is – and only now is she beginning to enjoy the fruits of her extensive labors.

Start Up Costs

Start-up costs can range from a few hundred dollars to several thousand or more. Wright invested around $3,000 originally but says people can start with much less; Barry estimates $15,000. Ron Perkin's book, *How to Find Your Treasure in a Gift Basket*, gives the following ball park figures for the low and high range of home-based start-up costs:

	Low	High
Initial Inventory (for sample baskets)	$300	$ 500
Wrapping Supplies	50	150
Business Licenses	100	150
Advertising	0	1,000
Business Cards	30	100
Work Bench	75	150
Phone Answering Machine	30	50
TOTAL EXPENSES	$635	$2,200

It's possible to spend much more on start up costs, of course. Other items you might reasonably want to add in include a shrink-wrap machine ($80-$200), a hot glue gun ($5-

$20), a computer and printer ($1,500), a two-color brochure or flyer ($100-$2,000), and a portfolio of photographs of your baskets, professionally taken, to show to prospective customers ($100-$500). You may also choose to invest more in your initial inventory, possibly earning larger discounts in the process.

It's not just the gifts that go into the basket that add up in inventory volume and price, but also what is used to decorate the basket – the cellophane, filler and bows. Though Wright started up with an investment of around $3,000, she says those who start out with corporate accounts can, ideally, receive a 50 percent deposit when the order is placed and use that money to purchase supplies needed for the order. She invested more because, "We wanted to start out with a fair amount so we'd have something to show," she says.

Licenses and Regulations

Business licenses vary by state, so check with state and local authorities for requirements. Also ask about zoning regulations in your neighborhood. Condominium or townhouse dwellers should check with their homeowner's association for regulations pertaining to operating businesses from individual units. If you plan to package any of your own food items, you'll need to contact the Health Department for their regulations. Wine and spirits require a separate license, so consult the local liquor control commission. When handling food products for gift baskets, a resale license is often required.

Targeting Customers

Giving some thought to the type of customer you want to reach will help you determine your inventory requirements. Will you target up-scale customers who are sophisticated and have gourmet palates, or those who might prefer more homespun gift items, or businesses that want to thank employees or clients? You may want to market to a combination of different markets, but the important thing is to visualize as clearly as possible what those different markets are, along with each

201

market's unique tastes, price considerations, and other characteristics. In fact, it may help to think of one individual (real or imaginary) as being representative of each market you intend to target.

Getting Organized

You'll also need to give some thought to organizing all the materials in your house in a specific room or turning part of the house into a showroom. Lighting is important, and is critical to both productivity in the work room and display in the showroom. Natural light is best for seeing true colors and coordinating the baskets. Fluorescent or track lighting works well to illuminate an area; an incandescent light from a single point is effective in accent lighting for displaying baskets.

Most people beginning in the home-based gift basket business will display sample baskets in their homes. In addition to setting aside an area as a "showroom," you can use your gift baskets in your own home decorating. "Your 'designer baskets' can be a beautiful embellishment to your home decor. These can generate sales not only from specific clients, but from friends and acquaintances who visit the house as well.

In setting up a work area you'll probably need the following: a desk and chair to do paperwork and make phone calls; space for a computer, typewriter, calculator and any other office equipment; space for filing cabinets, books and reference materials (including catalogs from suppliers); storage space for your inventory and working materials; a work bench for assembling your baskets, shrink wrapping them and preparing them for shipping. You'll also need a living room or other conversation area with chairs or a couch, where you can receive customers, hold business meetings, and "close the sale."

A Word about Telephones

Since the lifeline of the gift basket business is usually the telephone, there are a number of options to seriously consider that will help the business run more smoothly and efficiently, saving time and money: portable or cordless phones will keep you from running from one room to another while making baskets; a cellular phone for the car, though expensive, has the obvious advantage of allowing you to catch all your calls, even while making deliveries; call forwarding is an option that transfers calls to another number when you're away (such as to your answering service) which can prevent you from missing an order; call waiting allows you to put a customer on hold while you catch another incoming call. Sometimes a busy signal can drive away sales. There's also an option of having two numbers on one line that have different-sounding rings. That way, you can use one telephone line for both business and personal use and answer the phone appropriately according to the ring. This option offers the convenience of two separate telephone lines but at a much lower cost.

Have a Business Plan

"Whether planning to start a tiny home-based gift basket service or buy a franchised gift basket shop or other such 'turnkey' business opportunities, a business plan will greatly increase the chances of a business's success since it forces a person to research and take an objective look at the new business," writes Ron Perkins in *How to Find Your Treasure in a Gift Basket*. A basic business plan includes:

• Statement of Purpose: A short explanation of why the business plan was written and what the goals of the company are.
• Executive Summary: A one-page synopsis that describes the product or service and explains why this new company will succeed in the face of existing competition. When trying to get assistance from an investor, it's important to show how it will provide a high rate of return on his invested capital.
• Description of Business: A detailed explanation of how the idea for your particular gift basket service was conceived and developed. Discuss research and industry studies that relate

to your particular product and its potential for future growth.

• Marketing Plan: This represents the heart of a good business plan since you obviously can't stay in business for very long if no one buys your gift baskets.

• Competition Analysis: Find out exactly where other gift basket shops are located in your proposed market area, along with which type of their baskets sell the best, what time of the day they do the most business, if their business is profitable, etc. One way to investigate these otherwise confidential factors is to park across the street from the shop and watch.

• Pro Forma Profit and Loss Estimate: This will take into account every possible expense that is likely to arise during the first year or two of business. Sales projections should be very conservative and based upon research of similar operations, and not just an off-the-cuff guess.

• Management Qualifications: Summarize how the company's principal officers were recruited for this business and how their experience makes them especially useful to the company. At the end of this section include a complete resume for each of the principal officers.

"In addition to the usual elements of the business plan, it's good to have a critical path or timeline," says James Keegan of Keegan Capital Development. His company reviews business plans and helps ventures raise money through private investors and venture capital groups. "One of the most common mistakes I see in business plans is that there is only a vague idea of how much money is needed and how it will be used."

Lyle Bush of The Basket Case also espouses writing a business plan: "Before anybody decides to get into the gift basket business or any business, they should think seriously about doing a business plan – having a written plan of what they want to do and the goals that they want to accomplish. Have it as a one-year plan, a three-year and five-year. And work your plan, no matter what the economy does, no matter what your buying power is at the time, no matter what the response for your services is, work your plan and make the best of it." This plan will help guide you through the crises, Bush says – even good crises like an overwhelming number of orders.

Buying Inventory

When the time arrives for purchasing the baskets and merchandise to begin your business, select a company with a large selection of baskets in different styles, materials, weaves and colors. The more materials you order from one company the greater the discount and the lower the shipping charges – especially if it's a one-time freight charge.

More and more distributors are catering to home-business operators and allowing smaller wholesale orders – not the case five to 10 years ago. Most distributors allow a minimum of $250 on the first order and $100 minimum on reorders. There's generally a handling charge of $5-$10 on orders less than $50.

After establishing credit with a supplier, you can take advantage of further discounts, such as the 2 percent discount usually offered if you pay for your order within 10 days. To establish credit, suppliers usually require three trade references.

For other items check local discount stores, grocery stores and outlets – which can sometimes offer great bargains. Those in larger cities will find gift buyers' "marts" a great boon. Perkins' book lists marts in some major cities, for example, the Atlanta Merchandise Mart, the Dallas Market Center, the Denver Merchandise Mart, the Indianapolis Gift Mart, Kansas City Merchandise Mart, the New York Merchandise Mart and Marketcenter in New York City, the San Francisco Giftcenter and also the Western Merchandise Mart.

For food items, select products that have a long shelf life such as preserves, candies, cookies and condiments. Order fall/winter holiday items before the end of September to be well stocked. Perishable goods are obviously trickier to handle and include such items as breads, cheeses, packaged meats, cakes, fruits and chocolate. Freshness is imperative with perishable items, so you'll need to order smaller quantities and order more frequently. Also, be sure to ask suppliers how long the items have been in their warehouse and use the supplier with the freshest products.

205

Learning the Craft and the Business

Those with little design experience should consider taking a course in floral design at a community college or university extension program. Craft, novelty and gift trade shows can help provide ideas, and beginners should subscribe to "Gift Basket Review" magazine, which has monthly how-to articles on different aspects of basket assembly. The magazine also has video how-to tapes on such things as shrink wrapping.

Some adult education programs like the Learning Annex offer actual courses in starting a gift basket business. Talking with other people in the gift basket business can be of real benefit. Carol Onderdonk suggests interviewing non-competing gift basket business owners (outside of your marketing area) to get a sense of the business and learn the pitfalls. "It really doesn't take a lot of business sense as long as you remember to get your prices up there. Make sure you make a profit," Onderdonk says.

Advertising and Promotion

"People have to buy gifts for certain occasions. It's not a question of a gimmick item. Your job is to make them buy your basket instead of buying flowers. Buying gifts is a known commodity that you know people are going to spend money on. Promotional skills are the whole key to this business," author Perkins says.

Many gift basket proprietors begin advertising through word of mouth. That's a fine way to start and provides an opportunity to grow gradually. All along the way, referrals are the life blood of the gift basket business: often the receiver, who is delighted with the gift basket he or she has received, will order one for someone they know – and on and on. So it's important to always include a nicely designed tag or business card on every basket, preferably with an attractive logo, your business name, address and phone number on it.

"It's a referral business," says Lisa Hughes Anderson, who has operated Gift Basket Headquarters in Irvine, Califor-

206

nia since 1987 in a father-daughter partnership. "Often your best advertising is someone receiving a basket." By delivering a basket to someone who works for a big car manufacturer, for instance, you may land the company as a client. Individuals help get you into companies.

"The key is being visible." Don't sit back and wait after buying all the equipment and materials, because the business probably isn't going to come to your front door. You might have to do some cold-calling, actual pounding of the pavement going to office buildings, attorneys' offices and the like with your wares. "The best selling tool is an actual basket. And always make sure you have brochures and cards with you." Anderson hands these out in elevators while making deliveries or to anyone she passes along the way who admires or inquires about the baskets when she's delivering them. "It's real important not be timid." The key is also doing your homework: research your market, get business cards printed immediately and "Don't be too cutesy in the name."

"The best promotion I do is my brochure and I do that in a mailing," Onderdonk says. "But that's getting really expensive." She has a mailing list of 3,500 people and says that's probably the best return she gets on her advertising dollar. The second best advertising opportunity she gets is the twice-annual trade show at the Chamber of Commerce. "For $100 they'll give you a table and you can bring your wares. They have up to 500 local business people come through and she offers a free basket for putting their business card in her basket. "That's one of the way's I've built my mailing list. I've gotten some of my big hotel clients through that such as Holiday Inn and Homewood Suites."

Other ways to get business include networking and using personal contacts in organizations such as trade and business associations and church groups –and periodically providing a gift basket for a door prize at their meetings, calling on corporate and organization buyers (show your portfolio and leave sample baskets for decision-makers), obtaining publicity in local or regional publications about your unique baskets, giving your flyers or brochures to reps exhibiting at gift shows (who can place your baskets with retailers), and

207

exhibiting at craft fairs and home shows. As a result of your publicity and exhibits at shows, you can gradually build your own mailing list of interested people that you can mail flyers to. You can also talk about and display your baskets at home parties and open houses. One often-overlooked promotional idea is to donate baskets to nonprofit organizations for their fund-raisers in exchange for an acknowledgement in their printed materials and an announcement from the podium during the event.

"It's important to have a budget. There are so many different promotions you can do, you can really go overboard," Onderdonk says. "Especially if you work out of your home. I think advertising is second to inventory in your budget." Onderdonk has tried display ads in newspapers – "they have not been effective." She says one ad that really was effective last year was a holiday buying guide in the local paper's classified section. It was divided up into "gifts under $25, $50, $100." She put a little classified ad in – "I think it cost me less than $100, and I got tons of calls from it – much to my surprise." She says around the holidays she also puts an eighth of a page ad in the Chamber of Commerce newsletter, which costs $180. She also tried an ad in a local magazine that cost $500 and got only two calls from it. "So you just don't know."

Barry also names the Chamber of Commerce as a great place to network and find more clients, and also, the Board of Trade and the Washington Convention and Visitor Association. Those who live in cities of some size will have similar organizations.

Both Anderson and Onderdonk strongly recommend a listing in the Yellow Pages. Both say they get lots of calls from their Yellow Page ads, and they're worth the price (about $60 a month for a large color ad) – the bigger and more colorful, the better.

Tips and Advice

"Don't overbuy," is one of the most important warnings to heed. If you buy too many Valentine hearts or chocolate santas – and don't have enough orders – you're out of luck (and money). Other tips:

• "Find the nicest, lowest price baskets you can find. People are not all that interested in the basket, for the most part. Keep the basket price as low as possible so that you can have more things to put in it," Onderdonk advises.

• Cheryl Wright warns potential gift basket entrepreneurs to "Stay away from retail accounts." The markup makes the baskets too costly to sell well.

• Start by making some really beautiful sample baskets to show to potential customers.

• Go slowly, don't take on too much too soon. "Even if it's just one corporate account. That would get you going and you can work on building your business the rest of the time," Wright says. "Sometimes all it takes is for a customer to hear you're doing Apple computers, for example. That gets them interested and then you get another account. If you really do your best, they will refer you to others. Go that little bit extra."

• Buy Wholesale. "You're not going to make any money in this business unless you buy your supplies wholesale," all the gift basket business owners advise. If you pay retail prices for your supplies the baskets will be too expensive for people to buy at a price that would leave you a reasonable profit.

• "Try not to use your own funds," Anderson says. "It will eat up your savings."

• "Buy smart," she adds. "When you start your own business, don't go out and buy the top of the line computer, the top of the line answering machine – wait a while and see what your needs really are. We bought a used Xerox machine and a used fax machine, and they all work wonderfully for what our needs are. I think people put their dollars into some areas that really aren't necessary."

• Stay in the home as long as possible – don't try to get out as soon as possible. Once you locate in a rented space, overhead costs dramatically increase.

• As is true in a lot of sales businesses, says Anderson, "People are buying you as well as your product. Personalities and relationships – establishing relationships – and being real true to them, is tremendously important." For instance, she says a good working relationship is often more important than other factors: "You may get someone who will come in with a lower price – like someone who does your printing, for example, – but if you've got a really good relationship with someone, then you'll give them another chance or you'll continue to do work with them because you trust them."

• Those shipping baskets out of state should consider the daily pick-up service offered by United Parcel Service. For a small weekly charge of only $5 they will come daily, Monday through Friday, to pick up your outgoing packages.

What to Charge

Your costs for a basket and its contents should be roughly 25 percent of the final cost to the customer. Those who buy in small quantities, however, receiving only small discounts may find themselves paying 50 percent of the sales price for materials. Figure in overhead, which averages 20 to 40 percent of the sales price. For corporate customers or other large orders, most businesses offer quantity discounts. Pricing has to do with artistic quality and design, but the simplest designs don't necessarily have to be the least expensive.

Most people use what is known in the business as "keystoning" which is doubling the price of the materials. Then they add on other charges like shipping and "enhancements." Onderdonk adds on an additional 10 percent for "enhancements," which includes bows, colored shred, silk flowers and other decorative additions like flowers and calico fabric covers for jars.

Anderson says she started with the double markup on materials and goods, but now does a 2.5- and 3-time mark up based on the labor, materials and quantity. "It's real hard to increase the markup, but if you don't charge enough you won't get paid for your labor and you won't be able to make your ends meet. You can work your butt off in this business. The reward is creating a business that doesn't go under. It's our fifth year and we consider it a howling success because we're breaking even." She says she is reinvesting any profits she makes back into the business.

Earning Potential

Simple math shows that if you sell 25 baskets a week, 50 weeks of the year at $40 a basket, you can reach $50,000 a year in gross sales. In an hour, approximately 8 simple baskets can be assembled. More complicated baskets require more time–possibly averaging only three or four per hour. A reasonable gross income for one person doing a full-time gift basket business is $30,000. It all depends on how good your marketing skills are and how hard you want to work.

Disadvantages

Those who aren't careful can find their homes buried in shredded paper, cans of smoked salmon, chocolate, cellophane – and of, course, baskets. Gift baskets tend to be a seasonal business with a huge rush at Christmas and other holidays and slow periods in between, unless you do constant and creative marketing.

Extra help is a must at busy times, and they must be paid, too, taking their share of your profits. Then there's competition with the big mail-order companies like Harry and David.

Onderdonk says, "We don't ever get our own Christmas, and you've got to do your Christmas shipping early." Barry warns, "Be prepared to have a lot of headaches and to work a lot of hours. It's been real hard. It takes a lot of time, and there's a lot of frustration. It's fun, but often it isn't fun. It's a push all the time just making sure people are doing what they're supposed to be doing like getting the deliveries right; it's a push always pleasing people – some people you can't please no matter what, even though you think you're doing the best job you can."

Like other home-based businesses you have to do it all – the bookkeeping, accounting, marketing, promoting, billing, the basket making, delivering, supply ordering and inventory control.

211

Rewards

On the other hand, gift baskets are a positive, fun business and a unique service. "People like to get them and like to give them," Onderdonk says, "because it's not just one gift, it's like getting four or five gifts in one. It's a fun business and there are very few complaints if you do a decent job." The business allows for creative expression and can easily be done part time.

"Baskets are my therapy," says Onderdonk. "It's creative. I'm not particularly artistic, but it's just kind of fun to arrange things and have it look pretty. I also enjoy the relationships I have, particularly with my Colorado suppliers. They're just wonderful people. When I started this, there were two things that I really wanted to do in terms of supporting other people. One was to support other women business owners and the other was to support Colorado companies. A lot of them are women-owned, and it's fun to watch them grow and be successful."

Resources

The National Directory of Gourmet Basket Retailers is published by Telefood United Publications in Yarmouth, Maine; telephone: (207) 846-0600. This directory lists the different suppliers and retailers by state and city. Once listed in the directory, businesses get out-of-state customers who need baskets delivered in their area, or vice versa. The service is similar to the FTD or Teleflora flowers by wire in the floral industry. Generally the business that refers an order to another state receives 10 to 20 percent of the profit.

"Gift Basket Review" magazine is the magazine of the gift basket industry and is available in craft stores and larger magazine shops or through Festivities Publications in Jacksonville, Florida. It provides names of suppliers, design ideas and instructional articles such as "Building Better Gift Baskets." The magazine also sells video how-to tapes on different techniques—for instance, how to shrink wrap. The publisher also sponsors an annual trade show and gift basket convention.

Please see the appendex for additional resources.

Resource Guide

Note: the following are selections from THE WHOLE WORK CATALOG. To receive a free copy of the complete catalog, see page 236.

WORD PROCESSING

Word Processing Profits at Home: A Complete Business Plan
Peggy Glenn $18.95   **#0115**   ©92 pb   lg format

The fastest growing segment of the home business boom is data and word processing by computer, according to the U.S. Chamber of Commerce. This comprehensive handbook covers virtually every aspect of running a home-based word processing business. With candor, warmth and humor, Glenn discusses personal considerations, planning, advertising, pricing, equipment, marketing, legal aspects, customer relations, professionalism and much more. Recommended by the Small Business Administration.

Word Processing Plus: Profiles of Home-Based Success
Hodson $15.95 **#1951** ©91 pb

Marcia Hodson interviewed 44 women who successfully work at home and share their secrets on obtaining start-up funds, choosing equipment, pricing their services, reaching their market and more. We think this nicely complements Peggy Glenn's book by showing all the unique solutions *real* people have come up with–even showing the artwork and services listed on their business cards.

INDEPENDENT PUBLISHING

Desktop Publishing Success: How to Start and Run a Desktop Publishing Business
Kramer $29.95 **#1848** ©91 pb

This is an outstanding guide to starting a business providing desktop publishing services to businesses, organizations, etc. "If ever a book should be called The Bible of the Desktop Publishing Biz, this is it. Kramer and Lovaas walk the reader through every step of establishing and growing a business, from practical marketing and salesmanship to keeping the books, from bidding on a project to dropping an unprofitable client, from finding customers to expanding revenues.... It's all here, told by people who have done it all and genuinely know what they're talking about." –*Publish* magazine

How to Make $100,000 a Year in Desktop Publishing
Williams $18.95   **#1933**   ©90

Williams' company reached $1 million in sales after just four years of publishing regional magazines, a city magazine and other magazines, books and directories.   His large-format guide has chapters on Publishing a Quality of Life Magazine, Publishing a Tourism Guide, Publishing a newcomer's Guide, Publishing a City Magazine, Publishing Association and Membership Directories, Publishing a City or County History, Publishing a Weekly Newspaper or Shoppers' Guide, How to Sell information by Mail, and more. Does not cover businesses which sell DTP services (see *Desktop Publishing Success*).

Publishing Newsletters
Howard Penn Hudson $13.95   **#0157**   ©88   pb

Wherever there's a specialized, identifiable interest group there's a newsletter market, and newsletter publishing is now recognized as one of the fastest growing businesses in the U.S. The potential in this field is impressive, and Howard Penn Hudson, publisher of "The Newsletter on Newsletters," tells you everything you need to know to launch a newsletter: how to find and judge your market, determine editorial content, style, composition, advertising, goals, production, design, etc. This revised edition includes information on desktop publishing and a gallery of newsletters showing specific examples of how to use graphics. "It's like attending a $500 seminar on the subject of newslettering at less than 1/20th of that price. It's a great achievement." —Ed Brown, ATCOM

How to Publish a Parenting Paper on Your Kitchen Table
Grimm $19.95   **#2202**   ©91   pb

In the last few years there's been a boom in publications catering to the special needs of parents, focusing on local events and local people. This book, by the publishers of a parenting newspaper in Eau Claire, Wis., shows how to start and operate such a newspaper as a home business.   We're impressed by the amount of detail given, covering everything from layout and design to lining up local columnists to earning a profit (a well-run paper should become profitable within a year, according to the authors).   A unique desktop publishing opportunity, and a very attractive, well-executed book.

Is There a Book Inside You? How to Successfully Author a Book Alone or Through Collaboration   Poynter $14.95   **#0219**   ©91   pb

Using a step-by-step process this guide shows how you can author a book whether or not you have the time or ability to be a good writer.   How to pick your topic, break the topic down into easy-to-attack segments, evaluate your publishing options and find and work with co-authors, ghostwriters, contract writers, editors, researchers and clerical support, as needed. "...introduces the science of management to the art of writing."—Jan Nathan, PASA

The Self-Publishing Manual (7th Edition)
Dan Poynter $19.95   **#0423**   ©93   pb

If you're a writer you should consider self-publishing to make more money, to keep control of your manuscript, to get into print sooner and to make your manuscript a long-term asset. Poynter has self-published some twenty books, including several best sellers. He shares every detail of how he built an enormously successful one-man publishing company. "Expertly organized and chock full of hard facts, helpful hints, and pertinent illustrations."—*The Southeastern Librarian* "...indispensable"—*Self-Publishing Book Review*

How to Make a Whole Lot More Than $1,000,000 Writing, Commissioning, Publishing and Selling "How-To" Information
Lant $39.95   **#1898**   ©90   pb

Jeffrey Lant has built a one-person information empire, and he's adamant that anyone with motivation can do the same. This is a hefty volume with an impressive amount of detail on making money from books, booklets, audio cassettes and special reports. Full information is provided both for producing your own material and/or commissioning others to do the writing (while you concentrate on marketing). If you really want to ride the information-age wave—working at home with just your computer, fax machine and creative marketing imagination—you'll love this book.

Everyone's Guide to Successful Publications
Adler $28.00   **#1350**   ©93   pb

Written specifically for tight-budget operations using desktop publishing technology, Adler shows how to produce effective ads, brochures, flyers, posters, catalogs, directories, newsletters, reports, proposals, letters, letterhead, books and more. Includes 40 quick-reference sidebars filled with money-and time-saving tips as well as creative suggestions, practical advice and graphic examples on making the entire publication process work to grab and hold your reader's attention. As you would expect, this is a beautifully designed book–and it's guaranteed to improve the effectiveness of your publications.

EDUCATIONAL SERVICES

The Teaching Marketplace: Make Money With Freelance Teaching, Corporate Trainings, and On the Lecture Circuit   Brodsky and Geis
$14.95   **#1853**   ©91   pb

There's a huge, fast-growing market for non-credit education programs because they're fun and a great way to meet new people, in addition to their career advancement aspects. This unusual book shows how to turn almost any experience or personal enthusiasm into such a class—and an enjoyable source of part-time income for you. Covers choosing your topic, attracting students, organizing and selling your classes to schools and corporations—or freelancing on your own, the best times to teach, selecting a class space, keeping records, etc., plus fascinating profiles of freelance teachers.

CHILD CARE SERVICES

Start Your Own At-Home Child Care Business
Gallagher $12.95   **#2244**   ©89   pb

There are a number of books out on this topic, but in our opinion Patricia Gallagher's is clearly the best. Speaking from her own extensive experience, Gallagher covers getting started, cutting through red tape to get a license and zoning permit, promoting your business, establishing policies for payments and other matters, building good relationships with parents, plus suggested daily activity plans, stimulating play-and-learn activities, craft recipies and much, much more.

217

Kids Mean Business: How to Turn Your Love of Children Into a Profitable and Wonderfully Satisfying Business   Manning $9.95   **#0104**   ©85 pb

This is the age of the gourmet baby and the designer nursery, and very few fields currently offer as much potential for self-employment as child-related businesses. Manning's book explores a wide range of opportunities, from children's clothing boutiques to toys to day care, and from writing kids' books to teaching classes in everything from toddler gymnastics to computer programming. If you like children and you're considering self-employment, this is the book to read. There are truly exceptional opportunities in this field. "... a well-written, enthusiastic catalog of ideas." —*Library Journal*

RESEARCH & INFORMATION SERVICES

The Information Broker's Handbook
Rugge $29.95   **#2226**   ©92 pb

Information brokering is one of the hottest entrepreneurial fields of the 90s, and this is easily the most comprehensive, authoritative, up-to-date guide to the opportunities available. Starting from scratch, author Sue Rugge grew her own information brokerage company to the $2 million annual sales level, and she covers all the nuts and bolts here. Includes a free disk of business forms, information on all the search and retrieval options available today, details on establishing an office, marketing and selling your services, pricing and billing, etc. *Highly recommended.*

How to Make Money With Your Micro
Holtz $16.95   **#0066**   ©89 pb

This revised, updated guide provides ideas for money-making home ventures (including new possibilities in desktop publishing), worksheets and checklists that make it easier to set up your business, and all the nuts and bolts—setting fees and pricing, billing, legal and tax aspects, etc. "If you're interested in using your computer to make money, Herman Holtz's [book] will get you started in no time. Holtz gives solid advice on how to identify market needs, ways to fill them by using your micro, and what to be aware of when setting up your own business or free-lance venture."—*Family Computing* "We highly recommend this book . . . " —*Home Business News*

How To Be a Successful Computer Consultant
Simon $19.95   **#0159**   ©90 pb

A comprehensive, step-by-step guide for anyone who wants to build a successful career in computer consulting. Covers why people use computer consultants, the background you need, how to find clients, how much to charge, choosing your area of specialization (in systems design or custom software), marketing, getting publicity, staying current and more. Detailed, thorough advice.

900 Know-How: How to Succeed With Your Own 900 Number Business
Mastin $19.95   **#2574**   ©92 pb

This book shows how to start a business selling pre-recorded information—anything from pork belly prices to horoscopes— over the phone to a national market. According to the author, the 900 number industry has grown to $975,000,000 in just a few years and presents tremendous opportunities for anyone wanting to work part-time from home. "offers detailed advice on how to succeed with a 900 number"-*The Midwest Book Review*

How to Start and Profit from a Mailing List Service
Allegato/Edwards $19.95   **#1945**   ©91   75 minute audio program

This two-cassette program covers intriguing opportunities for working at home using a personal computer and mailing list software. Katie Allegato of Allegato & Associates explains how to create mailing lists from client-supplied data, monthly update services you can offer on a subscription basis, opportunities for compiling mailing lists on your own, and more. Covers getting started inexpensively, profitable special services you can offer, pricing and discounting techniques, ways to maximize your profits, how much you can expect to earn, and imaginative, offbeat and unusual ways to market mailing lists.

The Consultant's Calling
Bellman $15.95   **#2214**   ©90   pb

This is one of those books people fall in love with and rave about to all their friends. "Bellman presents consulting not merely as a way to work but rather as a way to live. Subtitled 'Bringing who you are to what you do,' this book covers the gamut from the practical (making money, creating a schedule) to the psychological (love of self, love of work). This is a very human work."–*New Age Journal* " I laughed and cried and hummed as I read ...It left me feeling affirmed..." –C. Bell

The Consultant's Kit: Establishing and Operating Your Successful Consulting Business   Lant $34.95   **#0124**   ©91   pb   lg format

We usually avoid carrying $35 books, but in a very few cases the expense seems justified. This is such a book—brimming with insights, tips and ideas, written by an acknowledged expert who quickly, easily and specifically shows you what works—and what doesn't. How to select a marketable skill, create a diversified service line, find and retain clients, get money each month from retainers, profit from commission contracts, spin off seminars and workshops, get free publicity and basically sell what you know in the most effective manner possible.

Infopreneurs: Turning Data Into Dollars
Weitzen $22.95   **#0265**   ©88   hc

Infopreneurs gather, organize and disseminate information for a profit, relying more on creativity than capital to launch their businesses. Weitzen gives a start-up plan for becoming an infopreneur, including finding an information-hungry market, leveraging data banks to create new opportunities, cost-effectively providing information 24 hours a day, customizing data for specific clients, repackaging information to produce information products and services for new markets, and obtaining instant payment for the information you supply. The profiles and examples are especially good.

Money Talks: The Complete Guide to Creating a Profitable Workshop or Seminar in Any Field   Lant $34.95   **#0160**   ©91   pb   lg format

"Workshops, seminars and lectures are a superb way of making money," begins Dr. Lant, who gives over 100 presentations a year himself. Creating programs that sell, training yourself to give effective presentations, breaking into the paying markets, identifying sponsors for your programs, mastering the college, trade and professional association markets, creating audio and video teleconferences, and much more. Highly recommended for anyone who knows how to do something that other people need and can use. "This seminar guide is by far the most complete I've seen."—J. L. Kennedy, syndicated columnist

Mastering the Information Age
McCarthy $12.95   **#2266**   ©91   pb

Knowing how to find, evaluate, organize and use information–without being overwhelmed by the shear volume of information available–may well be the critical skill for the nineties and beyond. McCarthy's new book shows how to control information rather than letting it control you, how to read faster and more effectively, find the information you need quickly, remember more, think more sharply, present information to others and use such advanced techniques as "grokking." There are some very clever ideas in this appealing, user-friendly guide.

GROWING SPECIALTY PLANTS

Backyard Cash Crops
Craig Wallin $14.95   **#2578**   ©89   pb

Subtitled "The Source Book for Growing and Marketing Specialty Plants," this is a guide to earning money growing any of 200 specialty crops including bulbs, culinary herbs, medicinal herbs, ornamentals, sprouts, small fruits, and much more. Covers deciding on the best specialty crop for you, how to sell all you can grow, how to buy wholesale seed and plant starts, where to get free expert advice for any crop, and much more. Very nicely illustrated, in-depth information.

Profits From Your Backyard Herb Garden
Lee Sturdivant $10.95   **#1242**   ©88   pb

Writing for the spare time gardener with a small space to grow in, Sturdivant describes exactly which herbs to grow, how to package, label, and sell them to local grocers and restaurants. She promises her techniques will bring an income of $50 to $250 a week, based on her experience growing herbs in her own backyard for the last five years. Also covers other herb businesses to consider.

Flowers For Sale: Growing & Marketing Cut Flowers
Sturdivant $15.95   **#2112**   ©92   pb

This book gives an easy, step-by-step plan for starting a flower growing and selling business either in your backyard or on a small acreage. Numerous successful flower businesses are profiled, including Saturday Market flower sellers and one grower who takes in $650,000 on less than an acre of flower production. Hundreds of plant varieties with potential as commercial cut flowers are listed, with seed sources and other information. Covers harvesting, pricing, displaying, selling, business and tax information, collecting flowers and greenery from the wild, more.

Christmas Trees: Growing and Selling Trees, Wreaths, and Greens
Hill $10.95   **#1234**   ©89   pb

Money does grow on trees, and Lewis Hill's book outlines in careful detail just how to gain the pleasure and profit of growing and selling trees, wreaths, and greens. Prospective growers will find complete information for developing and profiting from a continuously productive Christmas tree grove, with advice on selecting excellent strains, planting wisely, shearing, fertilizing, harvesting and selling both retail and wholesale.

How to Make Money Growing Plants, Trees & Flowers
Francix Jozwik, Ph.D. $19.95   **#2118**   ©92   pb

Dr. Jozwik, who has operated a successful greenhouse and nursery business for over 20 years, shows how to make a significant income growing special ornamental crops in your own backyard. He explains why these ornamentals are in such great demand and gives all the nuts and bolts for getting started without technical expertise or spending a lot of money. Detailed examples show the ins and outs of each type of business with actual economic data for specific operations. Photo illustrations throughout.

Ecopreneuring: The Green Guide to Small Business Opportunities From the Environmental Revolution   Steven J. Bennett $17.95 **#1774** ©91 pb

Bennett's guide shows how to take advantage of the many small business opportunities now developing with environment-related products and services. Covers opportunities in recycling, safe foods and food packaging, green products (e.g, personal and baby care products), green travel services, education and training services, and much more. Includes information on market size, growth potential, overhead, special equipment, marketing and public relations, etc., plus numerous case studies of successful ecopreneurs. A very comprehensive and up-to-date start-up guide.

WRITING AND EDITING SERVICES

How to Start and Run a Writing & Editing Business
Herman Holtz $14.95   **#2198**   ©92   pb

Writing and editing can be a viable business, and part of the trick is simply in knowing enough to position yourself as an editorial consultant. Holtz shows how to turn your writing skills into a steady source of income by servicing a variety of markets—including corporations, profit and nonprofit organizations, and the "vast" government market. Covers getting a full- or part-time writing business off the ground, matching your interests with real opportunities (writing everything from proposals and manuals to catalogs and newsletters), setting up your dream office, more. *Highly recommended.*

How You Can Make $25,000 a Year Writing (No Matter Where You Live)
Hanson $14.95   **#1905**   ©87   pb

How to cultivate magazine markets and write books–profitably–in the boonies, how to break into broadcast writing, how to develop a base of commercial clients, how to embark on a freelance editing career, how to set profitable yearly, monthly, and hourly rates, and much more. Hanson has authored hundreds of magazine articles and six books, worked as a PR practitioner, and served as editor for a variety of publications. Her experience shines through in this extremely detailed–and very well written–guide.

Secrets of a Freelance Writer
Bly $12.95   **#1264**   ©88   pb

The subtitle–"How to Make $85,000 a Year"–may be a slight exaggeration, but it's clear the type of commercial writing Bly advocates can be highly lucrative. This is a guide to providing the writing businesses need to promote their products, services, or ideas (including ads, annual reports, brochures, catalogs, and other promotional pieces). The author, an independent copywriter and consultant specializing in direct-response advertising, gives how-to tips and strategies for tapping these well-paying markets. "For inspiration alone, this book is well worth the price." —*National Home Business Report*

The Awful Truth About Publishing
Boswell $14.95   **#0015** ©86 hc

Subtitled "Why they always reject your manuscript–and what you can do about it." Boswell, a top publishing executive, demystifies book publishing with wit, humor and a great deal of first-hand insight. How to compose submission letters and proposals that actually get an editor's attention, research your market and understand your audience, and shape and focus an idea into a book that publishers will want to buy. "A good, sharp analysis of what it takes to get published today. Anyone interested in writing professionally needs to read this book."–J. Romanos, Simon & Schuster

The Resume Pro
Parker $24.95 **#2182** ©92 pb

We know of one woman who spends 15 to 20 hours a week writing resumes for people who makes $1,500 to $2,000 a month for her efforts. With the right know-how, other people can probably do as well—and finally there's a book that provides the right know-how. Yana Parker, author of *The Damn Good Resume Guide* and an acknowledged authority in this field, shows how to create resumes for people with a wide range of skills and experience and covers the nuts and bolts of setting up and operating a resume-writing service business. Large format, 416 pages.

A Guide to Travel Writing & Photography
Purcell $22.95 **#1861** ©91 pb

The Purcells are seasoned travel journalists who show how to travel the world and be paid for it in this beautiful book. The trick, according to the authors, is to deliver a complete package of pictures and text that's in ready-to-publish form. How to set up a travel journalism business, set realistic goals, get the word out about your services, find salable ideas, find strong images to support your articles, do the necessary research and create interesting articles that will excite editors. Very comprehensive information illustrated with 80 color photos.

How to Write Romances
Pianka $15.95 **#1299** ©88 hc

According to Phyllis Taylor Pianka (whose 12 romance novels have sold more than half a million copies), you can enter the intriguing world of the romance writer and be respectably paid for indulging your passions. How to find and develop strong story ideas, create believable characters, write dialogue that rings true, make your settings work storytelling magic, develop plots rich in romance, write romance into sensuality and sexuality, and submit your work for publication with good prospects of a happy ending.

Writing for Children & Teenagers
Wyndham $12.95 **#0184** ©89 pb

This guide to writing for and selling to the juvenile market will show you how to make time to write, get your story off to a running start, collect characters, spin a plot, build suspense, emotion and atmosphere, organize your book, prepare a professional manuscript submission packet and handle special writing projects such as biographies, mysteries and easy-to-read books. Based on actual, successful experience by the author of more than 50 books. Revised/updated.

CLEANING SERVICES

Cleaning Up for a Living
Aslett $13.95 **#0010** ©91 pb

Aslett, who has built a $12 million commercial cleaning business from scratch, gives step-by-step guidance for would-be cleaning entrepreneurs. He points out that cleaning is a fast growing industry and a relatively easy market to enter, requiring little start-up capital and no specific education ... but it does take specific know-how to succeed. His book gives all the charts, forms, business rules and information you need to get started. Large format, illustrated, index.

How to Start a Window Cleaning Business
Suval $14.95 **#1392** ©88 pb

Window washers are in high demand, says Suval, and you can expect to make $10 to $25 an hour once you build up speed. It's a skill that's easy to learn, pleasant to do, and has little competition. How to reach potential customers, obtain your equipment, wash windows the professional way, know what to charge, keep business records, and much more. Large format, illustrated, revised third edition.

LAWN AND GARDEN SERVICES

Lawn Aeration: Turn Hard Soil Into Cold Cash
Robin Pedrotti $19.95 **#2200** ©92 pb

This is one of those offbeat businesses that nobody's ever heard of—but that can produce a very good income when you know what you're doing. It costs about $6,500 to buy the equipment and supplies, but if you believe the author—and we think he's extremely convincing—you can make $35,000-$50,000 working full time only eight months of the year. It's also possible to get started with only $500 or so if you begin by renting your equipment. A good, thorough guide to an intriguing business opportunity.

MAKING AND MARKETING GIFT BASKETS

How to Find Your Treasure in a Gift Basket
Perkins $16.95 **#1964** ©91 pb

In the early 80's a few people found they could make a very good living putting together gift baskets for individuals and businesses (who give them to employees or clients). Over the years the popularity of these gifts–and the opportunities for gift basket services–has steadily increased. Perkins shows how to start a home-based gift basket service, starting with a minimal investment, and covers how to make beautiful gift baskets (filled with wine, cheese, fruit, candy, and other items), finding customers, the most popular theme baskets, more.

MISCELLANEOUS OPPORTUNITIES

Creative Cash: How to Sell Your Crafts, Needlework, Designs & Know-how
Brabec $14.95 **#0162** ©91 pb lg format

There's a good reason why over 70,000 copies of this book are in print: it is truly outstanding. As *Crafts and Things* Magazine puts it, "A practical (and witty) guide for the would-be entrepreneur that discusses the obvious—and not so obvious—ways of making money from crafts. This may be the best book on making money from crafts that we have ever seen." Informative, thoroughly enjoyable reading, with step-by-step how-to's.

Crafts Marketing Success Secrets
Brabec $9.95   **#0209**   ©91 pb lg format

This sequel to <u>Creative Cash</u> (above) is a collection of the best crafts marketing articles, letters, and how-to-make-money information from the author's periodicals. More than 100 crafts professionals are featured, with information on selling at fairs, to shops/galleries, wholesaling, marketing through trade shows, party plans, co-op shows and shops. Also covers networking, using finishing tags and labels, and insights into the successful operation of a handcrafts shop.

From Kitchen to Market: Selling Your Gourmet Food Specialty
Hall $24.95   **#2228**   ©92 pb

Hall shows how to become a freelance foodcrafter, taking advantage of America's insatiable hunger for new and different taste sensations by creating a profitable small-scale food business of your own. Whatever delicacy comes from your kitchen, this unique book shows how to sell it locally, nationally and internationally, with info on start-up costs, consumer demand, pricing, packaging, distribution and more. "Hall's guide may be the definitive manual in reaching…gourmet store shelves."—*Gourmet News*

Photo Business Careers
Art Evans $19.95   **#2272**   ©92 pb

This is a great-looking new book covering the ins and outs of starting your own photography business. All types of opportunities are covered—both full and part-time–from stock photo sales to photo franchises to running a custom lab in your own home. Includes ways to make money in PR without an investment, opportunities for owning your own one-hour lab, freelancing in your spare time, etc. Large format, photo illustrations. "some of the best advice you can find anywhere…"–Bob Shell, Editor, *Shutterbug*

How to Open and Operate a Bed & Breakfast
Stankus $14.95   **#0201**   ©92 pb

New Edition. The most comprehensive book on starting a B & B in your home we've seen, with complete start-up advice, an exclusive "Helping Hands Network" of current hosts from all over the country who are willing to advise newcomers, lots of charts and checklists and a "Should You Become a Bed and Breakfast Host?" quiz. "immensely readable and engaging"—*America's Bed & Breakfast*

How to Become a Professional Calligrapher
Stuart David $9.95   **#1926**   ©85 pb

With practice, almost anyone can develop the skills to make money from hand lettering envelopes (for weddings, parties, dinners, bar mitzvahs, etc.), fill-ins (all-types of certificates and pre-printed invitations), signs, menus, business cards and stationery, greeting cards, personalized T-shirts, etc., according to this very attractive, large-format guide. Covers how to find clients, how to charge, materials and procedures, developing your craft and more.

How to Start and Run Your Own Advertising Agency
Krieff $27.95   **#2242**   ©92   hc

Krieff did start his own ad agency...and it now has billings of over $32 million annually. Written in an easy-to-use, step-by-step format, he gives all the tools you need to develop your business plan, comply with all advertising and business regulations, lease office space, prospect for and keep clients, choose the right media, and create effective advertising. Includes checklists, glossaries, sample contracts, financial statements, legal forms and other materials to guide you every step of the way.

This Business of Art
Cochrane $19.95 **#0888** ©88 hc

This revised edition is a comprehensive guide to business practices for artists. Topics include contracts (and why they're essential), copyright and other rights, commission agreements, the artist as seller and exhibitor, bookkeeping made easy, the artist and the dealer, tax deductions you can take as an artist, royalties, how to prepare a proposal, consignment sales, law (libel, invasion of privacy, obscenity), insurance considerations and much more.

How to be an Importer and Pay for Your World Travel
Green/Gillmar $8.95 **#0187** ©93 pb

Completely updated for the 90s, this book shows you where to go, what to buy, how to pay for it, and how to get it home and then sell it. Includes current tariff schedules, the latest customs regulations, all the nitty-gritty details. Green is the founder of a hugely successful import company in San Francisco; Gillmar is an attorney experienced in import-export practices. This book has the kind of insights and wisdom that only comes from firsthand, hard won experience.

Playing for Pay: How to be a Working Musician
Gibson $17.95 **#2568** ©90 pb lg format

Whether you are a beginning or professional musician, you need two things to build a successful music performing career--a clear, honest view of the music business, and a plan of action. This book gives you both. Beginning with an overview of what freelancing in music really involves, Gibson moves on to show you how to create a strategic job-finding plan that will help you sell your music, regardless of where you live or what instrument you play. Includes checklists, worksheets, interviews with professionals, much more.

The Complete Caterer
Lawrence $14.95 **#2708** ©92 pb

How to get started, plan menus, shop effectively, meet schedules, price your services, market yourself, deal with insurance, taxes, client contracts and more. Includes recipes for a sampling of parties. "Anyone with a love of cooking ... can be a caterer. This book shows you how to get started, how to make your business grow, and, best of all, how to have a good time while giving other people good times." — Irena Chalmers

Massage: A Career at Your Fingertips
Ashley $19.95 **#2580** ©92 pb

"This comprehensive handbook covers everything the massage therapist needs to know:

225

education and certification, marketing, taxes, insurance, office management, and so forth. In addition, it provides extensive resources, including a directory of schools and licensing laws for all 50 states.... Schools offering advanced coursework in the different massage specialties are listed, as are suppliers, professional associations, and newsletters....An invaluable guide."–*Library Journal*

Small Store Success
Pittman $9.95   **#1177**   ©90   pb

This attractive book covers all the ingredients for starting and operating your own store, including store layout and design, promotions, advertising, buying merchandise, controlling inventory, customer service, computerizing your business, working with suppliers, and more. Pittman gives practical advice combined with insights from interviews with dozens of successful retailers. Highly informative without being overwhelming.

How to Make Cash Money at Swap Meets, Flea Markets, etc.
Cooper $14.95   **#1247**   ©88   pb

After Jordan Cooper was laid off from his job, he and his wife held a yard sale and then took the leftover items to a local swap meet. In one day, they took in several hundred dollars. He hasn't worked at a regular job since, and sometimes he makes more money in a single weekend than he made in an entire month at his former job. How to start with a minimal investment, select your merchandise, set your prices, advertise, and run a profitable cash business either part-time or full-time.

Making $70,000 a Year As a Self-Employed Manufacturer's Representative
Silliphant $10.95   **#0266**   ©88   pb

For a variety of reasons, more and more companies, both large and small, are turning to the independent representative as a way to effectively sell their products. How to get started and prosper in this very lucrative, rapidly growing field. Covers deciding what to sell, negotiating with the manufacturer, choosing travel or non-travel work, planning, locating clients, much more.

Build Your Own Network Sales Business
Kishel $14.95   **#2264**   ©92   pb

The Wall Street Journal predicts that 50-60% of all goods and services in the United States will be sold through multilevel or network methods during the 1990s. This new book shows you how to cash in on this billion-dollar phenomenon with your own self-replicating network. How to pick the multilevel marketing organization that's right for you, choose the right product or service, manage your time, address tax and legal considerations, attract and keep customers, more.

How to Make a Living in Antiques
Ketchum $22.95   **#1267**   ©90   hc

Ketchum explains all aspects of running a prosperous antique business including picking a specialty, making buying trips, bidding at auctions, buying from foreign sources, working out of your home, selling by mail, becoming a "picker-dealer," designing shop space, establishing a clientele, spotting fakes (and what to do if you're stung), and refinishing, restoration and other spin-off activities.

226

How to Recognize and Refinish Antiques for Pleasure and Profit
Peake $15.95 **#2110** ©84 hc

If you enjoy finding castaway treasures at garage sales and flea markets, Jacquelyn Peake's book is for you. By knowing what to look for and how to refinish and sell your finds, you can actually make a very enjoyable living as an antiquer. Includes solid information on the nuts and bolts of refinishing antiques plus insights on finding and recognizing the best buys and selling your projects from your home, on consignment, or at antique shows. Photo illustrations.

Home-Based Mail Order: A Success Guide for Entrepreneurs
Bond $14.95 **#1235** ©90 pb

As far as we know, this is the first book to approach mail order as a home business. Actually, it's an ideal home business, as we discovered first hand (our own business was started in a spare bedroom, then operated out of a converted garage for two years before we moved to commercial space). The author has 25 years of experience and gives advice that is upbeat and inspirational, yet highly practical. How to: select the right products or services, decide how to approach your market, develop a system for efficiently responding to inquiries and filling orders, expand your business steadily while avoiding uncontrolled growth, and much more.

Complete Direct Marketing Sourcebook
Kremer $19.95 **#1347** ©92 hc

Somebody had a good idea here–a book which brings together all the forms, sample letters, charts, formulas and procedures you need to run a streamlined, efficient mail-order operation. Some of the forms are masters, ready for you to copy and use; others only require that you add your letterhead at the top before copying. If you're going into the mail-order business this "swipe file" can greatly simplify your life. Highly recommended.

The Business of Sewing: How to Start, Maintain and Achieve Success
Barbara Wright-Sykes $14.95 **#2256** ©92 pb

This new guide to achieving success with your own sewing business shows how to overcome your fears and problems common to this type of business, design your office and sewing studio, find and retain clients, develop a profit-making price list, save money on supplies, and expand your business and your professional talents. "Barbara Wright Sykes has written an encouraging and very informative guide on how to put your love of sewing to work for you. She provides great inspiration to anyone with entrepreneurial spirit!" -P. Nilson, Simplicity Pattern Co.

The Independent Paralegal's Handbook
Ralph Warner, attorney $19.95 **#0169** ©91 pb

More and more people are saving money by turning to independent paralegals instead of lawyers to help them prepare routine legal paperwork. This updated guide shows how to open a legal form-typing business, with information on legal areas open to independent paralegals, where to get necessary training, what to name your business, how much to charge, how to market your services, strategies designed to avoid "unauthorized practice of law" charges, and interviews with six important figures in the paralegal movement. The potential for this type of business is simply enormous. An exciting opportunity.

How To Be a Weekend Entrepreneur
Ratliff $9.95   **#2208**   ©91   pb

This is a short-but-sweet guide to making money at craft fairs, trade shows and swap meets, written by the woman named Entrepreneurial Mother of the Year for 1989. Easy instructions, simple illustrations and checklists help you to find the best exhibiting opportunities, select the most profitable events, design and build a dynamic exhibit, and succeed at a relatively low-risk, low-investment business start-up.

How to Earn $15 to $50 an Hour With a Pickup or Van
Lilly $12.95   **#0246**   ©87   pb

If you're between careers or just don't want serious commitments for a while, this little guide can show you how to make a decent living with only a battered old truck or van and a willingness to work hard. A side bonus is the treasures you can find while hauling away people's "junk" (the author was paid to haul away a late 19th century oil painting, for example, later appraised at $400). There are some things we don't like about the book--the cover, amateurish layout and slightly inflated price--but overall Lilly covers the topic in a straightforward, honest, very thorough manner.

Pet Sitting For Profit
Moran $14.95   **#0916**   ©91   pb

Frankly, we were skeptical when we first heard about this. But when we learned the author started the business out of her home on a shoestring budget and now employs more than 30 part-time pet sitters, we decided to look more closely. Pet sitting is actually a good small-scale opportunity, thoroughly and competently covered by Moran's book. "... an absolute must. It covers everything from office procedures, legal structure, telephone techniques and customer complaints to advertising."—*Dog Week*

Turning Wool Into a Cottage Industry
Paula Simmons $14.95   **#0172**   ©91   pb

Simmons has thirty years of experience as a sheepraiser, spinner, weaver, teacher and author, and in this book she shows how a cottage industry involving wool can be the key to the good life. Beginning with raising and managing a flock of sheep or buying wool for resale, here is information on all aspects of home processing and selling raw and washed wool; carding as a cottage industry; the best equipment; business and merchandising tips; ideas for expanding a wool-based income; and descriptions of 18 entrepreneurs who've proved it can be done.

A Manual on Bookselling
$17.95   **#0142**   ©88   pb

Do you love books and dream of owning your own bookstore? This is the 4th edition of the definitive guide to the business of selling books, covering every facet of opening and running a bookstore. 60+ articles include "How to Become a Bookseller," "Promoting a New Store," "Retail Salesmanship," "Hardcover Bookselling," "Books About Books," much more. Indispensable information for anyone considering the book business, from the American Booksellers Association.

Complete Guide to Starting a Used Bookstore
Gilbert $14.95   **#1638**   ©91   pb

The author has owned and sold three extremely successful used bookstores. He shows why it's a good business to get into, what to look for in a site and a lease, how to lay it out and build it right, acquiring your opening stock, how to advertise, price, trade and buy, common mistakes and how to avoid them, and much more. "Sound first-hand information on those practices that make the difference between success and failure in the used book business."–*BookQuote*

Building an Import/Export Business
Weiss $14.95 **#0220** ©91 pb

Few businesses are as potentially lucrative as international trade, writes the author, an experienced import/export consultant. In step-by-step fashion, Weiss shows the types of businesses that offer the best opportunities, how to select products and suppliers, how to reach markets and customers, how to handle the nuts and bolts of international transactions and end up with a stable, profitable business for yourself. Very thorough, dependable advice.

Invest in Yourself: Put a Cash Business on Every Corner
Strauser $16.95 **#2246** ©91 pb

Florists are hard-pressed to keep up with demand on Mother's Day, Easter, Valentine's day and some other holidays. Strauser's book shows how to select high-traffic streetcorners, hire corner salespeople, buy flowers wholesale, and make a lot of money on these days. To a lesser extent this business can be worked every weekend on good corner locations. "I was amazed at the cash that I saw Jack Strauser make, between six and ten thousand dollars on any given weekend, any given holiday"-Tom Sterba, Banker, Chicago

HOME-BASED AND SMALL BUSINESS IN GENERAL

Earning Money Without a Job
Levinson $9.95 **#0108** ©91 pb

Hundreds of money-making ideas—some obvious, some surprising—all within the realm of immediate opportunity. Hardly any require much capital, and most can be done out of your home. This is an exceptionally well-written book that's a pleasure to read. "The real answer to being your own boss is many small jobs. This book is the best guide available."—*The Next Whole Earth Catalog*

Homemade Money: The Definitive Guide to Success in a Home Business
Brabec $18.95 **#0875** ©92 pb lg format

One of the foremost authorities on the boom in home businesses gives expert advice on getting started, selecting the right home business (and avoiding the wrong ones), planning for profits, resources for beginning entrepreneurs, strategies for diversification and expansion and more. As editor and publisher of the *National Home Business Report*, Brabec has unique insights to offer in this delightfully well-written, graphically appealing, very comprehensive guide. 3rd edition. "An invaluable tool for anyone starting, expanding, or maintaining a home business."--*Booklist*

National Home Business Report
Barbara Brabec, Ed. $24/year **#0200** Quarterly, 28 pages

Since 1981 this has consistantly been the most helpful, informative newsletter for those interested in running a home business. "One of the best publications in the field" – *Home Office Computing* "... a smorgasbord of information ... plenty of off-the-cuff advice from the editor" –*Changing Times* magazine

The Best Home Businesses for the 90's
Edwards $10.95 **#1932** ©91 pb

Paul and Sarah Edwards, the authors of *Working From Home,* interviewed over 300 home businesses while researching this new book. Provides very up-to-date information to help you decide which business is right for you, how much you can reasonably expect to earn from the business, how much competition you can expect, how much you can expect to spend in start-up costs, and much more. Each business is covered in a 2-page spread for easy viewing and comparison; graphics add visual appeal.

Working From Home
Paul & Sarah Edwards $14.95 **#0256** ©90 pb

This revised and expanded edition is subtitled "Everything You Need to Know About Living and Working Under the Same Roof," which isn't too much of an exaggeration. In 448 pages the authors cover all aspects of home businesses including presenting a business image at home, dealing with zoning, licenses and legal obligations and setting up an efficient home office. New chapters cover marketing your home business effectively, tips on how tax reform affects your home-office deductions, and a comprehensive A-Z listing of possibilities for home ventures.

The 50 Best Low-Investment, High-Profit Franchises
Robert Perry $12.95 **#1255** ©90 pb

Perry describes fifty lucrative, high-quality franchises available with investments starting as low as $2,500. Each franchise is described in detail, with advantages and disadvantages spelled out, start-up costs, the franchiser's package of services and products, support and training you can expect to receive, and potential earnings. Includes a step-by-step plan for finding the right franchise and cites warning signs to watch for. Carefully researched information.

555 Ways to Earn Extra Money
Jay Conrad Levinson $12.95 **#0913** ©91 pb

Whether you want to supplement a full-time job with extra earning projects or put together a network of part-time endeavors and give up the nine-to-five altogether, Levinson's book on moonlighting and "Patchwork economics" can help. Includes steps to get started, advertising tactics, suggested company names and unique—even surprising—ways to augment your income. Jay is one of our all-time favorite authors.

Franchises You Can Run From Home
Arden $14.95 **#1078** ©90 pb

"Great things happen when two trends meet," begins the author of this popular book. The two trends, of course, are the growth of working at home and the growth of franchising. Over 100 reputable franchises for home-based entrepreneurs are covered, including financial services, property improvement, domestic services, business services, desktop publishing, video services and employment services. Real-life success stories and helpful advice for a relatively inexpensive (and low-risk) way to go into business.

Running a One-Person Business
Whitmyer $12.95   **#0299** ©89   pb

Previously thought of only as a stunted version of a small business, one-person businesses are now a permanent—and rapidly growing—part of our new economy. The authors convey their excitement about this infinitely-versatile business form, presenting the idea that business can be a lifestyle and a statement of who you are and what you value. This book is a comprehensive guide to forming these unique enterprises, especially small businesses run from the home or the professional office.

Marketing Without Advertising
Phillips $14.95   **#0253**   ©86   pb lg format

"The first two chapters of this startling book argue convincingly, and with documented proof, that almost all advertising is totally ineffective and an utter waste of money....I guarantee you'll have an entirely new perspective on advertising. The rest of the book... explains clearly and in detail how you can promote your business without advertising, primarily by encouraging personal recommendations. The ideas are useful and well presented, of value to any business." -*The Whole Earth Catalog*

Starting and Operating a Business in . . .
by M.D. Jenkins and co-authors from each state
$29.95   **#0197**   loose-leaf binder

Very comprehensive, authoritative packages of how-to's. All the basics are in-cluded—setting up your business (with checklists), specific forms required for your state, condensed business overview and more. An up-to-date resource, consolidated in a loose-leaf binder for easy reference. Please specify which state you want.

The Entrepreneur's Guide to Doing Business With the Federal Government
Bevers $14.95   **#1418**   ©89   pb

This book shows small businesses how to cut through red tape and tap into the $240 Billion government market. According to the authors, even the smallest businesses actually can compete, provided they're willing to be patient and learn the details of federal procurement. How to identify the government markets that need your product or service, determine if you want to bid, respond to a solicitation, and negotiate and fulfill the contract.

Growing a Business
Hawkens $9.95   **#0260**   ©87 pb

Our choice for the best start-your-own business book. Hawkens is host of the **Growing a Business** PBS TV series and is founder of Erewhon, the natural food distributor, and Smith and Hawken, the mail-order garden supply company. Focusing on the fundamen-tal questions everyone should ask when starting a business, he shares his own start-up strategies and tells the stories of successful new businesses like Ben & Jerry's Home-made, Inc., Esprit, and Patagonia Outdoors. Hawkins has a refreshingly honest, whole-some yet realistic perspective that cuts through all the nonsense we hear about entrepre-neurship. *Highly, highly recommended.*

Free Money For Small Businesses and Entrepreneurs
Blum $14.95   **#0614**   ©92   pb

Second edition. This is a guide to the agencies, foundations, and other funds that offer outright grants to qualified new and existing small businesses. All totaled, this money tops $2 *billion,* and it's available for a wide range of uses—from start-up capital to research grants. Categorized by type of business, each of the more than 300 listings supplies the name and address of the grant source along with amounts available and special requirements. Includes details on how to apply as well as where to apply.

The Small Business Test
Ingram $8.95   **#1910**   ©90   pb   large format

Why do some small businesses succeed–often beyond anyone's wildest dreams–when so many others fail? Based on a detailed analysis of almost 100 small businesses, from bakeries to ad agencies–and from your own evaluation of your knowledge, experience, product and other factors– **The Small Business Test** gives you your actual chances for success in your new business. It's also interesting and fun to take. Includes advice on finding unique markets, calculating your business plan, getting the most from suppliers, preventing legal problems and more.

Master Forms & Contracts from Your Copierfor Entrepreneurs, Small Businesses & Landlords
Burns and Johnson $8.95   **#1843**   ©87   pb

Having the right form is the difference between painlessly getting the right information the first time and fumbling around wasting half a day trying to re-invent the wheel. In business, time is money, and this "swipe file" of essential forms can help you manage taxes, cash flow, employees, credit, collections, sales, estimates, repairs, orders, invoices, receipts, and, above all, time.

How to Form Your Own Corporation Without a Lawyer for Under $75
Nicholas $19.95   **#2234**   ©92   pb

The 20th edition of this classic guide with 900,000 copies in print. Using the forms in this book, just about anyone can begin realizing the valuable benefits of incorporating— tax-deductible automobiles and meals, medical insurance, limited personal liability, reimbursement of certain expenses and better access to capital.   "The book succeeds...because it fills a real need. Brought public information that previously had to be bought from an attorney."-*Publishers Weekly*

The Complete Small Business Loan Kit
Consumer Law Foundation $12.95   **#1278**   ©90   pb

If you can get the full amount of money you need to get your business started on a sound financial basis you'll be much less vulnerable to failure than most small business start-ups. This new book can help you do exactly that. Covers SBA loan opportunities, how to improve your credit rating enough to qualify for a loan, how to set up the best loan package with public or private institutions, how to make presentations that get results, special programs for veterans, the handicapped, and minorities, and more. Large format, very comprehensive.

SBA Hotline Answer Book
Berle $14.95 **#2035** ©92 pb

Each year, hundreds of thousands of people dial 800-368-5855, the Small Business Administration's hotline for information on starting a business. This book is a compilation of the 200 questions most often asked, covering a wide range of entrepreneurial concerns. We like the user-friendly question-and-answer format. All questions are conveniently arranged in alphabetical order by business topic. An appendix lists SBA field offices, SCORE major offices, minority business development centers, SBIC's, and more.

Finding Your Niche...Marketing Your Professional Service
Brodsky/Geis $15.95 **#2238** ©92 pb

Teachers, therapists, consultants, lawyers, artists and virtually every other professional in business or private practice can benefit from this guide to marketing your professional services. Gives excellent advice—with more than 120 options for marketing your service—in a friendly, intelligent format with lots of examples and antecdotes. *Recommended.*

Small Time Operator: How to Start Your Own Small Business, Keep Your Books, Pay Your Taxes, and Stay out of Trouble!
Kamoroff $14.95 **#0885** ©93 pb lg format

With a quarter of a million copies in print, this is the most popular small business guidebook in the United States. It's not hard to understand why—in a pleasant, upbeat way it's highly informative, nicely designed and extremely well written. It provides all the income and expenditure ledgers you'll need for your first year, along with clear step-by-step instructions for using them, and the examples given are both interesting and helpful. "The best of the genre...a remarkable step-by-step manual that is a delight to read. All the nitty-gritty of business is here." —*Library Journal*

Marketing for the Home-Based Business
Davidson $9.95 **#1239** ©90 pb

Most small business failures aren't caused by a lack of experience or even a lack of money but by the lack of an intelligent, consistent marketing strategy. This book covers marketing approaches that have worked especially well for home businesses. Includes chapters on Getting Started, Marketing With the PC, Getting Help, Marketing and Desktop Publishing, more. Davidson has a knack for making his material user-friendly and interesting.

The Contract & Fee-Setting Guide for Consultants and Professionals
Shenson $19.95 **#1899** ©90 pb

Fee-setting is the one area where otherwise-competent professionals and consultants frequently have problems—and often end up selling themselves short. Howard Shenson has lectured for many years on this subject and has a refreshingly clear approach with straightforward answers and carefully-calculated advice. Shows how to determine the market value for consulting and professional services, how to establish appropriate daily or per-project rates and calculate your overhead, pros and cons of various fee-setting and billing systems, 6 major goals of every contract, negotiating the contract and avoiding legal pitfalls, and much more. Includes sample contracts and forms.

How to Start a Business Without Quitting Your Job
Philip Holland $9.95   **#2222**   ©92   pb

Keeping your job while you get a business up and running on the side makes sense—a whole lot of sense, as you will see in this guide to the ins and outs of "the moonlight juggling act." Covers how to choose the right startup business, budget time wisely, and make sure neither job suffers, with firsthand accounts of successful moonlighters and the types of businesses that work for them. There are separate chapters on financing, liability, involving your family, and deciding when (or if) to quit your job.

The Start Up Guide: A One-Year Plan for Entrepreneurs
David H. Bangs, Jr. $19.95   **#2250**   ©92   pb

The real key to succeeding in a business is to work steadily toward your goals without becoming sidetracked or overwhelmed in the process. This guide, intended for those with no formal training, can help you do just that. "Provides a one-year, step-by-step timetable for organizing a business...all the while offering practical, realistic advice."-*Booklist* "shows entrepreneurs exactly what they should be doing at every important step"-*In Business*

The Great American Idea Book
Coleman/Neville $22.95   **#2706**   ©93   hc

Many, many fortunes have been made from someone's simple idea. This new book shows how to make money from your ideas—for movies, music, books, inventions, businesses and almost anything else. Covers securing the legal rights to your idea, developing it to the point where others will invest in it, promoting it effectively, defending it legally and financially, and—best of all—profiting by making the right deals. Individual sections cover TV, screenplays, books, movies, art and animation, inventions, franchising your business idea, much more. The success stories interspersed throughout are first-rate.

The Best Nonfranchise Business Opportunities
Andrew Sherman $19.95   **#2704**   ©93   pb

Everybody's heard of franchises, but most people know little or nothing about dealerships, license agreements, distributorships and other nonfranchise opportunities. All together, these opportunities represent a ten-billion-dollar industry that's frequently overlooked and includes some intriguing possibilities for anyone wanting a good small business. This new book is an independent survey of 75 of the best of these opportunities with capital requirements, advantages, etc. plus how to evaluate a nonfranchise opportunity, how to arrange financing, and what it takes to succeed.

Other Topics

Wishcraft: How to Get What You *Really* Want
Sher $9.95   **#1240**   ©79   pb

First published in 1979, this book has developed a very loyal following. "The most irreverent and refreshing self-help manual now on the market...Feisty, funny, and down-to-earth, this book is bound to benefit all those who sense they may have temporarily lost track of their true goals." —*New Age Magazine* "The best parts of this world were not fashioned by those who were realistic. They were fashioned by those who dared to look hard at their wishes and gave them horses to ride. . . Barbara Sher is to be commended, for making hope practical." —R. Bolles, author of *What Color is Your Parachute?*

Work-at-Home Sourcebook
Arden $14.95   **#0998**   ©92   pb   4th Edition

This is the only guide available giving detailed information on specific jobs that allow you to work from your home. Inside information is given on over 1000 companies that have home-work programs, with details on job descriptions, pay and benefits, how to apply and how to make the most of working at home once you get the job. Includes positions for home word processors, proofreaders, weavers, telemarketers, graphic artists, and many other types of work. This edition has a new section on home business opportunities, too. "Besides being a tremendous financial resource, this book is just plain fun to read. . . "—*Welcome Home*

How to Survive Without a Salary
Charles Long $12.95   **#1845**   ©92   pb

New edition. Some people decide that the benefits of a steady income come at too high a price. For them, a life of voluntary simplicity can be a richer, more rewarding alternative.   Long's book is a guide to the practicalities of such a life, as well as a manifesto for the freedom such a life can bring. How to analyze your true needs, find alternatives to buying, avoid consumer traps, make a casual income, and get along beautifully with less. Subtitled "Learning How to Live the Conserver Lifestyle."

College Degrees by Mail
Bear $12.95   **#0928**   ©91   pb

It's entirely possible to earn a legitimate college degree through home study. It can take as little as three months and cost as little as $500. The problem is that most colleges that offer such programs never advertise–and you don't want anything to do with many of those that <u>do</u> advertise.   This edition devotes an entire page to each of 100 colleges selected by Dr. Bear as being among the best offering home study programs. Subtitle: "100 Good Schools that offer Bachelor's, Master's, Doctorates and Law Degrees by Home Study." One of our most popular books, updated regularly.

The 10 Best Opportunities for Starting a Home Business Today
New Careers Center/Glenn $14.95   **#2710**   ©93

Please use the order form to order additional copies of this book.

ORDERING INFORMATION

Catalog Requests. We include a copy of "The Whole Work Catalog" with every outgoing order. If you only want to request a catalog, you may do so by calling us at (303) 447-1087 weekdays from 8-5, Mountain Standard Time, or you can drop us a note or fax.

Mastercard/Visa orders may be phoned/faxed in to the number above. $20 minimum on credit card orders, please.

Fax . Our 24-hour fax line is (303) 447-8684.

Our guarantee. We want you to be happy with everything you order from us. If you aren't satisfied with any purchase, please return it to us in new condition any time within **one full year** for a quick and courteous refund. Your satisfaction is our foremost concern.

Delivery. Your order will be shipped promptly, normally within 48 hours, by Bookpost (Special 4th Class Mail). Please allow up to three weeks for delivery, depending on where you live and the season. For much faster delivery, we can ship UPS (48 contiguous states). Add $.50 for each item ordered. UPS cannot deliver to a P.O. Box–street address required.

Foreign Shipping Charges. Please add 15% of the merchandise total (minimum of $6).

ORDER FORM
THE NEW CAREERS CENTER
1515 - 23rd Street, P.O. Box 339-CB, Boulder CO 80306

Name _____

Street /apt. no. _____

City/State/Zip _____

Daytime phone no. _____
(in case we need to contact you about your order)

Item No.	Title		Total Price	

Need more room? Just attach another sheet of paper.

Merchandise total			
Colo. residents add 3% tax			
Shipping (except foreign)		3	75
UPS delivery			
TOTAL (U.S. funds only)			

Please see facing page for ordering informating.

Method of Payment (Sorry, no C.O.D.'s)

☐ Payment enclosed: check or money order for the total amount of _____

☐ Visa ☐ MasterCard Acct. No. _____

Credit Card Expiration Date: _____

Note: $20 minimum on credit card orders, please

X _____
Cardholder's signature (required on all credit card orders)